THE 1066 NORMAN BRUISERS

BRUISERS

HOW EUROPEAN THUGS BECAME
ENGLISH GENTRY

THE 1066 NORMAN BRUISERS

BRUISERS

HOW EUROPEAN THUGS BECAME
ENGLISH GENTRY

HELEN KAY

PEN & SWORD
HISTORY

AN IMPRINT OF PEN & SWORD BOOKS LTD
YORKSHIRE – PHILADELPHIA

First published in Great Britain in 2020 by
PEN AND SWORD HISTORY
An imprint of
Pen & Sword Books Ltd
Yorkshire – Philadelphia

ISBN 978 1 52675 938 2

Typeset in Times New Roman 11.5/14 by
Aura Technology and Software Services, India
Printed and bound in Great Britain by TJ International

Pen & Sword Books Limited incorporates the imprints of Atlas, Archaeology,
Aviation, Discovery, Family History, Fiction, History, Maritime, Military, Military
Classics, Politics, Select, Transport, True Crime, Air World, Frontline Publishing,
Leo Cooper, Remember When, Seaforth Publishing, The Praetorian Press,
Wharncliffe Local History, Wharncliffe Transport, Wharncliffe True Crime and
White Owl.

For a complete list of Pen & Sword titles please contact
PEN & SWORD BOOKS LIMITED
47 Church Street, Barnsley, South Yorkshire, S70 2AS, England
E-mail: enquiries@pen-and-sword.co.uk
Website: www.pen-and-sword.co.uk

Or

PEN AND SWORD BOOKS
1950 Lawrence Rd, Havertown, PA 19083, USA
E-mail: Uspen-and-sword@casematepublishers.com
Website: www.penandswordbooks.com

Contents

Acknowledgements

As I write, Britain is renegotiating its relations with the European Union, a process that implicitly entails rethinking what it means both to be British and to belong to one of the United Kingdom's four constituent countries. National identities are a complex mix of history, culture, language, politics and landscape, and the concept of Englishness has evolved over time. But it has long struck me as ironic that the roots of one enduring image of Englishness – the county squire with his rolling acres – aren't really English at all. By and large, the landed gentry came from the Norman bruisers who crossed the Channel in 1066.

A number of people have helped me to flesh out the story of the ruffians who feature here. I must first pay tribute to Gwen Ashbaugh, lifelong friend and early beta-reader, who died before this book could be completed. Her wisdom, humour, kindness and courage were a source of inspiration.

I am also deeply grateful to Linda Ban, Ann Kottner, Peter Spring and Tess Tavormina, both for their incisive comments on various drafts and for their unstinting moral support. Peter provided invaluable input on military matters, while Tess shared her expertise on medieval medicine. No author could ask for better companions on the long journey from conception to final text. I am equally beholden to Kristina Bedford for deciphering many a faded manuscript on my behalf, and to Katy Parkinson for kindly taking me on a road trip around Cheshire. Katy, it transpires, is a descendant of one of the characters in this book.

My sincere thanks go to Jon Wright and Laura Hirst, my commissioning editor and production editor respectively, at Pen & Sword. I am also indebted to Professor J.J.N. Palmer, George Slater and opendomesday.org for providing the image from the Domesday Book that appears in the background on the dust jacket under a Creative Commons By-SA licence.

Above all, I want to express my gratitude to my parents. I owe my interest in history to my mother and this particular piece of history to my father. Like my friend Katy, he can trace his lineage back to eleventh-century invaders who were neither English nor landed nor gentle.

A Note on Money, Land and Names

Money

The standard unit of currency in medieval England was the pound (£). A pound was worth 20 shillings (s) and a shilling was worth 12 pence (d). Thus, a pound equalled 240d. The silver coin was the only coin in circulation until the thirteenth century, when the farthing (¼d) and groat (4d) were introduced. The gold noble (6s 8d) was added in 1344. Marks were also used for accounting purposes. One mark was worth two-thirds of a pound (13s 4d).

Land

Land was measured in terms of the yield it produced, so the actual area varied widely depending on the climate and quality of the soil. A virgate was the area of land a pair of oxen could plough in a year, while a bovate was the area one ox could plough in a year. Four bovates made up a hide – the amount of land considered sufficient to support a typical peasant family. This was nominally 120 acres. In 1305, parliament passed a law specifying the size of an acre (4,840 square yards), but many parts of England continued to use 'customary acres' until the early nineteenth century. The Cheshire acre was traditionally 10,240 square yards. Other measures included the selion (an open strip of land) and the perch (a unit of length based on the pole used to control a team of oxen).

Names

The languages of government were Latin and Norman French and the spelling of English wasn't standardised. Names therefore occur in many different versions in written records. Some surnames were toponymic and took the form 'de X', where X was a place. Hugh de Dutton was 'of' Dutton in Cheshire, for example. This clerical convention declined in the late fourteenth century. I have anglicised and modernised the spelling of all personal names and place names except those included in direct quotes, where I have kept the original spelling. I have also retained the preposition before toponymic surnames in the early part of the text.

List of Maps and Family Trees

The Boydells of Dodleston, Grappenhall and Handley

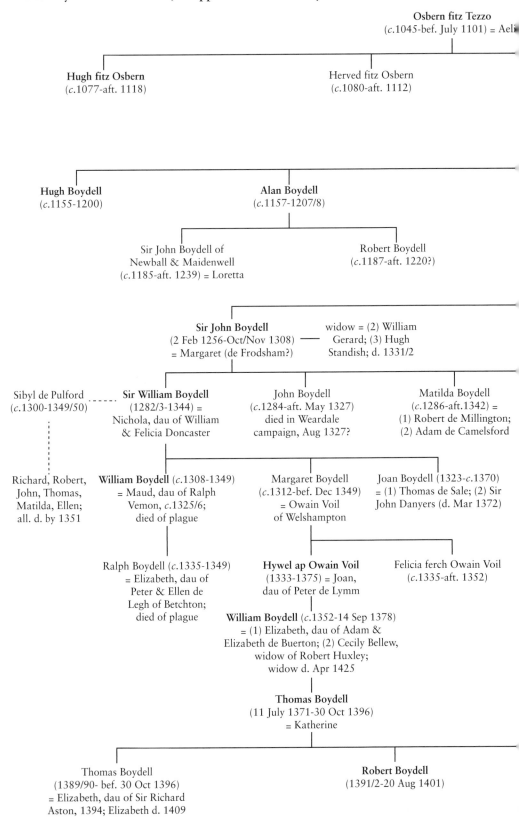

Osbern fitz Tezzo
(*c*.1045-bef. July 1101) = Ael

Hugh fitz Osbern
(*c*.1077-aft. 1118)

Herved fitz Osbern
(*c*.1080-aft. 1112)

Hugh Boydell
(*c*.1155-1200)

Alan Boydell
(*c*.1157-1207/8)

Sir John Boydell of
Newball & Maidenwell
(*c*.1185-aft. 1239) = Loretta

Robert Boydell
(*c*.1187-aft. 1220?)

Sir John Boydell
(2 Feb 1256-Oct/Nov 1308)
= Margaret (de Frodsham?)

widow = (2) William
Gerard; (3) Hugh
Standish; d. 1331/2

Sibyl de Pulford
(*c*.1300-1349/50)

Sir William Boydell
(1282/3-1344) =
Nichola, dau of William
& Felicia Doncaster

John Boydell
(*c*.1284-aft. May 1327)
died in Weardale
campaign, Aug 1327?

Matilda Boydell
(*c*.1286-aft.1342) =
(1) Robert de Millington;
(2) Adam de Camelsford

Richard, Robert,
John, Thomas,
Matilda, Ellen;
all. d. by 1351

William Boydell (*c*.1308-1349)
= Maud, dau of Ralph
Vemon, *c*.1325/6;
died of plague

Margaret Boydell
(*c*.1312-bef. Dec 1349)
= Owain Voil
of Welshampton

Joan Boydell (1323-*c*.1370)
= (1) Thomas de Sale; (2) Sir
John Danyers (d. Mar 1372)

Ralph Boydell (*c*.1335-1349)
= Elizabeth, dau of
Peter & Ellen de
Legh of Betchton;
died of plague

Hywel ap Owain Voil
(1333-1375) = Joan,
dau of Peter de Lymm

Felicia ferch Owain Voil
(*c*.1335-aft. 1352)

William Boydell (*c*.1352-14 Sep 1378)
= (1) Elizabeth, dau of Adam &
Elizabeth de Buerton; (2) Cecily Bellew,
widow of Robert Huxley;
widow d. Apr 1425

Thomas Boydell
(11 July 1371-30 Oct 1396)
= Katherine

Thomas Boydell
(1389/90- bef. 30 Oct 1396)
= Elizabeth, dau of Sir Richard
Aston, 1394; Elizabeth d. 1409

Robert Boydell
(1391/2-20 Aug 1401)

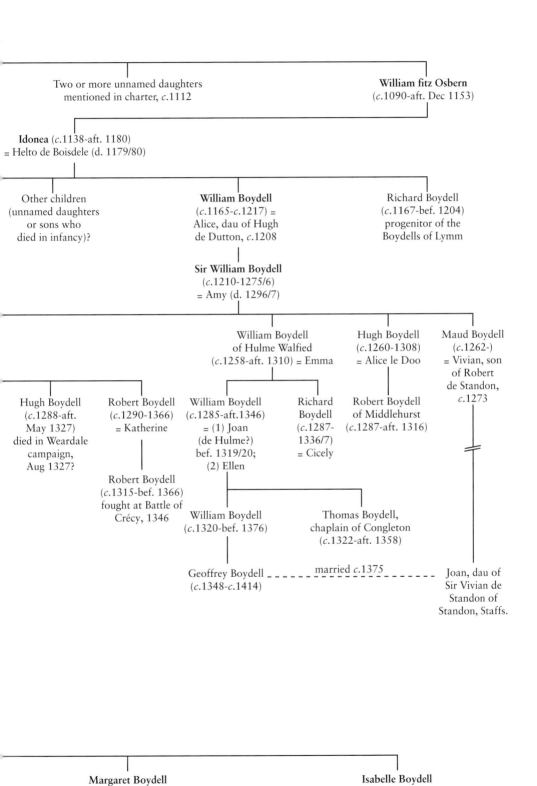

Introduction

When my paternal grandfather died, he bequeathed my father a knife and fork, a battered tin serving spoon and the bill for burying him: the meagre remnants of a long and troubled life. There was one other thing my grandfather left his son – and, ultimately, me – although we didn't know it at the time. He left us a story that stretches back thirty generations.

In 1066, William, duke of Normandy, invaded England, defeated the Anglo-Saxons in battle and seized the kingdom for himself. Some of the troops who fought for him were foreign mercenaries and adventurers. The rest were Norman nobles and the war bands they had raised from their tenantry to support the duke's daring enterprise. Most of the surviving mercenaries eventually returned home with jangling purses, but the Normans came to stay. They had risked their lives for a share of England's fertile earth.

This is the tale of one go-getting young Norman immigrant and the dynasty he established – a dynasty that played quite a prominent role in north-western England for more than three centuries. Osbern fitz Tezzo peeks out of the pages of the Domesday Book. Traces of his presence can also be found in charters recording religious endowments and in the ruins of the castle he built. His descendants, who assumed the name Boydell, left a bigger footprint. They served king and country, engaged in feuds and illicit love affairs and exercised considerable local sway. A junior branch of the family even produced two future queens.

The Boydells illustrate one of the strangest quirks in Britain's history – how a bunch of foreign thugs evolved into the quintessentially English gentry. The Conquest brought many social changes, the most significant of which was the creation of a new ruling class. Within twenty years of planting themselves on English soil, William and his compatriots held 95 per cent of the land. The barons of eleventh-century Normandy and

1

their followers had pulled off an extraordinary coup, with the wholesale transfer of territorial control – and the offspring of these men would form the bulk of England's late medieval nobility.

Defining the lesser nobility – or gentry, as they came to be known – is notoriously difficult, not least because the term itself wasn't used in the Middle Ages. The knights who formed the bedrock of the gentle class were originally just mounted soldiers. Moreover, good breeding and chivalrous conduct didn't necessarily co-exist with landed wealth. Many a local lord resorted to cheating, bullying and murder in the ruthless drive to enlarge his estates. However, the notion of gentility had certainly emerged by 1204, when one Somerset landholder who was involved in a territorial dispute tartly informed the county sheriff that he and his kinsfolk were 'natives and gentle men' within their community, whereas the sheriff was an outsider. The sheriff retorted that he was equally well born.

During the thirteenth and fourteenth centuries, the minor ranks of the nobility crystallised, as knighthood became a sign of honour rather than a profession and the ownership of land underwent a process of consolidation. By the early 1300s, two categories – knights and esquires – had materialised. There were roughly 1,250-1,500 knights, including Sir John Boydell, with annual landed incomes of at least £40. The remaining gentry owned no more than a single small manor apiece and had landed incomes averaging about £12 a year.

By 1400, the two ranks had become three. England's lesser nobles now called themselves knights, esquires or gentlemen, in that order. And, in 1413, parliament effectively recognised the last element in this trinity for legal purposes. The Statute of Additions specified that the estate, degree or trade of everyone who was named as a defendant in a lawsuit should be recorded, thereby drawing a line between gentlemen and yeomen (the highest of the non-noble classes). Nevertheless, the boundaries remained somewhat blurred.

They were also porous. Men migrated from one class to another. Those who were determined, able and fortunate rose in the world, while those who were inept or unlucky sank into obscurity. It was a risky business trying to climb the ladder. A pushy individual who put one foot wrong might be flattened by the hordes of other hopefuls snapping at his heels. Even so, every political upheaval brought a new batch of parvenus eager to reach the next rung.

Furthermore, without reliable birth or marriage records, it was relatively easy to forge a bloodline. In the mid-fourteenth century, for example, the Norwich family fabricated a pedigree that went back to a fictitious companion of William the Conqueror, using counterfeit deeds to reinforce their claim to ancient gentility And though the Pastons of Norfolk boasted of their knightly Norman forebears, they actually came of peasant stock – as their acquaintances were quick to note when they started putting on airs and graces.

So what distinguished the gentry from the rest of the populace? Most obviously, the majority of them held real estate. Land was the foundation of the medieval economy. It also conferred authority. Manorial lords were little gods within the realms they ruled. They presided over cases of petty crime and minor property disputes in their manorial courts, as well as being able to call on their tenants to provide them with labour and support them in private quarrels. In addition, many of the gentry held office as commissioners of the peace, tax collectors, county court jurors or as knights of the shire in parliament. That said, neither territorial assets nor a stint in public service were prerequisites for gentle status. Some merchants could claim to be genteel, even though they held no land.

It was their lifestyle and conception of themselves, as much as anything else, which separated the lesser nobility from the rest of English society. What made a man 'gentle' was his ability to live a life of leisure – as distinct from engaging in vulgar commercial activities like trade – to maintain a fine home, dress and dine well, comport himself with dignity and mix with like-minded people. The gentry had shared interests and concerns, married into families from the same station in life and called on each other to act as witnesses, trustees and guarantors. They saw themselves as a community, were obsessed with preserving their place among the upper crust and used heraldic emblems to display their credentials.

Thanks to the lands and offices they held, the readiness with which they invoked the law and their preoccupation with documenting their lineage, England's late medieval gentry left a remarkably copious textual legacy. Sifting through the evidence, it is possible to piece together an intimate account of Osbern and his kin: to conjure them up as creatures of flesh and blood and place them in the temporal and regional environment they inhabited.

I have grounded the tale of the Boydells in historical fact. However, my narrative ranges further than written evidence alone can support in an attempt to evoke the experiences of individuals who lived and died long ago. Medieval records generally say nothing about the emotions of the people who feature in them, although these can sometimes be inferred. The clerks who compiled the accounts were more concerned with charting debts, crimes, appointments to office and territorial transactions than they were with exploring hearts, minds or motives. The language they used is also largely formulaic. The court roll for a criminal trial will typically reveal *what* a man did or was accused of doing, but not *why* he did it – let alone what he was thinking or feeling when he committed the offence.

Manuscripts are equally limited in their ability to communicate the psychological impact of pervasive ideas and beliefs. Prayer books show how people worshipped, for example, but they cannot convey what it was like to occupy a world in which the calendar was marked out by saints' days, the Devil walked abroad and excommunication was a fate worse than death.

Much of the past remains hidden. So I have drawn on my imagination, informed by my research, to reconstruct key moments in the existence of the protagonists. Parts of the narrative take the form of fictional vignettes that stay faithful to what happened to the Boydells of Dodleston Castle insofar as it can be deduced from this distance in time. My aim is to bring the people who populate the following pages back to life for a few hours and to shed light on a crucial facet of English history in the process. For the story of the Boydells is not just a story about one specific family: it is, ultimately, a story about the shaping of the nation. The Norman bruisers who pulled themselves up by their sword arms may be long buried, but they made an indelible mark on the country they conquered.

1

Winner Takes All

Osbern stood in the middle of the green, directing his troops as they stormed into the hovels dotted around the edge of the settlement and dragged out the terrified villagers. One man resisted and was cut down, blood spurting from his chest as he collapsed. His woman screamed and started pummelling the soldier who'd stabbed him. She quieted when another soldier struck her hard with the flat of his blade, stunning her with the ferocity of the blow.

'Vite, vite,' Osbern shouted, waving his sword at the villagers and then pointing towards the hills. Men were pleading, women weeping, children wailing as they clung to their mothers' skirts. Osbern raised his sword and motioned towards the hills again. 'Allez,' he bellowed. Gathering their wits, the shocked villagers got the message, even if they didn't comprehend the words, swept up their children and fled.

When resistance to William the Conqueror's rule persisted in northern England, he had ordered the devastation of all the lands beyond the Humber. Everything – homes, food, crops, pigs, cows and squawking chickens – was to be destroyed. Osbern and his troops, acting under the command of Hugh d'Avranches, were helping to carry out the king's mandate.

Osbern watched as his soldiers rounded up the livestock, slitting the throats of the larger animals with their knives and wringing the necks of the hens with practised efficiency. Then he and his men hurled lighted brands onto the crudely thatched roofs. Flames licked the straw, crackling and hissing. Within moments the fire took hold. Crackles turned to deep-throated roar and orange sparks flew up into the sky as the village burned.

Satisfied that the settlement was beyond saving, Osbern summoned his troops. They had more ground to cover before nightfall and the sun was already sinking. They needed to hurry.

On the morning of 28 September 1066 – or possibly 29 September, since there are conflicting accounts of the date – William, duke of Normandy, landed at Pevensey Bay on the Sussex coast. He had set out on a dangerous mission to conquer England, the kingdom he believed his kinsman Edward the Confessor had promised him. The Anglo-Saxon king had died at the start of the year, but his brother-in-law, Harold Godwineson, had claimed the crown for himself. Edward had reputedly named Harold as his heir just before he died.

Whether England's ageing monarch had truly vowed to leave his throne to William is questionable. And even if he had, Anglo-Saxon law decreed that a deathbed bequest superseded previous gifts of the same property. However, Norman custom held that the promise of a post-mortem gift could never be revoked. The duke was determined to oust Harold and take the realm he thought was rightfully his. Many of the Norman nobles who sailed with him had been dubious about the idea of invading England when he first proposed it, but he had managed to bribe, browbeat and cajole them into giving him their support.

William's first steps on English soil were decidedly inauspicious, so the legend goes. As he leaped ashore, he stumbled and fell to his knees, eliciting cries of alarm at this evil omen, which seemed to confirm his nobles' earlier qualms. He immediately rose to his feet and called out that he had seized the country with both hands. His quick wits saved the moment; his skill, courage and good fortune were to win the day. While the duke stood on the beach at Pevensey, dusting the shingle off his palms, England's new sovereign was dealing with another invasion in the north. By the time the two came face to face on the battlefield, Harold fielded a force that was half its usual strength and his best warriors were exhausted.

William had been preparing to invade England for months. Normandy's forests had been stripped of timber to build a fleet of longships capable of carrying all the men, warhorses, food and fodder he required for his campaign. The duke had also assembled an enormous army by the standards of the eleventh century. The size of that army has been the subject of much speculation because the chroniclers of the time grossly exaggerated the figures. But the one near-contemporary source to provide a realistic number suggests that William may have set off with as many as 10,000 soldiers, supported by about 4,000 sailors and non-combatants (including cooks, smiths,

William the Conqueror's claim to the English throne

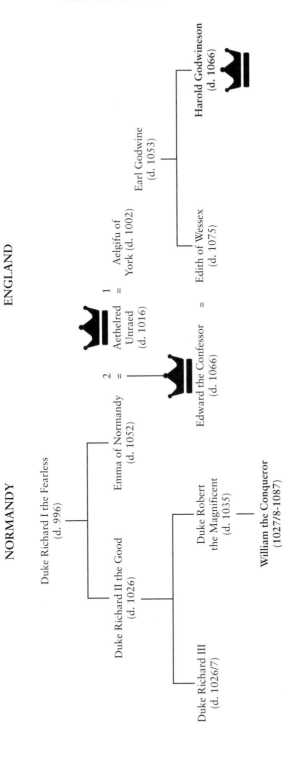

carpenters and clerics). Heavy winds blew some of his ships off course as they crossed the Channel. Even so, when he reached Pevensey, he could call on an exceptionally large assault force.

William's troops were also remarkably well trained. The backbone of the English army consisted of the housecarls who formed the king's personal bodyguard and those of his nobles. They were supplemented by the *fyrdmen* – free men who were required by virtue of the lands they held to serve in royal wars for up to two months a year, and farmers and artisans who could be mobilised to defend their shires when under attack. Many of the *fyrdmen* had neither swords nor armour: they marched to battle with spears, sickles, cudgels, knives and staves. So the English army comprised a small core of professional warriors and a large group of part-time conscripts with very little military experience, all of whom fought on foot. The Norman army, by contrast, included archers, infantry and cavalry. It was properly equipped and, under the duke's command, it had perfected the skills of war – performing mounted charges, besieging fortresses, raiding, burning and pillaging.

Among the soldiers in William's well-oiled fighting machine was Osbern fitz Tezzo, probably serving in the contingent of troops from Avranches in south-western Normandy. Most of the nobles whom the duke eventually rewarded for their aid in the Conquest drew their new tenants from the men who had served them in Normandy – and, since Hugh d'Avranches was the star to whom Osbern hitched his wagon, it is likely that Osbern came from Avranches. The d'Avranches family had helped to bankroll William's campaign. Richard le Goz, *vicomte* d'Avranches, and his son Hugh had provided sixty ships for the invasion. And either Richard or the teenaged Hugh was in charge of the Avranchin tenants who had volunteered to join William's expeditionary force.

Hugh was a wild youth, according to the *Ecclesiastical History* penned by Orderic Vitalis, an Anglo-Norman monk at the great Abbey of St Évroul. He loved hunting, feasting and games. He was 'a slave to gluttony', growing so obese in later life that he 'staggered under a mountain of fat, scarcely able to move'. And he was very promiscuous, siring numerous illegitimate children. As if this weren't bad enough, Orderic noted disapprovingly, he maintained a huge household swarming with rowdy young squires 'of both high and humble birth', whom he encouraged to behave with equal intemperance. But Hugh was not just a rich playboy who threw drink-fuelled parties and caroused through

Normandy in 1066

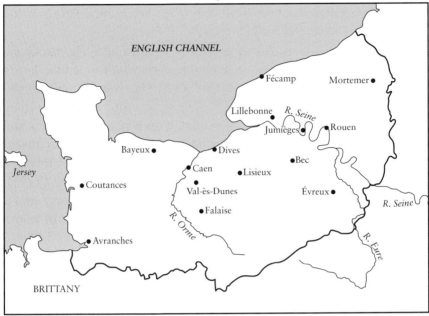

the night. He was also a formidable warrior and gifted commander, 'always in the forefront in battle'.

In short, Hugh was a contradictory person: rapacious and dissolute, yet brave, able and immensely generous. And what we know about him tells us something about Osbern fitz Tezzo. Osbern was probably one of the many Normans of modest stock whom Hugh welcomed into his household.[1] In all likelihood, he was much the same age as Hugh and may well have shared his overlord's penchant for wine, women and song. But he was also ambitious and jumped at the chance to advance himself by signing up to Hugh's war band.

So, when Osbern landed at Pevensey as part of William's invading army in September 1066, he was eager to prove himself in battle. He soon got his chance. On reaching England, the duke made his base at Hastings, 9 miles east of Pevensey, where he straightaway started assembling the wooden castle he had brought across from Normandy in segments and ravaging the surrounding countryside. Resisting pressure from his advisers to move inland, William concentrated on looting the area and terrorising the local populace. This was a standard feature of medieval warfare and enabled him to commandeer the food he needed to sustain his huge army. But he also wanted to goad his rival, King Harold, into coming to fight him, rather than leaving the security of his camp and leading a march into hostile territory. The lands he was laying waste belonged to Harold's family, and William hoped that the king would rush to the aid of his tenants. With his ships at his back, the duke knew that he could quickly re-embark and return to Normandy, if the English proved too strong to defeat.

William's tactics were brutally effective, but he had also been extraordinarily lucky. Bad weather had kept the Norman fleet pinned down in the port of Dives-sur-Mer for a month, leaving his soldiers kicking their heels in the nearby encampment.The duke issued strict orders that there was to be no foraging or brawling with the peasants. Bored and frustrated, Osbern and his friends doubtless spent their days training with other units and their evenings playing dice or sitting around a campfire, swapping ribald anecdotes.

Yet the delay was providential. While William was moodily waiting for the wind to change direction, the Norwegian monarch Harald Hardrada invaded northern England with Tostig Godwineson, King Harold's treacherous younger brother. Harold responded with characteristic vigour. He and his troops marched from London to Tadcaster in Yorkshire, a distance of 200 miles, in little more than a week. Surprising Hardrada's forces at Stamford Bridge, a small village near the city of York, they inflicted a crushing defeat on the Norwegians, just three days before the Normans landed at Pevensey. But the battle was fierce and both sides incurred heavy losses. So Harold's army was tired and depleted, and he himself was still in York burying his brother, when he learned of William's arrival.

Dismissing his foot soldiers, Harold immediately sent orders to the southern shires to muster a new army in London. Then he and his housecarls rode back to the capital at breakneck speed, taking just five days to complete the journey. His brothers Gyrth and Leofwine joined him there with another few thousand housecarls, while the *fyrdmen* trickled in over the next few days. However, the forces led by Edwin, earl of Mercia, and his brother Morcar were still recovering from a prior battle with Hardrada at Fulford on 20 September, where they had been badly beaten, and were too fatigued to make the long march south.

In early October 1066, William heard that Harold had returned from Yorkshire after vanquishing Hardrada. The duke paced fretfully around

The route of Harold's forced march

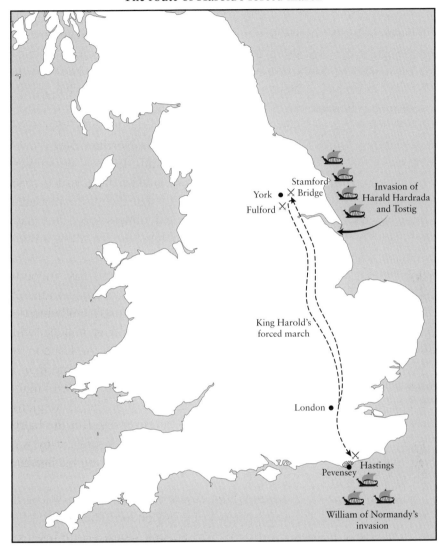

Stamford
York ● ✕ Bridge
Fulford ✕

Invasion of
Harald Hardrada
and Tostig

King Harold's
forced march

London ●

Hastings
Pevensey ✕

William of Normandy's
invasion

Source: G.S.P. Freeman-Grenville, *Atlas of British History* (1979), no. 33.

Hastings, inspecting his fortifications and wondering whether his scorched-earth policy would lure the king out of London or whether he would have to leave the safety of the coast. On 13 October, he discovered that Harold had risen to the bait. That evening, his scouts returned from reconnoitring the area with news that the first of the English had arrived. They were bivouacked on a ridge marked by a 'hoary apple tree', which overlooked a small valley with a stream running through it, about 7 miles north-west of Hastings.

William hastily ordered his entire garrison to stand to arms, donned his armour and draped the holy relics he had brought from Normandy around his neck. Then he delivered a rousing speech recalling previous victories. The next morning, as the sun was rising in a cold grey sky, he led his troops along the road out of Hastings. The archers and infantry marched in orderly formation in the vanguard. Behind them rode the cavalry, chain mail clinking, horses snuffling and pennants fluttering in the breeze.

Harold, himself a past-master of the lightning strike, had not been expecting the duke to use the same ploy. However, he had posted his own scouts and, when they warned him that the Normans were advancing, he deployed his housecarls in a long line to create a shield-wall. He took his place in the middle of the line and ordered his strongest warriors to stand in the first few ranks, with the *fyrdmen* behind them. When the housecarls angled their shields, the *fyrdmen* could run through the gaps and use their scythes and pitchforks to jab the unprotected legs of their opponents, before retreating. But when the housecarls stood shoulder to shoulder with overlapping shields, they presented an impenetrable barrier.

By nine in the morning, William's army was in position below the ridge. The duke had divided it into three groups: the Normans – including Osbern and his Avranchin companions – held the centre, flanked by the Bretons on the left and the French on the right. All three wings were arrayed in three lines, with the archers in front, the foot soldiers behind them and the mounted knights at the rear. Then trumpets blared and the waiting was over.

Maybe Osbern was frightened and muttered a quiet prayer, begging God to protect him. Or perhaps he was caught up in the moment, high on the adrenalin of impending battle. We can only surmise how he felt as he faced the English, with their mighty two-handed axes – row upon row of blond, moustachioed and long-haired housecarls so different from the dark, clean-shaven Normans with their hair buzz-cut at the back. What *is* certain is that the Battle of Hastings on Saturday, 14 October 1066, was horrendous even by the standards of the time. It lasted about eight hours, more than twice as long as most medieval mêlées. The primary sources are also consistent in claiming that the casualties were very high on both sides.

The Norman army began pushing up the slope and the archers launched their first volley. William was hoping to thin out the enemy, but Harold had chosen his location well. The bowmen had to shoot uphill, many of their arrows soaring over the heads of the English without inflicting any damage. In their light leather jerkins, they were also very vulnerable to the lethal hail of javelins, throwing-axes and rocks the *fyrdmen* rained down on them.

As the archers fell back, the foot soldiers advanced. Protected by their round shields, hauberks and metal helmets, Osbern and his comrades stepped slowly but inexorably forward, while the *fyrdmen* withdrew behind the shield-wall. Soon the two battle lines collided. Swords, spears and maces rang against Anglo-Saxon shields, great-axes crunched into Norman chain mail and men screamed in agony when weapons found their targets. Both sides fought savagely, until the slope was strewn with the bodies of the dead and dying.

Next, William brought his mounted troops into play. Yet still the English shield-wall held. Harold's hilltop position seemed virtually impregnable as the Norman cavalry struggled up the steep incline, horses stumbling on the rough ground. Eventually, recognising that his knights were floundering, the duke pulled them back and ordered the infantry forward again. When they were repulsed, he sent his horsemen thundering in for a second assault. The churned-up mud had become slippery with blood, guts and spilled brains. The stench of gore and excrement hung over the whole battlefield and both sides were tiring as the hours passed. At last, overwhelmed by the ferocity of the resistance, the Bretons broke. As they retreated, a rumour spread through the ranks that William had been killed. His panic-stricken soldiers turned tail and started fleeing, hotly pursued by some of the Anglo-Saxon *fyrdmen*.

William reacted swiftly. Brandishing his wooden battle mace, he raced ahead of the deserters. Then he tore off his helmet to show his face and galloped bareheaded down the broken line, yelling at his men to stand firm. Reassured that the duke was still alive, the Normans recovered their nerve and renewed their assault on the shield-wall. But though the English fought back as fiercely as before, William had spotted a weakness in Harold's defences. Realising that the Norman stampede had created a chance to kill the enemy, he decided to feign a retreat. As his troops started backing away, several thousand Englishmen rushed forward, jeering and screaming threats. This time the Normans were ready. The cavalry suddenly wheeled their horses around and rode down the pursuers, massacring them to the last man.

That, at least, was the version of events disseminated by William of Poitiers in his heavily biased history of the duke's deeds, although an alternative account suggests that what started as a ruse went badly awry and only William's speedy intervention saved the Normans. However, the result was the same: the English had been fatally weakened. As their numbers dwindled, William's mounted knights managed to break through the shield-wall and slay most of the royal bodyguards, who had formed a protective circle around their monarch, defending him till the last. Finally, when dusk was falling, they cornered Harold himself.

The Bayeaux Tapestry famously depicts England's last Anglo-Saxon ruler staggering as an arrow pierces his eye. In fact, over-zealous restorers, drawing on later chronicles, added the arrow in Harold's death scene during the nineteenth century. The *Carmen de Hastingae Proelio* – the only early source to describe how Harold died – suggests that his end was far more horrific. He was stabbed in the chest and gut, decapitated and castrated in a frenzied assault. It had taken the concerted efforts of four men, including the duke, to bring him down.

Utterly demoralised by their king's death and realising that there was no hope of resisting the Normans any longer, the remaining English turned and fled – although many were so seriously wounded that they could only crawl into the woods, where they were pursued and killed by the cavalry. William had won, but the cost had been colossal. When the sun crept over the battlefield the following morning, he surveyed the carnage. The ground was littered with the broken bodies of men and horses and drenched with blood. Several thousand Normans and perhaps twice as many Englishmen, including the flower of the Anglo-Saxon nobility, had lost their lives. Among the dead lay Harold, his corpse so badly mutilated that – by one account – only his lover, Edith Swan-Neck, could identify it.

Osbern fitz Tezzo survived. He was still one of the anonymous Normans whose individual acts of valour went unrecorded; other than the duke, only a few nobles are named in contemporary accounts of the battle. But Osbern would have many more opportunities to distinguish himself, for Hastings marked the beginning – not the end – of the Conquest.

The Normans remained in Sussex for a fortnight, resting, recuperating, tending their injured and burying their dead. Many of them were suffering from dysentery after weeks of camping in unsanitary conditions and all were bone-weary. While they recovered, William's chaplain held a Mass to give thanks for their great victory and the duke pledged the battlefield to God – a gesture the Almighty may not have welcomed much, since William had left the bodies of the English 'to be eaten by worms and wolves, birds and dogs'.

The duke was also waiting for what remained of the Anglo-Saxon high command to surrender. But only half of the English forces had fought at Hastings and the people of London refused to submit. Led by Earls Edwin and Morcar, the two northern lords who controlled Mercia and Northumbria respectively, and by the archbishops of Canterbury and York, they rejected William's demands and nominated Edward the Confessor's great-nephew, Edgar the Aetheling, as king. William responded by taking his army on a devastating march along the south coast to Dover and then inland to loop around London. The English were powerless to resist as Osbern and his fellow soldiers rampaged through the countryside. When the Normans reached Berkhamsted, William's opponents were forced to concede victory and swear their allegiance on bended knee. The duke progressed triumphantly to London, where he was crowned at Westminster Abbey on Christmas Day, 1066.

The coronation was a disaster. Dressed in his finest clothes, William promised to defend the Church, govern his subjects fairly and maintain the laws of the land. Then the two officiating prelates asked the mixed congregation of English and Norman nobles whether they would accept the new king's rule. The nobles 'shouted out', in English and French alike, that they would. However, the Norman guards posted outside the abbey, hearing raised voices in a language they didn't understand, immediately assumed that treachery was afoot and set fire to the nearby buildings. The flames spread rapidly and most of the congregation rushed out of the abbey, some to fight the fire, others to look for loot. Only a few terror-stricken churchmen remained in the sanctuary with the king and, by the time William had been consecrated, even he was trembling from head to toe.

It was an ominous start to his reign – and Orderic Vitalis, for one, blamed the Devil. But, by the spring of 1067, William felt sufficiently confident of his throne to return to Normandy, delegating the government of England to two of his most trusted confidantes. Yet though he had deliberately retained a number of English earls and sheriffs in an attempt to build an Anglo-Norman coalition, he was also sowing the seeds of discord. Angered by his decision to seize the lands of everyone who had opposed him at Hastings, resentful of the high taxes he had introduced and still grieving for dead kinsmen, the English believed that William was breaking the coronation oath he had made to rule his subjects justly.

By the autumn of 1067, the first of many uprisings against the new regime was underway. A powerful Midlands thegn, Eadric the Wild, joined forces with the king of Powys, in Wales, to attack Hereford Castle, one of the many wooden castles William and his followers had started building after the invasion. When the Normans repelled them, they retreated to Wales to plan further raids. Shortly afterwards, the people of Kent assaulted Dover Castle. The Norman garrison quickly suppressed the revolt, but William was sufficiently worried by the news reaching him from the other side of the Channel to return to England.

He was particularly alarmed by a rumour that the surviving members of Harold's family were hatching a plot to overthrow him – a rumour confirmed early the next year, when the citizens of Exeter rebelled. The ringleaders included Harold's mother, Gytha, burning for revenge on the man responsible for the deaths of three of her sons at Hastings, for Harold's brothers Gyrth and Leofwine had also been killed in the battle. Raising an army, William marched to Exeter and besieged it. Eighteen days later, when Gytha fled the city, the insurgents surrendered and a castle was erected to enforce the peace. Then the king pressed on to Cornwall, 'putting down every disturbance that came to his notice'.

By Easter 1068, William had established his authority over all of southern England, but northern England was proving far more difficult to subdue. In mid-1068, Earl Edwin rose up in protest against 'the injustice and tyranny' the Normans had inflicted on the English. His brother Morcar, and Earls Waltheof and Gospatric of Northumbria, joined him. Edgar the Aetheling also revived his claim to the crown and threw in his lot with the rebels.

William resorted to tried-and-tested tactics: he rode to all the remote parts of his kingdom and built yet more castles to repel enemy attacks, leaving a trail of destruction in his wake. When the walls of Warwick Castle went up, Edwin and Morcar reluctantly conceded defeat and sought the king's pardon, while their co-conspirators bolted to Scotland. William pressed on to York, where the terrified citizens handed over the keys to the city without a struggle. He stayed long enough to erect a castle in York before returning south.

Osbern probably played a part in quelling the resistance. The king had paused on his journey up to York to build a castle at Nottingham and it was then that he most likely granted Hugh d'Avranches lands in Tutbury, 26 miles west of Nottingham. Tutbury was the largest town in Staffordshire and Hugh wasted no time raising his own castle to help control the West Midlands. Osbern almost certainly accompanied his overlord north.

However, matters were far from settled and, in early 1069, Edgar the Aetheling launched another bid for the throne. William had appointed Robert de Comines, a man known for his cruelty, as the new earl of Northumbria. Comines had lived up to his reputation, sparking an uprising in which he and all but one of his soldiers were slain. Heartened by this display of resistance, Edgar swooped down from Scotland, rallied the Northumbrians and marched to York, where his supporters called for him to be crowned. But the Norman garrison in York managed to send word to William, who hurried north with a large army and drove out the rebels. Edgar fled back to Scotland, while William built a second castle at York, after sacking the city.

Yet even this was not enough to bring the stubborn northerners to their knees. In August 1069, the king of Denmark sent a fleet of several hundred ships to England. The Danes raided the coast before entering the Humber, linking up with Edgar the Aetheling and his supporters and advancing on York. When the Anglo-Danish army arrived, it took both castles by storm. Some 3,000 Normans were killed before the Danes returned to their ships, laden with booty, and the Northumbrians went back to their homes. Eadric the Wild simultaneously attacked Shrewsbury, with help from the people of Chester – and, cheered by events in the north, the men of Devon and Cornwall besieged Exeter. All of William's enemies, it seemed, were converging on him like hounds bent on bringing down a stag. He responded by sending troops to Exeter, while he marched north again to deal with the Danes and with Eadric.

As soon as the Danes heard that William was coming, they abandoned York and crossed the Humber to hide in the Lincolnshire fenlands. Satisfied that they were no longer an immediate threat, William turned

William's campaign routes, 1067–1071

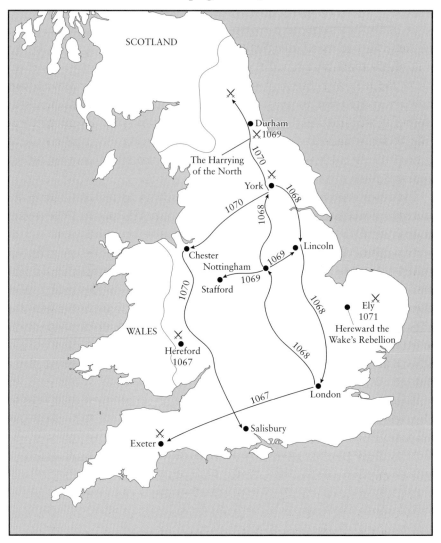

Source: G.S.P. Freeman-Grenville, *Atlas of British History* (1979), no. 34.

his attention to Eadric. He had little difficulty in crushing a large force of rebels at Stafford. However, as he was making his way to Lincolnshire to finish off the Danes, he learned that they had returned to York. The king turned back, but when he reached Pontefract he found that the bridge over the River Aire had been destroyed. After a three-week delay searching for a place where the river could be forded and a hard trek to York, he was furious to discover that the Danes had taken to their ships again.

William had spent three years trying to assert his authority over England. He had marched north three times in less than eighteen months, chasing enemies who repeatedly eluded him. And whenever he turned south, the garrisons he left behind were wiped out. He needed a 'final solution', something to end resistance to his rule forever. The course he settled on was horrific. Splitting his army into small raiding parties, he ordered the squads to scour the fells and forests where the rebels were hiding and burn them out. They were to reduce the entire region to ashes so that it could never again support a hostile force.

Even in an age renowned for its violence, this was an act of shocking brutality. Food was so scarce after the 'harrying of the north' that the English were reduced to eating horses, dogs, cats and human flesh, the twelfth-century chronicler John of Worcester reported with horror. Orderic Vitalis was also visibly distressed when he wrote his own account of the event. More than 100,000 people – 'helpless children, young men in the prime of life and hoary greybeards' – died alike of hunger, he lamented.

But William hadn't finished. Leaving Yorkshire a smouldering wasteland, he led his troops on a gruelling winter march across the Pennines, the great ridge running like a spine through northern England. Lashed by rain and hail, Orderic Vitalis tells us, the Normans stumbled 'over steep mountains and precipitous valleys, through rivers and rushing streams and deep abysses'. They were weighed down by their armour and weapons, soaked to the skin and half-starved because there was no food to be had by foraging. Yet still the king drove them on, chivvying, encouraging, persuading – always ready to reach out with a helping hand when his foot soldiers slipped on icy paths or struggled to wade through streams swollen with meltwater.

At last the army reached Chester, where the citizens surrendered without a fight, recognising that further resistance was futile. William swiftly followed up by defeating the rebels at Shrewsbury, building yet more castles at Chester and Stafford and ravaging the area. Then he returned to Winchester to celebrate Easter in the spring of 1070. But for some of his mercenaries the hardships had proved too much to endure. Complaining that they could not obey a lord who commanded them to do the impossible, some of them asked to be discharged from his service. Others simply deserted. All William could do was promise that those who stuck it out would be handsomely rewarded for their efforts.

In fact, the end was very close. Although the devastation of northern England didn't completely crush armed opposition to the Normans, only a few vestiges remained. In 1071, Earls Edwin and Morcar escaped from court. Edwin was betrayed and killed, while Morcar fled to the Isle of Ely, where he found an ally in Hereward the Wake, a local freedom fighter who had aligned himself with the Danes. William quickly eradicated this one remaining obstacle. He bought off the Danes and attacked the isle. In October 1071, Morcar surrendered and was carried off to Normandy in fetters. Meanwhile, Hereward decamped to the continent. Five years after the Battle of Hastings, the Conquest was finally over.

The English had suffered horrendously. Thousands had perished in battle and thousands more had starved to death. Many had been dispossessed of their lands, their womenfolk raped, their infants murdered and their homes burned to cinders. Their king had been erased from the records, their greatest warriors destroyed and their way of life shattered.

The Normans, including Osbern, had also endured terrible times. They, too, had died in their thousands, braving Saxon shield-walls and Danish broadswords and defending their castles. They, too, had lived in misery and squalor as they campaigned the length and breadth of the country, struggling across hostile terrain in harsh winters, hunting rebels hidden in mountains and forests, waiting – nerves taut as a bowstring – for a knife in the side or an arrow in the back. But the outcome was quite different. For the English, the Conquest was an unmitigated disaster. For the Normans who survived, it brought territory and treasure. They had played for the highest stakes and prevailed in a world where the winner took all.

2

The Wages of War

Osbern felt a surge of pride as he rode towards Dodleston and saw his castle squatting on the horizon, a dark smudge against the streaky blue of the noontime sky. It was tiny by comparison with some of the fortresses the king had erected. The conical earthen motte on which the keep stood was only ten feet high and forty-three feet wide at the flattened top. Even so, it had taken twenty-five men more than forty days to move the soil.

Osbern had pressed all the peasants in Dodleston and as many as he could spare from some of his other manors into working on the castle. They had begun by digging a deep circular ditch and piling the earth from the ditch in the middle of the circle, but it was slow going when all they had were wooden shovels tipped with iron. Eventually, once Osbern was satisfied that the motte was high enough, he ordered the men to cover it with a thick coat of clay to keep out water and stop the earth from slipping. Then he set them to felling and carting trees to build the keep. He had decided on a simple two-storey tower with a hall for storing arms, food and water on the ground floor and a sleeping space above it, capped by a lookout post on the sloping roof to provide a clear view of the surrounding countryside.

Now the men were digging the bank and outer ditch around the bailey enclosing the motte. Osbern planned to put a well, granary and stable inside the bailey, together with some huts for the servants who would be working at the castle. He also wanted a garden for herbs and vegetables, some fruit trees and a small meadow for a few cows and sheep, so that the castle would be self-sufficient if it came under attack. However, that would have to wait. It was more important to finish the outer ditch and erect a palisade to make the castle secure.

The oats in the fields had already turned yellowish-brown, although the ears hadn't yet started drooping to release their seeds. But Osbern knew that he would soon have to let the men go to bring in the harvest. They would be delighted. He was aware that they resented working on the castle, even though he didn't understand most of what they said.

When William the Conqueror defeated the Anglo-Saxons, he confiscated their estates and introduced a new tenurial system, under which he owned all the land. The king retained some of it for his own use, awarded some of it to the Church and granted the rest to his barons on condition that they swore an oath of loyalty to him and provided him with men for his armies. The barons, in turn, granted part of the land they held to a select group of knights, who likewise pledged their loyalty to their overlord and promised to fight for him. The knights then granted little strips of ground to large numbers of peasants, who worked their lord's fields and gave him a share of their produce. Villeins might farm a hide of land. Bordars held smaller plots, while cottars might have just a few acres with a vegetable patch. At the bottom of the pile were the serfs, who held no land and could be bought or sold like possessions.

Within a decade of the Conquest, William had given much of the country to his barons and they had doled out part of their winnings among their own followers. But it was the threat of another war that produced proof of just how well Osbern fitz Tezzo had fared. In 1085, William learned that Cnut IV, king of Denmark, was planning to invade England. Cnut was reputed to be assembling a huge fleet of longships with the help of his father-in-law, Robert, count of Flanders.

William was in Normandy when he got wind of Cnut's plans. Deeply alarmed, he sped back from the duchy, bringing a large force of mercenaries with him. As soon as he landed, the king called an emergency council. After consulting his advisers, he decided to disperse the troops around the country. He also ordered that all the coastal defences should be strengthened and the terrain near the sea razed to prevent the Danes from pillaging for food. The Danes were a terrifying foe. They could navigate their dragon-prowed ships through water just a few feet deep, jump out and launch hit-and-run raids, inflicting horrific damage.

Shortly before Christmas, William's spies brought news that Cnut had been forced to delay his invasion, so the king let some of the mercenaries go home but kept the rest in England for the winter. He and his advisers also remained on high alert. The festive celebrations at Gloucester Castle, where he was staying, were muted – although he still held a formal 'crown-wearing' ceremony, as he did almost every Easter, Whitsuntide and Christmas. On such occasions, William dressed in a richly embroidered knee-length tunic and wore a gold crown – possibly the diadem encrusted with twelve different gemstones that he had commissioned for his coronation. The king was no dandy, but he understood the importance of ritual: displaying himself in all his majesty, like Christ on his heavenly throne, was a visible reminder of his role as God's representative on earth. And that winter it was more important than ever to assert his authority, since his crown looked so insecure.

Eight days after Christmas, during which he held court and dealt with church business, William reconvened with his counsellors. Next, he sent commissioners 'over all England into every shire and had them find out how many hundred hides there were in the shire, or what land and cattle the king himself had in the country, or what dues he ought to have in twelve months'. He also ordered the commissioners to record how much land and livestock every tenant held and how much it was worth. The Domesday survey (as it was later known) was completed by August 1086 and 'not one virgate of land . . . not even one ox, nor one cow, nor one pig' was omitted, according to the disgruntled author of the *Peterborough Chronicle*.

Ironically, the threat of a Danish invasion had disappeared by that point, with the assassination of Cnut in July 1086. But the lone scribe who collated all the commissioners' findings and drafted the report pressed on with his task. He spent at least a year summarising the returns from six of the seven regions, or 'circuits', into which the country had been divided. Then he stopped, possibly because William was dead. The king had been leading an assault on the French town of Mantes on the frontier with Normandy when he had a riding accident. He had grown very fat and slipped in his saddle while jumping over a ditch. The pommel pierced his stomach, causing internal injuries. William lingered in agony for six weeks, before expiring on the morning of 9 September 1087, and the reek from his bowels was so awful that he was buried with indecent haste. 'He who was once a mighty king, and lord of many a land, was left . . . with nothing save seven feet of ground,' the *Anglo-Saxon Chronicle* rather sanctimoniously reports.

The anonymous author of the Domesday Book simultaneously halted his labours, but he had already accomplished something quite remarkable. Great Domesday, which summarises the first six circuit returns, covers thirty-one counties between the Channel and the Tees.

Little Domesday, which represents an intermediate stage in the drafting process, includes Essex, Norfolk and Suffolk. The two volumes collectively describe the assets of about 8,000 feudal landholders, including Osbern fitz Tezzo.

The Domesday Book reveals the vast redistribution of England's assets that had taken place since 1066. The aggregate value of the area covered by the survey was about £73,000. The Church had managed to retain most of its pre-Conquest possessions and held about 26 per cent of this land, but almost everything else was in Norman tenure. The king was by far the richest person in the country, with estates covering 17 per cent of England. Another 150-200 barons held roughly 54 per cent between them. Native landholders, by contrast, controlled less than 5 per cent – and most of them held only a single manor.

The bulk of England's propertied wealth was now concentrated in the hands of a small circle of Normans who held their territory directly from the crown. However, there was an elite within the elite. Some seventy men held estates worth £100 to £650, while the ten greatest magnates controlled enormous fiefdoms worth £650 to £3,240. Hugh d'Avranches was in this top tier. The king had initially granted him the lordship of Whitby, a desolate spot on the east coast of Yorkshire. But a far bigger prize was soon to fall into his lap. William had originally given Gerbod the Fleming the earldom of Chester. When Gerbod became embroiled in a civil war in Flanders, the king made Hugh earl of Chester instead.

William had already established two new earldoms in Shrewsbury and Hereford and granted them to two of his most trusted advisers. He wanted to form a buffer zone in the Welsh Marches, both to protect his realm from attacks on its western flank and to prevent the Welsh from providing support for any remaining English rebels. With the creation of a third earldom in Chester, he hoped to bolster these defences. Hugh was the ideal man for the job. He soon moved onto the offensive, penetrating deep into the heart of Snowdonia, where he and his knights spilled the blood of numerous Welshmen.

But for all that the earldom carried serious military responsibilities, it was a lucrative source of money. Chester had suffered badly during the Conquest. In 1066, it was a thriving metropolis of about 3,000 people, many of whom earned a living from trade with Ireland. By 1086, more than two-fifths of the 487 houses that were standing 'in the time of King

Edward' had been destroyed. Even so, Hugh netted £70 and a mark of gold per year from leasing out the administration of the city's property rents and taxes, tolls and court fines. As earl of Chester, he also enjoyed a remarkable privilege – the right to hold Cheshire 'as freely by the sword' as the king himself held England by the crown.[1] This meant that he could rule the county as a semi-independent state, although he still had to swear allegiance to William.

Moreover, the earldom was just a fraction of the bounty the king had bestowed on Hugh. He held land in twenty English counties and the Welsh Marches, bringing his combined wealth to more than £1,000. Coffers overflowing from the estates he had received, the earl promptly rewarded his own henchmen by subletting part of his territory. Osbern was among those who benefited from his overlord's munificence – and he must have been a particularly competent soldier to earn the lands he received. He wasn't in the premier league; the best warriors were headhunted by more than one magnate and often held land directly from the king as tenants-in-chief. Hugh also rewarded a handful of men, including his cousin, Robert of Rhuddlan, much more lavishly. Nevertheless, Osbern was certainly in the second echelon.

The Domesday Book shows that Hugh granted him three manors – Newball, Maidenwell and Stainton-by-Langworth – in the prime wool-producing terrain of the Lincolnshire uplands. Osbern also held seven manors in Cheshire – Handley, Golborne, Poulton Lancelyn, Winnington, Appleton Thorn, Grappenhall and Dodleston (which came with fifteen houses in Chester's city centre) – as well as portions of the manors of Dutton, Lymm and Warburton. In addition to this, he held 6½ hides and some woods in Gresford and had leased another hide of land in Edritone, in the Welsh Marches.[2]

But though Osbern's Cheshire holdings were far larger than his Lincolnshire estates, they accounted for only 38 per cent of his total wealth. Much of Cheshire consisted of fells or lowland marshes, which couldn't be put under the plough, while heavy rains combined with claggy soil to reduce the agricultural productivity of the rest. Part of the territory Osbern held had also been completely ruined, reflecting the high price England's northerners had paid during the great battles of 1066. Many of the local men had died fighting Hardrada and his Norwegians at Fulford, leaving their estates unmanaged. The depredations inflicted by William's soldiers – including Osbern himself – had made matters

Osbern fitz Tezzo's Domesday holdings

● Lands Osbern held as Earl Hugh's subtenant   ○ Lands Osbern held as a sub-subtenant

Source: Prosopography of Anglo-Saxon England.

even worse. Appleton Thorn, which had been worth 16s in 1066, was still 'waste' twenty years later.

Like most of his fellow manorial lords, Osbern farmed out the bulk of his land, retaining relatively little 'in demesne', for his own use. He invested in two mills, which were prized as both a symbol of lordly authority and a steady source of income, with a monopoly over the milling of locally grown grain. He also owned a salt-pan – another valuable asset – which was attached to the manor of Maidenwell. Salt was needed for preserving meat and fish; before the discovery of rock salt in 1670 it could only be obtained by evaporating water from inland brine springs or the sea. Lastly, Osbern held a stake in 'two eyries of hawks' in Gresford and hawks' nests were even more precious than salt-pans. A number of rents recorded in Domesday were payable in birds of prey; cash payments made in lieu of hawks show that such birds could fetch as much as £10.

All in all, then, Osbern was a very affluent man. More than 80 per cent of the secular subtenants named in Great Domesday were small fry, with lands worth £5 or less. Osbern's holdings were valued at £19 15s 6d, placing him among the 15 per cent with estates worth between £5 and £45. To put this in context, an unskilled worker earned about 25s a year. So, while Osbern hadn't profited as much as the magnates, he was still wealthier than he could ever have imagined as he sat dreaming of the future in the hot summer evenings of 1066.

Like many a nouveau-riche Norman, he marked his social elevation by splurging on a fortress. The first written reference to Dodleston Castle occurs *c.* 1190, but archaeologists date its construction to the early years of the post-Conquest period, when Osbern was alive. The stronghold he built was a motte-and-bailey castle. A timber keep stood on a flattened mound encircled by a ditch, which was surrounded by a roughly rectangular bailey enclosed by a bank and outer moat. Two fields edged by earthworks formed an additional protective ring around the bailey.[3] There were several advantages to this form of construction. It was quick and cheap. The resulting castle, if it was well sited and carefully built, could also be quite strong. On the downside, wooden keeps were flammable. Moreover, timbers rotted and towers collapsed, so constant maintenance was required.

Modest though it was by royal standards, Osbern's castle occupied a site of considerable strategic significance. Dodleston was the head manor of Atiscros, one of the twelve 'hundreds' into which Cheshire was divided for administrative and judicial purposes. It had previously belonged to Edwin, earl of Mercia. The manor lay on the main road from Chester to Wrexham in north Wales, while the keep itself overlooked the marshlands between the River Dee and the Welsh foothills, forming part of a defensive line of fortifications designed to safeguard Cheshire.

Earl Hugh may have charged Osbern with building Dodleston Castle as part of the military service he owed for his lands. However, the keep was also proof of how far Osbern had climbed; castles were not just a means of defence, they were also a demonstration of might and material success. By 1100, the Normans had erected more than 500 motte-and-bailey castles, most of them in the years immediately after the Conquest. Yet there were relatively few fortresses in Cheshire, compared with other frontier counties. Hugh, it seems, was cautious about giving his tenants too much power. And Osbern had obviously earned a place in the earl's inner circle to be trusted with such a vital military bastion.

Fate had been kind to him in other ways as well. His wife Aeliz had borne him at least five children, including a son to whom he could bequeath his gains when he died. Osbern was suitably grateful. He named his eldest boy Hugh as a tribute to his overlord, and his youngest William as a token of respect for the king. In 1081, when Earl Hugh gave some land to the Abbey of St Évroul, where he was sending his natural son Robert to become a monk, Osbern also granted the abbey the tithes from Newball, the richest of the manors he had received.[4]

The gift served a dual purpose. In 1070, the bishops of Normandy had devised a set of penances for those who fought under William's banner. The papal legate Erminfrid had endorsed the document and the king had almost certainly given it his stamp of approval behind the scenes. The Penitential Ordinance covered acts of violence perpetrated at the Battle of Hastings, during the period preceding William's coronation and immediately after he had been crowned. It decreed that anyone who knew he had killed a man should perform one year's penance for each man he killed, and anyone who had wounded a man but didn't know whether he had killed him should do penance for forty days for each man he had struck. Additional clauses specified the atonement required for homicide committed while foraging for food or looting, rape, violation of church property and other such sins, with heavier penances for those who were motivated solely by greed when they erred.

Given the blood the Normans had spilled in the course of subjugating England, they should probably have spent the rest of their lives on their knees. But those who had fought at Hastings doubtless had no idea how many men they had slain in the heat of battle, so there was a get-out clause. Anyone who didn't know how many people he had killed could do penance one day a week until he died. Alternatively, he could build or endow a religious institution. Thus, in bestowing the tithes from Newball on the Abbey of St Évroul, Osbern presumably hoped both to please his earthly lord and to shed a tiresome burden of contrition.

Osbern also continued to accompany Hugh on his periodic incursions into Wales. In 1081, the earl captured and imprisoned Gruffudd ap Cynan, one of the grandsons of a former king of Gwynedd, who was spearheading resistance to Norman rule in the region. By 1086, Hugh controlled much of north Wales, including Gwynedd, with Robert of Rhuddlan, who held north-east Wales as his vassal. But these spectacular advances ground to a sudden halt in July 1093, when Robert was butchered in a skirmish with a band of Welsh marauders.

The Welsh had landed beneath the Great Orme, a massive promontory at the north-western tip of Caernarfonshire. Leaving their ships beached on the shore, they pillaged the countryside before hurrying back to the coast with their spoils. Robert was taking a midday nap in his castle at Deganwy, about 3 miles from the headland, when word of the raid reached him. He immediately sent messengers to summon help and rushed to the promontory, without even pausing to put on his hauberk. As he reached the top of the headland with the few soldiers he had been able to gather at short notice, he could see the Welsh on the beach below. They were still loading their prisoners and plunder, but the tide was rising fast and it was clear that they would be able to refloat their vessels before reinforcements arrived.

Robert urged his troops to climb down to the beach and attack the Welsh before they could escape, but the men refused, pleading that they were outnumbered. So, enraged beyond reason, he scrambled down the slopes with the one soldier who was brave – or foolish – enough to follow him. As the Welsh saw Robert running across the sand, unarmed and accompanied by a single retainer, they launched a volley of spears and wounded him. However, Robert had a daunting reputation as a fighter and the Welsh were wary of taking him on at close quarters. Keeping their distance, they harried Robert with their javelins until he was brought to his knees. Then they fell on him, hacked off his head and nailed it to the mast of one of their ships, in full view of the horrified locals watching from the cliffs.

Robert's death – and the indignity to which his body had been subjected – came as a painful personal blow to Earl Hugh, since the two had been close friends as well as kin. He had his cousin's remains brought back to Chester and buried in an imposing stone tomb at St Werburgh's Church, where he had recently established a new Benedictine monastery. The loss of one of his strongest commanders was also a serious setback to Hugh's military plans and a major morale-booster for the Welsh, who had suffered greatly at Robert's hands. In 1094, they rose up against the Normans. Gruffudd ap Cynan and his ally, Cadwgan ap Bleddyn of Powys, destroyed the Norman castles in Gwynedd and routed a relief expedition. Meanwhile, the Welsh in the south demolished the new castles at Ceredigion and Dyfed.

The rebellion checked the Normans' progress. In 1095, the Welsh destroyed Montgomery Castle and slew all the soldiers who were garrisoned there. That autumn, William Rufus – who had succeeded his father, William the Conqueror, as king of England – retaliated by leading an army into Wales, but the Welsh hid in the highlands. With neither the resources nor the time to do more as winter approached, Rufus reluctantly abandoned the campaign. In 1096, Hugh, earl of Shrewsbury, led a second army into Wales, although nothing came of it. A third expedition the following year, under the king's command, proved equally fruitless.

Finally, in the summer of 1098, Earls Hugh of Chester and Hugh of Shrewsbury joined forces in a concerted effort to subdue north Wales. They succeeded in pushing the Welsh back as far as Anglesey. Gruffudd and Cadwgan fled to Ireland, leaving the two earls apparently triumphant – until Magnus Barelegs, king of Norway, unexpectedly appeared on the scene. Magnus had been plundering the Hebrides and Isle of Man. But seeing Anglesey besieged as he sailed past with his fleet of six ships, he decided to investigate. The Normans were preparing to defend themselves when the Earl of Shrewsbury, arrayed in full armour, made the mistake of getting too close to the Norwegians as he rode through the shallows. Various reports allege that Magnus took aim, pierced the earl through the eye with an arrow and slew him, although one chronicler rather unkindly claims that it was another man who killed Shrewsbury and then threw his bow to Magnus, saying, 'Well shot, sir!'[5]

The dispirited Normans retreated from Anglesey and Rufus – who was preoccupied with affairs in Normandy – abandoned any further attempts on Wales. When Gruffudd and Cadwgan returned from Ireland in 1099, Gruffudd was allowed to keep Anglesey, while Cadwgan kept parts of Ceridigion and Powys.

The perennial conflict with the Welsh may be one reason why Osbern wasn't among the donors or witnesses listed in the charter in which the monks of St Werburgh's Abbey eventually recorded the endowments Earl Hugh of Chester and his followers had made. Between the foundation of his new monastery in late 1092 and his death in 1101, Hugh showered the abbey with gifts, as well as encouraging his men to give generously. During the mid-twelfth century, the monks compiled a list of the grants they had received.

Osbern's neighbour, Scirard, one of the rare Englishmen to prosper in the early years of the Norman regime, was among those who made donations. Scirard gave the monks various assets, including 'the chapel of Bebington' and 'four bovates of land and the tithes from the same manor'. Bebington bordered Poulton Lancelyn, which Osbern held. Indeed, the chapel lay only a mile north of Osbern's lands and the cleric who served it probably lived in Poulton Lancelyn, where the Domesday Book records the presence of a priest.

Osbern had demonstrated his willingness to support Hugh's pious endeavours when he granted the tithes from Newball to the monks at St Évroul. He had also, as it happens, given some land to St Werburgh's Abbey, showing that he was still alive in the early 1090s when the monastery was established. Yet he wasn't among the retainers who witnessed Scirard's grant. So perhaps he was garrisoned in Wales at the time, or perhaps he had died – killed in combat or felled by disease. The Welsh were redoubtable adversaries. 'The entire nation [is] trained in war. Sound the trumpet for battle and the peasant will rush from his plough to pick up his weapons as quickly as the courtier from the court,' the chronicler Gerald of Wales later noted. Whether Osbern was among the 'great losses of men and horses' the Welsh inflicted on the Normans is impossible to determine. What we *do* know is that when Earl Hugh was laid to rest at St Werburgh's Abbey in July 1101, Osbern was already in his grave.

3

An Undone Land

The interior of the new church at Burwell Priory was a fine piece of work, with plastered walls covered in lively illustrations of biblical scenes and a wooden roof like an inverted ark. A round arch edged in bricks led from the nave, where the congregation stood, to the altar, where the priest celebrated the sacred moment when mere bread became the body of Christ.

The Benedictine monks from the priory attended the daily recitation of the full Office and the principal Mass, clad in their distinctive black habits, but on Sundays everyone in the community came to worship. That Sunday in about 1112 the church was especially crowded. Word had spread that Hugh fitz Osbern planned to settle his disagreement with the sheriff over a meadow in Carlton by giving the disputed land to the priory. The sheriff insisted that the meadow belonged to Burwell Manor. Hugh was equally adamant that it formed part of his own estates, but he had decided it wasn't worth pursuing the argument any further. A number of villagers from Maidenwell had made the three-mile walk across the fields to witness the proceedings on Hugh's behalf – or simply to gawp.

Hugh had asked his mother to perform the ritual placement of the charter recording the endowment on the altar, and Aeliz had dressed carefully for the occasion. She was wearing her best gown, a green robe with embroidery on the cuffs of the sleeves. The rosary of polished agate that Osbern fitz Tezzo had given her as a wedding present hung around her neck. She was still a pretty woman, Hugh thought affectionately, even if she was no longer the slender young bride whom his father had married more than thirty years previously.

Once the service was over, the prior called Aeliz by name. She walked reverently, head bowed, to the altar and laid the charter on it, as tradition prescribed. Robert, a monk from the priory, had drafted the deed and Hugh's two younger brothers, Herved and William, had witnessed it. Josce, Bernard, Ulf, Usquil, Odo the smith and some of Hugh's other tenants had also agreed to attest it for the family, while William the steward, Agemund the forester and various parishioners from Burwell had promised to stand witness for the priory. Robert had inscribed their names in the charter, which he now read aloud in sonorous tones so that the witnesses could hear the details, sniffing self-importantly when he reached the end.

As the congregation filed out of the church, Hugh thanked the men who had come from Maidenwell to bear witness for him. He made a point of talking to them in English. Although his father had only picked up a smattering of the language he himself was fairly fluent, having grown up surrounded by native servants. Of course he wouldn't dream of using anything other than French with family and friends, but being able to converse with his tenants in their own tongue made it easier to oversee his estates.

Ansgot of Burwell founded Burwell Priory in about 1110, after making a pilgrimage to the shrine of St James the Apostle in Santiago de Compostela. On his way back to England he stayed at the Abbey of La Sauve Majeure, near Bordeaux, and was so grateful for the charity the monks accorded him that he decided to set up a daughter house in Lincolnshire. With his wife Eda's approval, Ansgot gave the new priory four churches, a chapel and a cottage in Burwell. 'Hugh of Newball' – Osbern fitz Tezzo's eldest son – attested the endowment.[1]

Ansgot was one of a number of Norman nobles, knights and manorial landholders who established priories in the realm they had conquered, revolutionising the religious face of Britain. In 1066, there were some forty-five Benedictine monasteries in England, concentrated in the southern and eastern parts of the country. Between 1066 and 1150, ninety-five Benedictine and Cluniac houses (where the monks followed a more rigorous version of the Benedictine Rule) were founded, nineteen of them in Wales.

The new monasteries helped to promote a sense of community between lords and their tenants. They also offered a path to redemption. The Church taught that life in the world was sinful, particularly for warmongering knights. One way to be saved was to become a monk. Another was to found or endow a religious house. This secured the prayers of the monks for the donor's soul and comprised a generous act of alms-giving, which atoned for the donor's sins.

Several years after Ansgot founded Burwell Priory, Hugh fitz Osbern made his own gift to the monastery. The record shows that Hugh's 'lady mother', Aeliz, laid the charter on the altar on behalf of her sons and daughters and herself. The sheriff also agreed to abandon all claim to the land 'for the love of God'.[2] Hugh could afford to feel pleased; he had simultaneously managed to mitigate his sins, reinforce his status as a member of the Norman elite and end a quarrel that could have proved very costly.

He wasn't alone in using such a stratagem. A disproportionate share of the assets endowed to the Church in Anglo-Norman England were the subject of litigation, for obvious reasons. The Church was in a much stronger position to take on legal challenges than most individual landholders, Hugh included. He was no baron, even though he had inherited Osbern's estates in accordance with the law of male primogeniture imported by William the Conqueror, which was slowly taking hold among the lesser nobility.

The king had not only redistributed England's landed wealth after seizing the throne, he had also changed the basis on which that wealth cascaded down the generations, a change with almost equally far-reaching consequences. In Anglo-Saxon society, a man's land was typically split among his sons under the principle of 'partible inheritance'. In Normandy, by contrast, there was a dual pattern of inheritance. An ordinary man could divide his estate. However, a noble was required to pass all his inherited property to his first-born son, although he could dispose of his acquisitions – in the form of conquests, purchases and land obtained through marriage – as he wished.

William adhered to Norman custom. In a writ issued shortly after his coronation in December 1066, he assured the burghers of London that 'every child [should] be his father's heir after his father's day'. But when he himself died, he left Normandy (which he had inherited) to his eldest son, Robert Curthose, and England (which he had acquired) to his second son, William Rufus, making no territorial provision for his youngest son, Henry, who simply received 5,000lbs. of silver. Most of the barons copied William's example. Where there was more than one son in the generation after the Conquest, the inheritance generally went to the first-born and the acquisition to the second-born, while any other sons had to provide for themselves or pursue a career in the Church. Alternatively, the Norman inheritance and English acquisition descended as a single estate.

This pattern soon spread to the knightly ranks. The territory bestowed on a noble by his ruler carried the duty to defend it – and preserving an estate intact, rather than dividing it into ever smaller units, made it easier to protect. Moreover, the fewer the men who controlled the nation's military reserves, the more quickly it could muster an army. The leading magnates therefore began to pursue a similar policy with their own followers and, within a century of the Conquest, the law of primogeniture applied to even the humblest military tenancy.

Osbern fitz Tezzo left almost all his acquisitions to his eldest son. A local survey of Lincolnshire landholders conducted between 1115 and 1118 shows that Hugh held the manor of Newball.[3] He also held Maidenwell, which fell outside the scope of the survey but clearly remained in the family because it passed to his heirs. However, Stainton-by-Langworth, the third of Osbern's Lincolnshire manors, was now in other hands. By the late twelfth century, knights enjoyed hereditary rights to the land they held through military service, but in earlier years a lord might stipulate that it be returned when the tenant died. Earl Hugh had obviously made some such proviso regarding Stainton-by-Langworth and when the manor reverted to him on Osbern's death he gave it to Roscelin, one of his other retainers.

So Hugh fitz Osbern had inherited the two Lincolnshire manors that his family still kept. He also seems to have inherited his father's key Cheshire holdings. Sometime before dying in April 1109, Anselm, archbishop of Canterbury, allegedly confirmed the endowments St Werburgh's Abbey had received. His 'testimony' is suspect, but if the monks forged it they were almost certainly drawing on earlier deeds recording genuine bequests. Anselm's charter refers to a house in Chester donated by Hugh fitz Osbern in exchange for half of the manor of Warburton, which Osbern fitz Tezzo held in 1086. The most plausible explanation for this arrangement is that Osbern made the abbey an unrecorded gift of his share of Warburton and that Hugh swapped it for one of the fifteen dwellings in Chester which came with the manor of Dodleston, when he succeeded to his father's lands.[4]

However, neither Hugh nor his brother Herved appears to have had any surviving children. By the mid-twelfth century, the family estates belonged to William fitz Osbern. Given Norman naming conventions, this can only have been Hugh's grandson, a great-nephew or his youngest brother. As the population of England grew, distinguishing labels had become more important. One common way of singling out a man from others with the same first name was to combine his name with his father's; as X son of Y he could be easily differentiated from X son of Z. Thus, if William was Hugh's grandson, his father would have been called Osbern fitz Hugh. Similarly, if he was Hugh's great-nephew, his father would have been called Osbern fitz Herved or Osbern fitz William. But there is no sign of an Osbern fitz Herved or fitz William in the archives, and the only man named Osbern fitz Hugh to feature in contemporary records was the son of Hugh Blundus, baron of Pulford. The absence of any reference to an intermediate generation suggests that William was Hugh fitz Osbern's brother.

William was probably born at least ten years after Hugh. Women were fertile for about two decades – the Conqueror and his wife had nine or ten children over a span of sixteen years, for example – and the deed recording Hugh's gift to Burwell Priory shows that William had at least two sisters as well as two older brothers. Aeliz may also have had other offspring, born between these children, who died as babies. Infant mortality rates were high by modern standards, even in the royal family. Between 1150 and 1500, England's queens produced roughly ninety-six living children. Thirty-four died in their first year, while another twenty-two died before the age of 20. Only forty reached adulthood, despite the better medical care royal progeny enjoyed.

William supported St Werburgh's Abbey, as his father and brother had previously done. In a charter drafted in about 1140-50, he granted the abbey a house in Fleshmonger Lane, one of Chester's main roads and the chief place where the butchers conducted their trade. Some years later, he also gave St Mary's Nunnery in Chester 'two parts of the tithe of his demesne of Golborne [which Osbern held in the Domesday survey] for the remission of his sins and for the soul of Randolph the earl'. The gift was made on the day the earl 'was entombed before the bishop'. Among the witnesses was 'Matilda, the countess', widow of Ranulf de Gernon, fourth earl of Chester, who died on 16 December 1153.[5]

Earl Ranulf – like William – had lived through one of the most turbulent periods in English history as Henry I's daughter, the Empress Matilda, battled with her cousin Stephen for the crown. The Conqueror had passed

England intact to the next generation. The generation after that ripped it asunder in a royal succession dispute. Rightful monarch and righteous usurper, perfect knight and perfidious rogue, the untried young king who finally healed the schism: these were the main players in the 'game of thrones' unwittingly started by Henry himself.

Henry was intensely ambitious and the sudden death of his elder brother, William Rufus, cleared his path to power. On 2 August 1100, Rufus was hunting in the New Forest when his friend Walter Tirel accidentally shot him with an arrow. His body was brought back, blood dripping from the cart, for burial at Winchester Cathedral. Meanwhile, Henry, who had been hunting elsewhere in the forest, rode to Winchester as fast as his horse could carry him and seized the royal treasury. On 5 August, just three days after Rufus's demise, he was crowned king of England, cutting out his eldest brother, Robert Curthose, duke of Normandy.

Robert was away on crusade when Rufus died. As soon as he returned to Normandy, he started mustering an army to enforce his own claim to the throne. In July 1101, he and his troops landed at Portsmouth, but Henry was ready for him and Robert had no stomach for a full-blown fratricidal battle. Much to the disgust of his supporters, the duke caved in without a fight. He agreed to let Henry keep England in return for an annuity of 3,000 marks a year and various other concessions, while Henry promised that Robert should hold Normandy.

The truce quickly fell apart. In late 1103, Robert sailed to England to complain that Henry hadn't honoured his pledge to forgive the duke's vassals for backing his claim to the throne. Henry countered by accusing Robert of other breaches and forced him to surrender his annuity. Then, two years afterwards, Henry reneged on his oath that Normandy should be Robert's and invaded the duchy. In September 1106, he defeated his brother at the Battle of Tinchebray. Robert was captured and kept in confinement for the rest of his extraordinarily long life, while Henry assumed control of Normandy. The landless youngest son had reunited the Anglo-Norman realm and taken all his father's estates for himself.

Henry devoted the remaining twenty-nine years of his reign to defending the dominions he had acquired and the twenty or more illegitimate children he fathered played a major part in his machinations. However, he had only two legitimate offspring: a girl called Matilda and a boy called William. On 25 November 1120, his plans for the empire he had built were wrecked when Prince William drowned while sailing back from Normandy.

Henry had been visiting the duchy and had already organised his return journey. But when Thomas fitz Stephen offered the royal family passage on the *White Ship*, the king encouraged his son to accept the invitation. With its square sail billowing in the wind and its crew of fifty oarsmen pulling on their blades, the *White Ship* was said to be the fastest vessel in the world. According to William of Malmesbury, it could fly 'swifter than a feathered arrow . . . skimming the sea's curling top'. The 17-year-old prince was thrilled at the prospect of sailing on such a magnificent craft.

William and his entourage crowded on board in high spirits, followed by servants staggering under the weight of all the wine they carried. The booze circulated liberally as the prince and his friends partied and, when some of the sailors asked if they could toast William, he blithely ordered fitz Stephen to broach three casks. By the time the *White Ship* weighed anchor night had fallen and everyone was roaring drunk. Then the prince decided to race his father home. Henry had left port several hours earlier and his fleet was already on the open sea, so William urged fitz Stephen to sail as quickly as possible. The inebriated captain needed little encouragement to demonstrate what his mighty vessel could do. But either it was too dark to see or the helmsman was too intoxicated to steer; the *White Ship* hadn't even cleared the harbour when it crashed into a submerged rock. The timber hull shattered, freezing water gushed through the gaping planks and the ship sank within minutes, taking the prince, two of his half-siblings and many leading young nobles with it. Richard d'Avranches, Earl Hugh's only legitimate son and the heir to his earldom, was among the dead.

Hugh and William fitz Osbern must have known Richard reasonably well. But if they mourned his passing, it was with the quiet regret of loyal liegemen, not the wrenching anguish of a bereaved parent. Two days passed before anyone dared break the news to Henry, as he waited increasingly anxiously in England for the prince's arrival. When a tearful young boy finally flung himself at the king's feet and told him about the shipwreck, Henry collapsed. The loss of three of his children was devastating. However, William's death wasn't just a personal tragedy, it was also a dynastic catastrophe.

With no legitimate son to succeed him and no heir from a second marriage hastily arranged in 1121, the grief-stricken king cast around for alternatives. He started by promoting his nephew, Stephen of Blois, who had narrowly escaped sailing on the ill-fated *White Ship*. Stephen was the son of Henry's sister Adela, but with two older living brothers he was hardly an obvious candidate for the English throne. In May 1125, another option emerged. Henry's legitimate daughter, Matilda, who had married the Holy Roman Emperor Heinrich of Lorraine, was widowed. The couple had no children, so the emperor's lands passed to his sister's nephew. Matilda returned to England and during the Christmas of 1126, while the court was at Windsor, the king made his choice. He gathered 'all the most important men in England' around him and made them swear to accept Matilda as their queen when he died. Stephen was amongst the first to promise that he would uphold her claim.

In 1128, Henry also arranged for his daughter to marry Geoffrey Plantagenet, son of the count of Anjou, hoping to forge an alliance that would secure Normandy's southern border. The match was not a happy one. In mid-1129, the couple quarrelled and Matilda left Geoffrey, although Henry eventually persuaded her to return to him. But, in 1135, she fell out with her father as well. Thus, when Henry died in Normandy that December – after eating a dish of lampreys, so the gossip went – Matilda was sulking elsewhere.

Stephen saw his chance and seized the throne, ignoring his oath of fealty to Matilda. His supporters claimed that a woman couldn't rule the country effectively and that it was more important to preserve the nation's stability than it was to honour a forcibly extracted pledge. But far from keeping England on an even keel, Stephen had just fired the opening salvo in a civil war that would last almost two decades.

When news of her cousin's coup reached Matilda, she was pregnant with her youngest son and embroiled in another political dispute. Four years passed before she was ready to invade England, intent on claiming her crown. With the help of her half-brother Robert, earl of Gloucester, Matilda managed to secure south-western England and part of the Thames valley, while Stephen retained control of the south-east. However, neither side could prevail. Then, in February 1141, Stephen suffered a major setback, thanks to the earl of Chester's Trojan-horse tactics. Ranulf had initially supported Stephen, despite the fact that he was Robert of Gloucester's son-in-law. But he was much more interested in preserving and expanding his own power base than he was in resolving the royal feud.

Ranulf's main territorial interests lay in Cheshire and Lincolnshire. He had inherited lands in both counties from his father, who had succeeded to the earldom of Chester when Richard d'Avranches drowned. He and his half-brother, William de Roumare, had also inherited lands in Lincolnshire from their mother, Lucy of Bolingbroke. And Ranulf had long harboured hopes of acquiring Lincoln Castle, where Lucy appears to have held hereditary rights. In late 1140, the earl pounced. He and Roumare sent their wives to the castle when the garrison was nearly empty, under the pretence of paying a social call on the constable's wife. While the ladies 'were laughing and talking', Ranulf arrived, ostensibly to escort his wife and sister-in-law home. Once inside the castle, he and the three men he had brought with him admitted Roumare and his soldiers, who were waiting outside, and forcibly ejected the king's guard.

Hiding his fury, Stephen visited Ranulf and his half-brother in Lincoln, heaped further honours on them and returned to London for Christmas – only to march back to Lincoln secretly before the festivities were over and besiege the castle. Ranulf was taken completely by surprise. But the earl was as resourceful as he was duplicitous. Creeping out of the castle one night, he rode to Chester and sought his father-in-law's help. Together, he and Robert of Gloucester raised an army and returned to Lincoln, where his half-brother was still holding out. On 2 February 1141, they crushed Stephen's troops. The king was captured and carried off to Robert's fortress in Bristol, while Ranulf clinched his victory by sacking Lincoln.

William fitz Osbern must have been among those who rode to Ranulf's aid. The hard-pressed earl called on all his tenants to honour their feudal obligations and brought 'a brave contingent of foot soldiers from Chester to give battle', as well as recruiting a 'fierce mob' of Welshmen. Indeed, William must have been in the thick of the fighting, since it was the knights from Cheshire who finally overwhelmed the king. Led by Ranulf, they dismounted and surrounded Stephen, cutting him off from the rest of his army. Although the king fought ferociously, he was forced to surrender when his sword and battle-axe shattered.

Stephen's captivity brought a brief upturn in Matilda's fortunes. She was proclaimed 'Lady of England' and entered London, planning to have herself crowned queen. However, she soon antagonised the citizens with her hard heart, insufferable arrogance and failure to display 'the modest gait and bearing proper to the gentle sex'. Had Matilda been a man, her autocratic treatment of London's merchant leaders might have passed for a display of regal strength. Lacking that crucial Y chromosome, she was condemned as a harridan.

In July 1141, the hostile Londoners drove Matilda out of the capital. She fled, first to Oxford and then to Winchester, where she found herself besieged by Stephen's wife – another Matilda, but a woman far shrewder than the empress. Queen Matilda had hired an army of Flemish mercenaries to rescue her husband. On 14 September 1141, they routed the Angevin forces – the name by which the supporters of the Plantagenet royal house were known because Geoffrey came from Anjou. Although the empress managed to escape, her half-brother Robert was captured while covering her retreat. Earl Ranulf and his men, reaching the battlefield 'late and ineffectively', hastily withdrew to Chester. Robert was subsequently exchanged for Stephen and, by November 1141, Stephen had resumed the throne.

Meanwhile, Matilda returned to Oxford, which she made her centre of operations. But, by the autumn of 1142, she was in trouble again. Stephen had recovered from a brief bout of sickness, rallied his supporters and was now planning to attack Oxford. Trapped in the castle with a tiny garrison and very little food, Matilda knew she couldn't hold out for long. By December she was desperate – and, determined not to fall into Stephen's clutches, she came up with a bold getaway plan. There was snow on the ground and the River Thames had frozen solid, so Matilda and four of her most trusted knights were lowered from St George's Tower by rope in the middle of the night. Dressed in white to blend in with the snow, they stole across the ice-covered river and walked to Abingdon, where they were able to buy horses and ride to Wallingford. The empress had once again eluded Stephen's grasp.

Ranulf, unreliable as ever, eventually returned to the king's camp, lured by the promise of additional lands – although his reconciliation with Stephen proved very brief. While the Anglo-Norman nobility were tearing England apart, the Welsh had been making marked gains. In 1146, Owain ap Gruffudd, prince of Gwynedd, destroyed Mold Castle, which guarded the pass through the mountains from the Clwyd valley to Chester. The earl called on the king for aid, but Stephen's advisers feared a trap. Ranulf's refusal to return the royal estates he had acquired or to provide hostages for his good conduct reinforced their suspicions. So Stephen had the earl arrested, whereupon the Welsh invaded Cheshire.

Ranulf was forced to surrender several key castles to secure his release, but he clearly believed that Stephen had betrayed him; thereafter, he became one of king's most implacable enemies.

Ranulf's final break with Stephen coincided with several other significant developments. In October 1147, Robert of Gloucester died, removing Matilda's champion from the scene. Robert had proved a brave soldier, honourable adversary and true statesman. He had also been unswerving in his loyalty to his half-sister. With his demise the empress's cause seemed all but extinguished. In 1148, weary and demoralised, she retired to Normandy, leaving her 15-year-old son – named Henry after his grandfather – to carry on the fight.

Henry was precocious. His boyhood had been dominated by his parents' struggle – Matilda in England and Geoffrey in Normandy – to secure his mother's patrimony. Raised in a world of war and intrigue, the young prince had learned to be cunning and cautious, yet courageous and 'constant in adversity'. He was also energetic, fiery and fiercely intelligent, equally at ease in the saddle and the council chamber.

Henry was resolved to recover his ancestral rights. He had already made one attempt in 1147, which failed for lack of resources. In 1149, he made a second bid. At a meeting in Carlisle, he secured David of Scotland's support. Ranulf joined them and swore to help. True to form, the earl struck a hard bargain, extracting a promise that Henry would grant him extensive holdings in the Midlands, including the estates of several lords who had sided with Stephen. But while the prince was preparing to launch an assault on York, Stephen learned of his plans and hurried north with a large force. Dismayed by the strength of the opposition, Henry's new allies refused to do battle and he was forced to flee for his life. The prince had failed again, yet he had acquitted himself very creditably. He had secured two powerful allies. He had also shown that he was brave, quick-witted and a worthy leader, bringing new hope to the proponents of the Angevin cause. In late 1149 or early 1150, Geoffrey of Anjou implicitly acknowledged his achievements by ceding him the duchy of Normandy.

Henry had secured half of his maternal inheritance, thanks to Geoffrey's unflagging efforts; the other still eluded him, but he hadn't given up. For the next few years he was involved in an intermittent war with Louis VII of France and in stamping his authority on Anjou after Geoffrey's death in 1151. Then, in May 1152, he married Eleanor of Aquitaine, whom Louis had divorced only two months earlier – a move that simultaneously scandalised Europe's ruling houses and massively enriched the young prince.

Eleanor was eleven years Henry's senior. Smart and spirited, she had joined Louis on crusade in 1147 and was whispered to have enjoyed amorous liaisons with various men, including Saladin, the Saracen leader. There is nothing more than circumstantial evidence (and even that is slight) to substantiate these colourful stories, but they are indicative of the queen's high profile at a time when women were expected to stay in the background. Eleanor was a medieval celebrity. She also brought Henry immense political power. The marriage – contracted in secrecy because Louis was Eleanor's overlord and feudal custom dictated that she secure his consent – gave the prince control over the whole of south-western France from the Loire to the Pyrenees.

In January 1153, Henry invaded England again, determined to settle the succession dispute once and for all. Both factions had expended huge resources on the conflict and the country was in bad shape after eighteen years of civil war. The full extent of the damage is difficult to assess, but contemporary accounts paint a bleak picture. 'The land was all undone and darkened,' the *Anglo-Saxon Chronicle* tells us. 'Men said openly that Christ and His saints slept.'

Stephen was equally eager to reach a decisive conclusion; however, bad weather and his barons' reluctance to fight obstructed his efforts to face the prince. In the end, it was bereavement – not battle – that brought the king to the negotiating table, when his warlike son Eustace died in August 1153. That November, the two parties hammered out a deal: Stephen would keep the crown for the rest of his life, but Henry would succeed him. On Stephen's death only a year later, Henry assumed the throne of England without challenge.

By then Ranulf was dead – allegedly murdered by William Peverel, constable of Nottingham Castle and one of the people whose holdings Henry had sworn to grant the earl when he acquired the crown. Ranulf and Peverel were longstanding rivals and Peverel was understandably irate at the prospect of losing his lands. Pretending that he wanted to discuss various matters, he invited the earl to his house and served him with poisoned wine. According to the anonymous author of the *Gesta Stephani*, three of Ranulf's retainers 'died on the spot', although the earl recovered after 'long agonies', because he had drunk quite sparingly.

Another contemporary chronicler, Gervase of Canterbury, claims that he succumbed to the lingering after-effects of the poison.

Ranulf's constant scheming had caught up with him, yet William fitz Osbern remained faithful to his overlord till the last. He chose his final tribute carefully; in giving a share of the tithes from Golborne to St Mary's Nunnery, he was supporting the religious house the earl had founded. But the state of his own soul was much on his mind, too. By 1153, he was an old man in his sixties, staring death in the face himself. One thing alone sustained him, his daughter Idonea – the child conceived in his maturity, the child whose birth had come as a bitter disappointment when he longed for a son, the child who had somehow crept into his heart, beaming up at him from her cradle and bewitching him with her gummy smile.

4

What's in a Name?

The great hall was festooned with ribbons and garlands of flowers. A rectangular, two-storey chamber on the ground floor of the manor house, it served as reception room, dining room and administrative centre. In winter, when the fire was lit, smoke curled up from the central hearth to the blackened beams in the roof and the air could become quite stuffy. But that day the weather was glorious and the air redolent with the mouth-watering scents of a feast.

Idonea had walked to the church in her new blue dress, the traditional colour of purity. Helto and his brothers were already waiting by the lichgate, enjoying the sunshine. Bride and groom exchanged vows outside the church door, with Helto standing on the right and Idonea on the left – because woman was 'formed out of a rib in the left side of Adam'. Then they entered the church and knelt at the altar to receive the priest's blessing.

Afterwards, the wedding party ambled across to the manor house for the banquet. Helto and Idonea sat with their families and the guests-of-honour in chairs at the high table at one end of the great hall, while less important people squeezed onto benches at trestle tables set up around the perimeter. When everybody was finally seated, after much good-natured jostling, the house servants started bringing in the food. They'd been cooking for days – cutting, chopping, slicing and pounding, baking, boiling, smoking and roasting, until the kitchen sweltered. But what a meal they'd produced! There were jellies, pies, fritters and stews; chickens, rabbits and hares; a hog, spiced with cloves and ginger; whiting, plaice and pike; several different kinds of cheese; and fresh and preserved fruit.

The guests tucked in greedily, spooning portions of food onto wooden plates – or trenchers of stale bread, if they sat at the lower tables. Meanwhile, two servants walked around the room filling the visitors' cups from large pitchers of wine and ale. Both flowed freely and by the end of the meal many people were tipsy. There were appreciative belches and one man farted, earning himself an elbow in the ribs. It was considered rude to break wind, pick one's nose or scratch one's flea bites at the dining table.

Later, as night was drawing in, Idonea's female friends escorted her to her chamber, where they undressed the nervous bride, combed her hair and put her to bed. Helto's brothers helped him strip down to his shirt in the solar before bringing him to Idonea's room. There was much teasing and bawdy advice before they departed, leaving the couple alone.

The Anglo-Norman rules of inheritance favoured men over women. At a time when the ability to defend one's land and provide military service was crucial, a single woman or widow was vulnerable; she could be abducted and forced to marry or dispossessed of her estates altogether. A few intrepid women took up arms. In 1090, Isabel de Conches 'rode armed as a knight among the knights', when her husband Ralph went to war with William, count of Evreux. Similarly, in 1119, Juliana, one of the natural daughters of Henry I, fired a crossbow at her father when she was defending the citadel at Bréteuil. And during Stephen's chaotic reign, the doughty Dionisia de Grauntcourt unhorsed a knight 'with one blow of her spear'. But such women were rare – and often regarded with ambivalence. Even as Isabel was praised for her courage, she was blamed for fomenting the war with William of Evreux by making disparaging comments to his wife. And when Juliana leapt from the tower in which her father had confined her after she surrendered Bréteuil Castle, Orderic Vitalis gleefully reports that she 'fell shamefully, with bare buttocks' into the frozen moat.

For obvious reasons, then, most women didn't hold land in their own right. In a world where men were assumed to be strong and women weak, it was patently undesirable to entrust the 'fair sex' with the defence of territory. However, if there was no legitimate son, a daughter could inherit her father's estates – and, by 1166, about fifty-four baronies had descended through the female line.

Idonea was among the small group of women who held land themselves. In the decades immediately following the Conquest, the military duties a vassal owed his lord were decided on an individual basis. But by the mid-twelfth century 'knight service' had solidified into a quota system under which landholders were obliged to provide a specified number of knights for forty days a year, when summoned by their lord. A list of feudal fiefdoms shows that Idonea held the manors of Newball and Maidenwell for 'three knights' fees'. Further evidence of her status comes from a grant made after she was widowed. Idonea gave the nuns at Barlings Abbey in Lincolnshire 'two perches of land' and asked them to pray for the souls of her family, including her parents, her husband, 'lord Helto', and his ancestors. She expressly stated that the endowment was part of her 'patrimony and heritage'.[1]

There is no record stating precisely what that patrimony was and there were no hard and fast rules on female succession. Nevertheless, there *were* certain norms. Firstly, daughters usually inherited before collateral male kin (uncles, nephews or male cousins). Secondly, if there was one daughter, she inherited everything; and if there were two or more daughters, the estates were divided between them. Idonea succeeded to all the lands held by Hugh – and subsequently William – fitz Osbern, suggesting that she was William's only child.

She was born in the late 1130s. But although she was affluent, Idonea's position in life was still very restricted. She had grown up in an era when the Church and aristocracy defined the place of women and the one point on which they agreed was that women were inferior to men. For the clergy, woman was both Eve and Mary: the temptress responsible for man's expulsion from Paradise and the mother of Christ the Redeemer. For the aristocracy, she was both an ornament and an instrument for managing its chief asset, the land.

That said, women were slowly becoming more conspicuous as they played a growing role in the transmission of territory. The preservation of the main line at the expense of younger sons had increased the likelihood of female succession. The daughter of an upper-class family could also expect to receive land or other assets as her marriage portion and a bride acquired certain rights in her husband's estates. Her husband could assign a particular piece of property as her dower. Otherwise, she was entitled to one-third of his holdings at the time of the marriage, when he died. Widows retained their marriage portions where there were children from the union and could claim their dower irrespective of whether the union was fertile. If an unscrupulous husband disposed of his wife's dower while she was alive, his heir was required to recover the lands on her behalf or give her 'reasonable lands' in exchange.

So single heiresses and widows were increasingly useful bargaining chips, as Henry I recognised. At his coronation in 1100, he made several significant concessions to his magnates to buy support for his precarious hold on the throne. Rights over women, and the limited rights they could claim for themselves, featured heavily in the so-called Charter of Liberties. Henry wanted his tenants-in-chief to consult him before marrying off their female relatives, but he promised that he wouldn't forbid any marriage unless it was to one of his enemies. He also vowed to grant custody of minors to their widowed mothers or next-of-kin and to seek advice when arranging the betrothal of orphaned daughters – an allusion to the feudal rule under which the crown acquired guardianship of the underaged heirs of deceased tenants-in-chief, including the right to dispose of them in marriage. This was a valuable privilege, since the hand of a wealthy girl could be sold for a lot of money. In addition, Henry undertook to let all childless widows keep their marriage portions and dowers and not to force them to remarry against their will. Lastly, he exhorted his magnates to treat the daughters and widows of their own tenants in the same way.

The civil war, which had formed the backdrop to Idonea's childhood, reinforced the growing prominence of landed women within the political elite. The war hinged on whether a woman could rule the kingdom directly and the opposition this idea engendered explains much of the bad press Empress Matilda elicited. But the empress wasn't the only strong woman to emerge from the wings. When Stephen was incarcerated at Bristol Castle, it was his wife who kept his wilting cause alive. Queen Matilda possessed more tact than her rival, although she was quite prepared to use violence when required – and because she was acting in her husband's name, she was perceived as a paragon of wifely virtue. Thus, Idonea must have grown up hearing stories about two indomitable women, even if the one was reviled and the other revered.

However, well-bred young ladies in twelfth-century England still had just two options: marriage or the nunnery. The second of these routes could bring a woman considerable influence, if she managed a convent with large estates. Abbesses exercised much the same legal powers as other landholders. They could preside over manorial courts, approve the sale and lease of lands and litigate on matters pertaining to the property under their control. They also reigned supreme inside their own walls, with the right to punish the nuns for any infractions and authority over both the servants and the priest officiating in the abbey.

A few brilliant women, such as Hildegard of Bingen and Héloïse of the Paraclete, even earned great esteem as intellectual heavyweights. Hildegard wrote nine books, including three massive volumes of visionary theology, composed music and invented an alternative alphabet. She preached openly before mixed audiences of clergy and laity, with the full approval of the Church authorities, and was consulted by bishops, popes and kings. Meanwhile, Héloïse developed the Paraclete into a thriving convent with six daughter houses and conducted a scholarly correspondence with her former lover, Peter Abelard.

But though the religious life offered women far greater freedom from male authority than they could enjoy in the secular sphere, they were still constrained. The female orders were enclosed and many convents were poor. Moreover, while some women chose to become nuns, many had no alternative. Younger daughters of the nobility often ended up in convents because their fathers couldn't afford the dowry needed to marry a member of their own class. Other women were banished to nunneries because they were illegitimate, disfigured or backward, because grasping relatives wanted their wealth or as a form of punishment. Predictably, a number of those who had been forced to take the veil strayed from their vows; in 1177, for example, the convent at Amesbury was dissolved because the abbess had borne three children and the nuns had fallen into 'evil ways'.

Idonea's path in life was already determined. As an only child, she would have been expected to carry on the family line and prepared for marriage. All girls learned spinning, sewing and weaving, as well as domestic skills such as how to cook, brew, preserve fruit and make herbal remedies. In addition, those of well-to-do parentage were taught etiquette and household management. They needed to understand the dictates of hospitality, oversee the production of food and clothing, supervise childrearing and organise the movement of the household when it was required. They also had to be able to run the manorial estates, since this task fell to a wife when her husband was away fighting.

Some nobles sent their daughters to convents to be educated, but most girls learned at home by watching and copying their mothers. Those of gentle birth frequently married before adolescence, with matches arranged by their parents. Girls might be as young as 12, boys as young as 14 – although a marriage wasn't legally binding until it had been consummated and this was usually delayed until the girl was 15.

There were often big age gaps between husband and wife, too. Many teenaged girls were wedded to men in their thirties, but the age difference could go either way. Empress Matilda and Eleanor of Aquitaine were both more than a decade older than their second husbands, for example. Political expediency produced toy boys and trophy wives alike.

Idonea probably married in about 1153, while William fitz Osbern was still alive, and the husband he chose for her was Helto de Boisdele. Helto's parentage is obscure, but the surviving records suggest that he had four brothers: Alan, John, Osbert and William. Alan and John witnessed a deed in which Idonea purchased some land in Reston, near Maidenwell. Osbert and William were monks at Poulton Abbey, a small Cistercian monastery founded by Robert Pincerna, Earl Ranulf's hereditary butler (one of several important household offices that passed from father to son). They both attested a deed in which Robert's daughter, Matilda, gave Poulton Abbey an annuity. A fifth family member features in the next generation. Ralph – possibly Alan's son – was also on good terms with Matilda; he witnessed the charter in which she endowed Poulton Abbey as well as the marriage settlement she subsequently made for her daughter Margery.[2]

So Helto's family was socially connected with one of the leading members of Earl Ranulf's *ménage*. Indeed, the earl may have had a hand in arranging his nuptials. Ranulf had entered the marriage market in a big way in the 1140s, as the civil war weakened royal control over the sale of wealthy brides. He brokered various matches to consolidate his power base and reward his most loyal supporters. And he would certainly have wanted to ensure that Idonea married someone who could provide the military service he required.

But though the marriage was arranged, it seems to have been quite successful. Idonea gave birth to the couple's first child, Hugh, named (like Earl Ranulf's son and heir, Hugh de Kevelioc) after Earl Hugh of Chester, in the mid-1150s. A second boy, called Alan after Helto's brother, followed. Two more sons, William and Richard, brought up the rear. William's name harked back to the Conqueror (and thus to Idonea's father), while Richard was probably called after Henry II's third legitimate son, Richard. Naming children after their senior godparent of the same sex or a member of the royal family was common practice.

Helto, Idonea and their growing brood divided their time between Lincolnshire and Cheshire, although the journey from Newball to

Dodleston was long and difficult. It entailed crossing the desolate, windswept moors of the Peak District at the southern end of the Pennines, leading packhorses along steep dirt trails, or taking a protracted detour around the fells. In winter, snow often blocked the passes, but even in summer the weather was changeable. Heavy rain or clouds might suddenly descend, blanketing the hills in mist.

Between 1154 and 1157, Helto made a gift to the nuns at Sempringham Priory in Lincolnshire, a tiny community of monks and nuns established by Gilbert of Sempringham in 1131. Some years later, Helto granted the Abbey of Louth Park, a small Cistercian house located at the foot of the Lincolnshire Wolds, the right to 'twelve cartloads of branches' a year from the woods in Newball 'for fuel or fencing'. He and Idonea also gave St Werburgh's Abbey 2s a year out of the rents they received from their estate in Chester. And towards the end of his life, Helto donated another 8s a year to St Werburgh's, 'with his body' – as a post-mortem gift to accompany his burial at the abbey. Two shillings were to come from the tithes of Handley Church and the rest from his goods.[3]

Apart from making various religious endowments himself, Helto witnessed several charters on behalf of other men anxious to pave their way to heaven. In the mid-1150s, he affirmed a grant by Richard fitz Alvred to St Mary's Nunnery, when Richard's daughters Beatrice and Joetta joined the convent as postulants – the first stage in preparing for life as a nun. And, in about 1174, he attested a deed in which Roger de Mowbray gave Fountains Abbey the forest of Nidderdale.[4]

Helto also witnessed a charter for Hugh de Kevelioc, who had inherited the earldom in December 1153 at the age of 6.[5] And when Welsh raiders invaded his lands in 1170, the earl came to his defence. The *Annales Cestrienses* – a chronicle compiled by the monks at St Werburgh's Abbey – relates how Hugh 'slew a great multitude of Welshmen' in a bloody skirmish 'near the bridge of Baldert' (Balderton, a mile north of Dodleston Castle). Then the elated earl had their heads lopped off and piled in a mound outside the leper hospital south of Chester, as a demonstration of his military prowess and a warning to other Welsh brigands.

However, there is no evidence that Helto supported Hugh when the discontented young earl joined the baronial revolt against Henry II in 1173. The rebellion began as yet another squabble within the dysfunctional royal family. Henry planned to split his dominions between his four surviving sons. England, Normandy and Anjou were to go to the eldest, another Henry, who was crowned king of England in 1170. Richard was to get Aquitaine, Geoffrey, Brittany and John, Ireland. But Henry didn't give the boys any real power and, by 1172, the Young King (as his eldest son was known) was clamouring for his heritage.

In March 1173, the Young King fled the English court to join his father-in-law, Louis VII, in Paris. His brothers, Richard and Geoffrey, soon followed him, egged on by their mother. Eleanor had repeatedly spoken up for her sons, but she had her own reasons for feeling aggrieved with Henry. After John's birth in 1166, Henry had taken other women to his bed. He had also ignored his wife's rights in Aquitaine, most notably when he held court in Limoges in February 1173 and accepted the homage of the count of Toulouse, as if Eleanor didn't exist. The queen resented being sexually and politically sidelined.

The mutinying princes provided a focal point for Henry's enemies, the earl of Chester among them. Hugh de Kevelioc had never succeeded to the lands and castles Henry II had promised his father, Ranulf, before coming to the throne. Two decades later, Hugh was simmering with anger. A number of other magnates with similar complaints were equally ripe for revolt and flocked to the Young King's cause. But though the uprising was initially successful, Henry was far richer, more experienced in warfare and more politically astute than his adversaries. Hiring a large force of mercenaries, he crushed the opposition in a series of campaigns conducted over the next year. He also captured Eleanor, who was making her way to the French court disguised as a man. Richard tearfully submitted to his father in August 1174, while the Young King and Geoffrey surrendered the following month.

Henry was lenient in victory – to everyone except his wife. He kept Eleanor in custody until he died, apparently unable to forgive her disloyalty, despite all he had done to alienate her. But he pardoned the unruly barons and granted his sons a bigger income. Hugh de Kevelioc, who had surrendered when the castle of Dol-de-Bretagne fell to the king's forces in August 1173, was imprisoned for a while. Henry also confiscated his lands, although he restored them to the earl in 1177, after deducting a fine.

Helto seems to have distanced himself from the earl's actions. The deed he attested for Hugh de Kevelioc is undated, but the list of witnesses suggests that it was drafted between 1163 and 1173, before the revolt took place. Thereafter, Helto didn't attest any documents on his overlord's behalf. He had survived one civil war and probably had no desire to see another; indeed, his various appearances in the Pipe Rolls imply that he now preferred the law to the lance.

The Pipe Rolls were annual summaries of the king's income and expenses, written on large parchment sheets that were then stitched together and rolled up tightly so that they resembled organ pipes. They record a wide range of payments to the crown, including feudal dues and taxes, 'offerings' for the right to pursue legal disputes and penalties imposed by the itinerant justices. The Rolls show that, between 1169 and 1171, Helto was involved in a disagreement with Ralph de Normanville, who held the manors of Fulstow and Stainton-by-Langworth. Normanville's wife was a descendant of Roscelin and his sons, who had acquired Stainton after Osbern fitz Tezzo's death, but Osbern's heirs obviously still begrudged its loss. By 1174, Helto was back in court suing Conan, son of Elias, another Lincolnshire landholder. And in 1175-76, he was at odds with 'Stephen the chamberlain'. Stephen agreed to pay the royal treasury '100 marks and one destrier' – or war horse – to resolve the argument. Helto settled his own bill the following year.[6]

In 1174-75, Helto also entered into a protracted tussle with William de Percy over a debt of £5. The treasury was chasing Helto for the money, but he claimed that it was Percy's liability. Helto lost the case, although he was clearly reluctant to pick up the tab. It was still outstanding in 1179-80, when the Pipe Rolls state: 'Helto de Boisdele owes 100s for two knights' fees against William de Percy. But he is dead and he was not in the right.'[7]

Helto's body was presumably interred at St Werburgh's Abbey, as he had requested. Idonea also paid the nuns of Barlings to pray for his soul, attaching a wax impression of her seal depicting the Lamb of God to the charter. Meanwhile, her brother-in-law William vacated his cell at Poulton Abbey to help wrap up Helto's worldly affairs. He gave 'the lands which belonged to Helto de Boydell' to Thomas Golborne in a deed witnessed by Alan and Ralph. The wording of the charter implies that Helto owned the lands in his own right – although, if this was the case, they must have been very modest, since Idonea's estates formed the bulk of the family's fortunes.[8]

Yet Helto left a legacy that was to prove far more lasting than material wealth. By the 1130s, most Anglo-Norman families had begun using surnames as a means of self-identification. A few families used patronyms (names beginning with the word 'fitz'), which evolved into true surnames as a single ancestor's name replaced the switch of names from one generation to the next. Others used bynames, some of which were distinctly unflattering. So, for instance, William Belet – literally, 'William the weasel' – founded the line of Belets who became the king's hereditary butlers, while Thomas Becket, archbishop of Canterbury, derived his appellation from his 'beaky-nosed' father, Gilbert Becket, and one Domesday tenant went down in history as the unforgettable Humphrey Goldenbollocks. However, the majority of families used toponyms, often recalling their Norman roots even as English gradually became their mother tongue. Helto adopted this last approach. His ancestors probably came from Bois d'Elle, a hamlet on the banks of the river Elle, just north of the town of Saint-Lô in Normandy. And his surname – eventually anglicised to Boydell – was the moniker by which the family would henceforth be known.

After her husband's death, Idonea retired into the background, although feudal custom and the law both entitled her to recover control of her patrimony. In fact, medieval wives enjoyed greater independence as dowagers than at any other stage in their lives. Well-heeled widows might come under pressure to remarry, since neither Henry I nor his barons always kept the promises made in the Charter of Liberties. But those who had enough money could buy permission to remain single or choose their next husbands. In 1130, Lucy of Bolingbroke paid the king 500 marks for the right not to wed for five years. Earl Ranulf's wife, Matilda, who had played the decoy in his ruse to take Lincoln Castle, also remained single when he died; indeed, she was a widow for thirty-six years. And during her son's minority, she acted as his representative on various occasions. However, there is no further sign of Idonea in the records, suggesting that she died shortly after Helto or ceded her estates to her eldest son.

Hugh was now about 25 years old. He had already witnessed the deed in which his mother bought some land in Reston. He had also attested two charters for Hugh de Kevelioc and his retinue, while he was still a minor.[9] Youth wasn't an obstacle to witnessing. If anything, it was an advantage, since one problem with relying on the testimony of witnesses to prove the authenticity of a deed was the fact that such evidence was only available while the witnesses were alive.

Some Anglo-Normans tried to overcome this drawback by including boys among the witnesses – and whipping them to create an enduring memory of the occasion!

Like his father, Hugh didn't attest any of the earl's later charters. But Hugh de Kevelioc's tenure was very brief; he was only 34 when he died in June 1181, to be succeeded by his 11-year-old son, Ranulf de Blondeville. Mindful of the earl's treachery, Henry II kept the boy under close supervision in Normandy. Nevertheless, by 1 January 1189, when the king knighted him at Caen, Ranulf had been recognised as earl of Chester (the third to be called Ranulf) and had taken formal possession of his estates.

The Boydell family simply transferred their loyalties to their new overlord. During the next two decades Hugh and his brothers witnessed at least ten charters for Ranulf III, including a deed in which the earl guaranteed the citizens of Chester 'all the liberties and free customs' they had enjoyed under his ancestors. Hugh attested seven charters, Alan and William two, and Richard five (with more than one sibling attesting some deeds).[10] The brothers also witnessed various charters for senior members of Ranulf's household.[11]

These included a deed in which John de Lacy, hereditary constable of Cheshire, gave Hugh de Dutton authority over the county's lowlife. Ranulf had been fighting the Welsh and, finding himself besieged at Rhuddlan Castle, managed to send John a message requesting aid. There were only a few men-at-arms in Chester – too few to rescue the beleaguered earl – but it was fairtime in the city. And the annual summer fair, held for three days at the Feast of St John the Baptist (20-22 June), was a major event. Hundreds of people from all over Cheshire had flocked to Chester to buy the more exotic items that were unavailable at weekly markets and to have some fun. Musicians, acrobats, jugglers, fire-eaters, sword-swallowers and rope-walkers were performing in the marketplace before the abbey gate and an excited crowd had gathered to watch them. So the resourceful John de Lacy marshalled a ragtag band of 'coblers, fidlers, merry companions, whores and such routish company'. Then he led the rabble on a 28-mile march to Rhuddlan Castle to liberate the earl. When the Welsh saw a large relief force bearing down on them from the rear, they took fright and fled.[12]

Ranulf, as amused as he was grateful for this unorthodox rescue, rewarded the constable by granting him hereditary command of all the fiddlers and shoemakers in Chester. And John divided the spoils with his steward, Hugh de Dutton: he retained control over the shoemakers and their business but gave Hugh power over 'all the lechers and whores'. As late as 1498, the Duttons still claimed an annual payment of four bottles of wine, a lance and 4½d from every minstrel and 4d from every whore in Cheshire at the Feast of St John the Baptist.[13]

However, the Boydells had also provided the earl with faithful service and their turn was soon to come. In the mid-1190s, Ranulf granted 'Hugh Boydell of Dodleston' the right to build a road at Latchford and levy a fee for passage across the River Mersey between Runcorn and Thelwall. This wasn't as picturesque a perk as the one Hugh de Dutton had received, but it was nonetheless valuable. In 1349, the tolls from the river crossing at Latchford and a fishery there were worth 13s 4d – enough to buy twenty gallons of Rhenish, the costly white wine from the Rhineland favoured by the upper classes.[14]

Hugh Boydell made a number of grants as well. In about 1190, he gave Robert Lancelyn all the lands in Bebington Poulton, Appleton and Hale that Robert's father had previously held. In return, Robert promised to help defend Dodleston Castle by providing two soldiers for forty days in wartime, and four men for six days every third year to repair the earthworks at the castle. Several years later, Hugh also gave Adam de Dutton all his land in Warburton in exchange for his homage and military service. His brothers Alan, William and Richard all attested the deed, as did John Boydell (probably Hugh's nephew). Hugh had already leased the manors of Grappenhall and Latchford to William fitz Sampson, but William was in arrears for the military service he owed. So the two men came to an amicable arrangement under which William resigned the manors to Hugh for 7 marks.[15]

But by 1200 Hugh was dead and, since he had no children of his own, he left everything to his brother Alan. Soon afterwards Alan settled a dispute with Bullington Priory in Lincolnshire concerning a gift from his parents. He confirmed the endowment Helto and Idonea had made, on condition that he could exchange three fields for some meadow land in 'Miklehale'.[16] He also gave the churches of Handley and Dodleston to St Werburgh's Abbey and, sometime before 1204, he attested a grant of lands to Lincoln Cathedral with his brother Richard.[17] According to the twelfth-century chronicler Roger de Hoveden, a massive earthquake worse than anything 'since the beginning of the world' had split the cathedral 'from top to bottom' in April 1185. The following year, the new bishop – Hugh of Avalon, a Carthusian monk from Burgundy – had begun a huge reconstruction programme that would transform the cathedral into one of the tallest buildings in Europe.

However, Alan's health was now deteriorating. In late 1204, when the Abbott of Louth Park sued him, claiming that the monks were no longer receiving the cartloads of wood Helto had promised them, Alan failed to appear in court. In January 1205, the sheriff of Chester reported that he was ill in Yorkshire, so the case was postponed until May. Alan's attorney then asked for permission to view the wood and, in the Michaelmas term, Alan gave half a mark for royal consent to reach an agreement with the abbot. The case was finally settled on 3 November 1205, when Alan confirmed via his attorney that he acknowledged the validity of Helto's charter. The Abbott of Louth Park agreed to pay him 3 marks of silver in return.[18]

By then, Alan was on his last legs and wondering how best to dispose of his lands. Rather than keeping them intact, he took the unusual step of dividing them – having concluded, perhaps, that managing such a scattered estate was too troublesome. He left his lands in Lincolnshire to his elder son, Sir John Boydell. But in an undated deed witnessed by Sir Ralph Mainwaring, justice of Chester (who left office *c.* 1207), he granted Dodleston 'in fee and mastery, with all its appurtenances in Lymm', to his brother William.[19] Then he, too, died. Thus, by 1206 or 1207 at the latest, William Boydell had inherited the family's Cheshire estates – and this presented him with a serious dilemma.

5

Family versus Flock

Handley Church was empty, save for the solitary figure kneeling on the packed-earth floor in front of the altar, arms raised above his head in supplication. William's knees were sore and the muscles in his shoulders were burning, but he tried to ignore the pain as he prayed to God for guidance. Was it really so sinful, he wondered, to want the material pleasures manorial lordship would bring. He knew what Gilbert of Sempringham had done in the same situation, as both a parish priest and the heir to his family's estates. When his father died in 1130, Gilbert didn't abandon his flock. On the contrary, he had used his wealth to found a religious order – which William's parents, Helto and Idonea, had supported when they endowed Sempringham Priory. But Gilbert was a man of exceptional piety. In fact, he had just been canonised.

William had become a clergyman because he was a younger son lacking lands and military talent. Now, with the death of his brother Alan, he had acquired the family holdings in Cheshire and the chance to live the sort of life he desired, not the life imposed on him by order of birth. He sighed deeply and dropped his arms to make the sacred sign of the cross, thankful for the relief it brought his throbbing shoulders. He had to believe this opportunity was part of God's divine purpose, not the Devil's doing – for he was not, he admitted to himself, the stuff of which saints are made.

The Normans had reinvigorated England's monasteries after the Conquest, but they had effected an equally big change in the structure of the secular clergy who cared for the souls of the populace. In Anglo-Saxon times a fairly small network of minster churches served large territories. By the middle of the twelfth century there were numerous little parishes, each typically serving a single village. Since it was often the local lord who had built or endowed the church, he retained the advowson. In other words, he decided who should hold the living.

Most patrons, including the Boydells, regarded the advowson as an item of personal property they could sell or use to support their relatives. As lord of part of the manor of Warburton, Hugh owned half of the advowson of Lymm. When the benefice fell vacant, he arranged for his brother William to become one of the two rectors there. By 1200, William also held the benefice of Handley, another living within the family's control. While he was 'clergyman and parson of Handley', William confirmed the grant of 8s that his father had made to St Werburgh's Abbey, presenting the charter before the altar at the abbey in person.[1]

Neither Lymm nor Handley was a rich benefice. In an ecclesiastical tax assessment conducted in 1291-92, Lymm was valued at £4 13s 4d, while Handley didn't feature on the list at all, possibly because it was too poor to warrant a levy. Moreover, Alan had already given the church at Handley to St Werburgh's Abbey, which meant that most of the tithes from the parish now went to the monks. However, despite the fact that he held no lands, William maintained his standing amongst the local lords. Apart from witnessing various charters for Earl Ranulf III, he attested a grant from Simon de Messingham to Lincoln Cathedral, probably made soon after the earthquake had devastated the minster in 1185. He also witnessed a charter in which Richard de Lyons confirmed a grant made by Adam, the chamberlain of John de Curcy, earl of Ulster, to St Mary's Nunnery in Chester.[2]

But when his brother Alan died, William's fortunes were transformed. Alan's sons, John and Robert, had both settled in Lincolnshire, where they gave generously to Barlings Abbey. John and his wife Loretta donated a large tract of wood in Maidenwell and part of the forest of Newball, together with a meadow, some pasture land and free passage through the forest. Meanwhile, Robert granted the monks two bovates of land in Newball, which his brother had given him, in return for their prayers and 1lb of pepper, to be paid to John and his heirs every year. Neither John nor Robert showed any sign of wishing to return to Cheshire.[3]

William's younger brother, Richard, was probably dead as well by 1207. Richard had witnessed a grant by Bertram de Verdun, one of Henry II's key counsellors, sometime before 1192, when Verdun perished in the Holy Land. He had also attested a gift to Lincoln Cathedral in about 1202-04.[4] But there is no further trace of him, suggesting that he

The Boydell estates in Cheshire

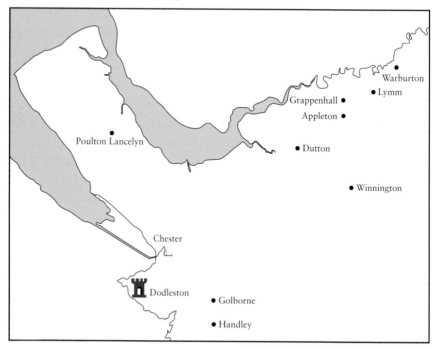

Source: Prosopography of Anglo-Saxon England.

died soon afterwards. Thus, William now held the whole of his mother's Cheshire estates, uncontested.

Richard had left a son, John, who was still a minor[5] – and life was fragile, as the calamities that had recently befallen the royal family clearly demonstrated. Henry the Young King had succumbed to dysentery in 1183, while his brother Geoffrey had been trampled to death by a horse in a tournament three years later. So, when Henry II died in July 1189, the throne went to his son Richard, whose military feats had earned him the accolade 'Lionheart'. But Richard had also died in April 1199, when an arrow wound, incurred while he was besieging the castle of Châlus in the Limousin, turned septic. The kingdom had accordingly passed to his youngest brother, John.

If three of the king's adult sons could die within sixteen years, placing the future of the entire Boydell family on the shoulders of a single youngster would be risky. Besides, even if William loved his nephew, he may well have wanted a son of his own – a son to whom he could bequeath the lands that had at last come his way. So William faced a quandary. On the one hand, he was a clergyman responsible for the spiritual care of his flock. On the other, he was a manorial lord with earthly duties and a family name to preserve. How could he reconcile these demands?

Most parish priests in eleventh-century England were married, even though canons requiring priests to be celibate had existed since the fifth century. But William the Conqueror was determined to stamp his authority on the Church. He wanted both to consolidate his grip on England, believing that heaven and homeland were intimately connected, and to improve the moral conduct of the clergy. In 1070, William persuaded Pope Alexander II to send the Benedictine monk Lanfranc to England as archbishop of Canterbury.

Lanfranc had resisted the appointment, pleading that he couldn't speak English and that the natives were barbarous, but Alexander II overruled him – and Lanfranc was nothing if not dutiful. Resolving to be 'a new Englishman', as he put it in a letter to the pope, he embarked on the task of reforming the English Church. Between 1070 and 1076, he held five councils to correct various ecclesiastical wrongdoings and, at the Synod of Winchester in 1176, he made a first cautious move to enforce clerical chastity. The synod decreed that parish priests who were already married could keep their wives. However, unmarried priests could no longer marry and any man who wanted to be ordained would have to publicly declare that he was celibate. Lanfranc hoped to ease the transition by gradually eliminating clerical marriage, but he was rapidly disabused of his hopes. The clergy continued as before.

Lanfranc's successor, Archbishop Anselm, made several other, equally vain, attempts to enforce clerical celibacy. Archbishop William de Corbeil renewed the attack at the Councils of Westminster in 1125 and 1127, and the Council of London in 1129. In August 1129, Corbeil also threatened to remove married priests from their benefices. But he left Henry I to enforce the decree, with predictable results. When the diocesan bishops dispersed, the *Anglo-Saxon Chronicle* notes, the priests 'kept their wives by the king's permission', completely ignoring the archbishop's diktat.

Many priests deeply resented these attempts to alter the rules, as they saw it. Henry, archdeacon of Huntingdon, was an especially eloquent critic. As the son of a priest himself, he had particular reason to feel aggrieved by the slur on his parentage, but he was by no means alone in his opposition. Some priests simply disobeyed the order to put aside their wives; others went on strike. The outraged families of the abandoned wives also caused trouble in a number of instances – and where protestations failed, bribery often worked.

Yet sentiment in England and Europe was slowly changing. In 1123, Pope Celestine II had passed a decree invalidating all marriages contracted by clerics in higher orders. This decree was repeated at all three of the councils Corbeil convened and, in 1175, Archbishop Richard of Dover took up the cudgels once more. At the Council of Westminster in May 1175, the synod issued a definitive prohibition on married clergy. The ban drew on a decree recently issued by Pope Alexander III and was worded in extremely uncompromising terms: 'If any priest or cleric in holy orders, having a church or ecclesiastical benefice, openly has a whore and after being warned once, twice and thrice, does not dismiss his whore, and does not expel her from his presence completely, but rather marries her, persisting in his filth, then he shall be stripped of every office and ecclesiastical benefice.'[6]

The increasingly harsh language used by the Church authorities and the fact that they had widened their target from married priests to the partners of those priests – now vilified as harlots, not wives – was finally taking effect. There was more still to do in eliminating marriage among the lower parish clergy, as distinct from those serving in cathedrals; between 1200 and 1300, clerical celibacy was a recurring theme at English synods. Even so, the Church had made great progress in imposing chastity on a defiant priesthood.

It had simultaneously, of course, robbed many clergymen of their sexual appeal, particularly ordained priests from the upper classes hoping to find partners from their own circle. There were exceptions, like Hugh Puiset, treasurer of York and later bishop of Durham, who conducted a long-term affair with Alice, daughter of William de Percy, lord of Topcliffe (with whom Helto Boydell had wrangled over two knights' fees). But Alice herself was illegitimate and such exceptions were infrequent. Moreover, a liaison of this nature could never produce a legal heir. Before 1100, many wealthy priests publicly acknowledged their sons in charters and other documents. Between 1150 and 1200, the number of upper clergy known to have had children declined dramatically – although the number of other young male relatives they claimed to have rose significantly. Pope Alexander III wasn't fooled. According to Gerald of Wales, he responded sardonically: 'The Lord deprived bishops of sons, but the Devil gave them nephews.'

So, if William wanted to perpetuate his line, what could he do? There was, in fact, a process via which monks, nuns and ordained clergy could be released from their vows: they could apply to the Apostolic Penitentiary in Rome. Alexander III had set up this 'tribunal of conscience' to deal with sins deemed so heinous that only the papacy could absolve those who had committed them. But it also considered requests for release from certain vows.

The pledges a Christian made fell into two categories: simple vows, such as an undertaking to fast for a certain period; and solemn vows intended to last a lifetime. While simple vows were a matter for the local ecclesiastical authorities, solemn vows fell under papal jurisdiction. Vows of chastity came into this second category. A petitioner could ask the Apostolic Penitentiary to be released from his commitment or have it commuted to some other kind of pious work. He had to show that he was unable to observe the original vow because of an impediment such as sickness, or for political or ecclesiastical reasons. If he could do so, the Penitentiary had the power to commute even the most serious of oaths.

However, applying to the Apostolic Penitentiary was not for the faint-hearted. And what was already a difficult procedure was about to become even harder, as relations between the pope and king of England reached an all-time low. The two had quarrelled over which of them had the authority to choose a new archbishop of Canterbury after the death of the previous incumbent in July 1205. Lay rulers had traditionally made such appointments, but the reformist agenda had bolstered the power of the papacy. King John wasn't about to cede his rights – and in Pope Innocent III he faced a man every bit as intransigent as himself.

John was autocratic, spiteful and an abject failure as a monarch. Almost immediately after the death of his brother Richard, he had renewed hostilities with France, but he wasn't the military superstar his brother had been. By August 1204, the French had seized his parents' dominions in Anjou, Maine and Poitou. Worse, they had occupied Normandy, the land of the Conqueror himself. The fates of England and Normandy had been entwined for 138 years. John's failings as a war leader had severed that link. For the Boydells and many other descendants of Norman immigrants who held no estates in the duchy, the loss of the motherland was symbolic. William had never even set foot there. But a number of magnates still had strong political and territorial connections with the duchy. These were the king's intimates and they made no secret of their rage. Mortified by the capture of his family's continental possessions, John was in no mood to see his authority in England eroded.

The king favoured John Gray, a clerk who had served him loyally since his accession to the throne and whom he had made bishop of Norwich. The monks at Canterbury Cathedral preferred their sub-prior, Reginald. They secretly elected Reginald and sent him to Rome to be confirmed. When the king discovered what they had done, he was furious. He immediately went to Canterbury and bullied the monks into choosing Gray as their new archbishop. Then he sent letters to Rome informing the pope that Gray had been elected.

In May 1206, John learned that Innocent had cancelled Gray's election. Concerned by the conflicting accounts he had received, and by rumours of John's browbeating tactics, the pope had decided to review the situation himself. That December, he finally heard the case, after summoning some of the monks from Canterbury, as well as representatives of the king, to present their respective sides of the argument. He concluded that the monks, alone, had the right to choose a new archbishop. But when he asked which man they wanted, they were divided. Some still supported Reginald, while others now backed Gray. Since they couldn't agree on a candidate, Innocent appointed his own nominee, Stephen Langton, instead.

John reacted swiftly. He issued a proclamation declaring that anyone who acknowledged Langton as archbishop would be considered an enemy and ordered that the monks of Canterbury be expelled from England. Four days later, the sheriff of Kent sent the monks packing. Innocent promptly excommunicated the offending sheriff, but in a bid to end the conflict he asked three leading English bishops to visit the king and beg him to change his mind. If John stuck to his decision, they were to impose an interdict on the whole country. Confronted with the threat of an ecclesiastical go-slow, John hit out even harder. He swore to evict all the prelates from his realm and confiscate their property. Indeed, according to the thirteenth-century monk Roger of Wendover, anxiously observing events from his cell at St Alban's Abbey, the king even threatened that he would send England's prelates to Rome 'with their eyes plucked out and their noses slit'.

The bishops temporised, knowing that the king was quite capable of appropriating their estates, even if he didn't dare mutilate them. In January 1208, John also backed down and offered to accept Langton's appointment, provided that the pope guaranteed his right to approve all future episcopal elections. But when the papal emissary came to London in March, he made it clear that Innocent would never accept such a compromise.

On Sunday, 23 March 1208, the interdict was announced from every pulpit in every church in England and Wales. No priest was to conduct any service, apart from baptisms for the young and absolutions for the dying. There could be no celebration of the Mass, no marriages in church, no anointing of the sick, no burials in consecrated ground. And even though baptisms could be conducted, they could only take place behind closed doors. These stringent terms were eased slightly over time. Nevertheless, for the next six years, most people were deprived of all but two sacraments, their churches sealed and silent.

More to the point for any man who wanted to be released from his religious vows, the climate was hardly conducive to a favourable hearing by the Apostolic Penitentiary. In 1210, Innocent stopped one case before the Papal See until the conflict with the king had been resolved, and there is no evidence that any English suitors took their cases to Rome during the interdict. Thus, if William Boydell was an ordained priest, his chances of securing permission to leave the religious life and marry were looking bleak.

However, many parsons never bothered to become ordained, preferring to stay on the lower rungs of the clerical ladder as doorkeepers, readers, exorcists or acolytes (the so-called minor orders). Precise numbers are impossible to determine because ordination lists weren't kept in the twelfth century. But in fourteenth-century Yorkshire only half of all rectors were ordained and there is no reason to think the situation was very different 200 years earlier.

Clerics in minor orders could marry, as long as they weren't members of cathedral communities. But only ordained priests could celebrate Mass and most parishes couldn't afford to support an acolyte as well as a priest. Since William came from a well-to-do family, this wasn't as big an obstacle as it would have been to a man who was wholly reliant on his benefice. So it is feasible that he deputised to a rector and never took orders himself.

However, if William wasn't ordained, another question arises. Masculinity was closely linked with sexual virility in twelfth-century England. Why, then, did a man who was free to wed choose not to do so until he was in his early to mid-forties? One possibility is that William's relatives put pressure on him to stay single. Landowning families struggled to preserve the integrity of their holdings and sometimes forced their younger sons to delay or shun marriage. True, Richard, the youngest of the four Boydell siblings, had married. But William may have been willing to strike a deal with his older brothers, such as promising to remain a bachelor in return for the right to a future share of the family's estates.

Alternatively, William may have been homosexual and, though the Church was cracking down on clerical marriage, it often turned a blind eye to same-sex relationships. At the Third Lateran Council in 1179, the papal authorities outlawed 'that unnatural vice'; guilty clerics were to be 'expelled from the clergy or confined in monasteries to do penance', while laymen were to be 'completely separated from the society of the faithful'. Yet there was no real change in ecclesiastical practice regarding homosexuality throughout the thirteenth century.

One way or another, then, William was in a difficult position when it came to safeguarding the future of his family line. If he was an ordained priest, he had to secure permission to put aside his vows and the only jurisdiction with the authority to do this lay in Rome. If he was an unordained cleric and single because of his sexual preferences, he had to wed and bed a woman. And if he was single as a result of family pressures, he had to find a suitable wife – fast. Fortunately, this was a much easier challenge for a man who had just inherited half of the family estates. For William *did* marry, with or without dispensation, and neither the legality of the marriage nor the legitimacy of his offspring ever came into question.

William's bride was Alice, the teenaged daughter of Hugh and Agatha de Dutton. Hugh was a neighbouring manorial lord and the great-grandson of Odard de Dutton, another Norman bounty hunter. Hugh d'Avranches had granted Odard part of the manor of Dutton. By 1086, Odard also held the manors of Aston by Sutton and Higher and Lower Whitley, together with a moiety of the manor of Weston and lands in Halton.

Dutton was about 8 miles south-west of Grappenhall as the crow flies and the two families were already friendly. Earl Hugh had given Osbern fitz Tezzo the other part of the manor of Dutton, so the Boydells and Duttons had a mutual stake in the area. Hugh Boydell had subsequently granted Hugh de Dutton's youngest brother, Adam, his half of the manor of Warburton, in exchange for a payment of 12s a year and help in manning Dodleston Castle. And various family members on both sides had witnessed a number of charters together.[7]

Thus, Alice was a logical choice – and she came with a generous marriage portion, as two subsequent lawsuits show. The first case explicitly states that Hugh de Dutton gave William 'the manor' of Nether Whitley, while the second refers to '13 messuages [dwellings], 100 acres [of arable land and] 20 acres of wood in Nether Whitley which Hugh de Dutton gave to William Boydell in free marriage with Alice, his daughter'.[8]

Seen from the viewpoints of Hugh and William, this was a very satisfactory deal. The two families were cementing their alliance with ties of kinship and William was getting a bride young enough to bear children. Alice, of course, had been brought up to expect such an arrangement, although how she felt privately at the prospect of marrying a man at least twenty-five years older than her is another matter. Nevertheless, William was still capable of begetting an heir; within the next few years the couple had a son called William.

Now that he was ensconced as head of the Boydell family, William also endorsed several agreements made by other family members. He confirmed the donation of Handley Church that his brother Alan had made to St Werburgh's Abbey. He reiterated his father Helto's grant of lands to Thomas fitz William (Thomas son of William Golborne), which his brother Hugh had likewise sanctioned. And he gave Liulf de Twemlow, the English sheriff of Cheshire, part of the manor of Winnington in return for his homage and military service.[9]

In addition, William made a number of religious endowments of his own. He granted Poulton Abbey, where his uncles Osbert and William had been monks, a farmhouse in Dodleston, with a field in Balderton attached to it. Some time later, he added 'pasture for 40 mares, 40 cows, two teams of oxen, 200 sheep and a place of safety for all [the monks'] cattle feeding in Saltney for four days and nights'.[10] Both these gifts must have been made before 1214, when Earl Ranulf III moved the monks to the newly founded Dieulacres Abbey, just outside Leek in Staffordshire. Isolated as it was on the very edge of the boundary with Wales, Poulton Abbey had come under repeated attack from the Welsh.

William continued to support the monastery when it transferred to Leek. Soon after the monks moved there, he granted them another piece of land in Balderton. He also witnessed a deed in which the abbot gave some land in Pulford to Richard fitz Richard in exchange for a toft – or homestead – and other property.[11] By then, however, the interdict had been lifted and the king was treading more carefully in his dealings with the Church.

John had alienated many of his magnates with his brutality and licentious behaviour; it was one thing to grope their hapless maidservants, quite another to molest their wives and daughters. He had also become increasingly nervous about the risk of a French invasion, particularly after uncovering a baronial plot to murder him in August 1212. The two leading conspirators had fled to France – where Philip II was preparing a great offensive.

Under mounting political pressure, John realised that he had to settle with the pope. On 13 May 1213, he agreed to accept Stephen Langton as archbishop of Canterbury. Two days later, he ceded England and Ireland to the papacy for a feudal service of 1,000 marks, declaring that he wanted to hold the two countries as the pope's vassal. Some of his magnates were appalled by John's decision to surrender sovereignty to a foreign power, but the climbdown was politically astute. Innocent immediately called on Philip of France to halt his plans for invasion – and he obviously had God's ear. When Philip, infuriated by the pope's change of heart, pressed on with his plans and attacked Flanders, John responded by sending English forces to help. On 30 May 1213, the earl of Salisbury and count of Boulogne surprised Philip's entire fleet lying at anchor in the Zwyn estuary and destroyed it.

Another year passed while the king negotiated with the papal authorities over the compensation he owed the Church for the revenues he had expropriated. After months of haggling, they agreed on the sum of 100,000 marks of silver – although, predictably, John later reneged on his promise. Finally, on 2 July 1214, Innocent formally removed the interdict on England and Wales. At long last the church bells could peel again, the general populace could attend Christian services and the dead could be buried in hallowed soil.

John was soon to need a Christian burial himself, as his reign drew to its disastrous close. Between 1214 and 1216, the French had defeated his forces at the Battle of Bouvines and the English barons had clipped his royal wings, demanding that he agree to the political reforms embodied in what would later be known as Magna Carta. The king had also become embroiled in a baronial war when he tried to wriggle out of the pledges he had made and had seen French invaders land in England at the invitation of the magnates who opposed him.

On the night of 18 October 1216, John arrived at Newark Castle in Nottinghamshire. Wracked by dysentery and exhausted by the unremitting pace at which he had been riding on campaign around the country, he had to be carried in on a litter. A great gale was howling around the castle walls as the abbot of Croxton was summoned to the king's bedside to hear his confession and administer the last rites.

Far away in Cheshire, William Boydell was also failing. He was probably dead by 1217, at which point his in-laws stepped in to sort out his widow's future. Alice was still a young woman. She was also entitled to a dower of as much as one-third of William's estates and was thus an attractive asset. Yet her second husband, Hugh de Brexes, was much less affluent than her first. Hugh witnessed a grant of lands in Brimstage *c.* 1200-08, but the paucity of references to the Brexes family suggests that it was among the lesser local gentry.

So why did Alice marry 'down'? Her kinsfolk hadn't come under pressure from the earl of Chester to wed her to one of his retainers, for Ranulf III had just pledged that he would do no such thing. Shortly after King John had been forced to seal Magna Carta, the earl issued a charter granting his subtenants their own set of rights. In the Magna Carta of Cheshire, drawn up between March 1215 and October 1216, he promised that when a man died, his widow could 'peacefully occupy his house for 40 days' and 'neither the lady nor the heir shall be married where this would involve loss of rank, but by the favour and assent of their family'.

Presumably, then, the Duttons agreed to the match – albeit with reservations. The marriage went ahead after Hugh's brother, Richard de Brexes, covenanted to treat Hugh's heirs 'by Alice, daughter of Hugh de Dutton', as his own heirs. The line-up of witnesses to the deed included Alice's uncles, Adam de Dutton and Hugh de Massey, and her first cousin Geoffrey, as well as Philip de Orreby, justice of Chester.

Alice's family had clearly twisted arms and come out in full force to protect her interests.[12]

It is tempting to wonder whether Alice also demanded a say in choosing her next spouse. Hugh de Brexes may have been less prestigious than William Boydell, but he had one crucial advantage over his predecessor: he was much the same age as Alice. Hugh was still alive *c.* 1245-50, when he attested a charter recording the sale of some land in Hulme Walfield, suggesting that he was born *c.* 1190-95 – long after William. Having buried one decrepit husband, Alice doubtless had no desire to be forced between the sheets with another.

6

The Path of Chivalry

Gringolet's tail swished back and forth. The stallion was a magnificent beast, easily the equal of his namesake, the great destrier belonging to Sir Gawain in the stories about King Arthur and his knights of the Round Table. But he was restive, sensing his master's tension. William Boydell had recently turned fourteen and been promoted from page to squire. Now he was learning how to wield a lance – and though he was an accomplished rider, he was struggling with the quintain. In theory, it was simple: you galloped towards the post in the middle of the tiltyard, hit the shield fixed to one end of the revolving crossbar at the top of the post and then raced away to avoid being walloped by the weighted sack on the other end, as the crossbar swung round. In reality, it was fiendishly difficult.

William and his fellow squires had been taught how to hold the lance properly, aligned with the forearm and tucked close to the body so that it didn't slide back under the armpit on impact. They'd also practised on the wooden training horse with wheels, dragging each other around the tiltyard until they were panting for breath. But they'd soon discovered that striking the shield without getting clouted by the sack and knocked out of the saddle was even harder when they were mounted on highly strung stallions than it was when they were perched on the training horse.

Gringolet snorted, pawing the earth restlessly. Then the master-of-arms beckoned to William, signalling that he was next. Swallowing hard, William kicked his horse forward, reins loosely gathered in his left hand and lance locked in place. Gringolet hurtled towards the quintain, the powerful muscles in his hindquarters bunching and flexing as he accelerated, and William struck the shield with a satisfying thunk. He spurred Gringolet on, but from the corner of his eye he could see the sack veering towards him. A few seconds later, a thump between his shoulder blades sent him flying through the air and crashing to the ground.

William lay dazed and winded. He could hear the master-of-arms yelling at him and the other squires jeering, but black spots were dancing before his eyes. Eventually he staggered to his feet, fighting off a wave of nausea, and looked around for his horse. Gringolet was studiously investigating a clump of weeds at the foot of the fence enclosing the bailey.

Sometime between 1229 and 1232, Sir William Boydell witnessed a deed in which Einion de Burton gave a plot of land in Pulford to Dieulacres Abbey in Staffordshire.[1] More than a decade had passed since the death of his father – years William had spent completing the strenuous training required to win his sword and spurs. In the late eleventh century, the term 'knight' simply denoted a mounted warrior. A man who could afford to keep a horse enjoyed a certain cachet; he was one of the cavalry, not just a grunt. But many knights were landless and made a precarious living as mercenaries in the retinues of greater men. By the early thirteenth century, several forces had transmuted knights into members of the social elite.

The changing attitude of the ecclesiastical authorities was one factor. Where, formerly, the Church had condemned knights as men of violence, it increasingly saw them as defenders of the faith – a sentiment that was reinforced by the First Crusade. In 1095, Pope Urban II launched a campaign to recover Jerusalem. Princes and knights from all over Western Europe took the cross and voyaged to Palestine. On 15 July 1099, they captured the Holy City, bringing it back under Christian rule for the first time since 637.

A growing sense of knightly solidarity contributed to the ennoblement of the profession. Knights gradually became more fashion-conscious, copying aristocratic modes of dress and participating in military games. Tournaments were popular in England by the 1140s, although they were illegal until 1194. But that didn't stop illicit gatherings: in 1186, for example, the future King John presided over a joust outside the walls of Chester, while he was waiting for a ship to Ireland, and the excited citizens rushed out to watch. Knights also developed their own rite of passage – a ceremonial 'girding' and blow with the flat of the blade on the candidate's shoulder – strengthening perceptions of knighthood as an exclusive order.

The idealisation of the knight in literature had a similar effect. The bloodthirsty brute of the past was transformed into a chivalrous warrior. Brave, courteous and gallant, he protected Christians, upheld justice and always strove to do the right thing. Indeed, in the romances of Chrétien de Troyes and Marie de France, the knight was indelibly recreated as an Arthurian hero who battled monsters, rescued damsels in distress and searched for the Holy Grail.

The increasingly prominent role knights played in service to the crown completed this metamorphosis. Originally, the knight answered to the baron who employed him – and thus only indirectly to the king. But at the Assize of Clarendon in 1166, Henry II explicitly acknowledged knights as a distinct social faction. Ten years later, at the Assize of Northampton, he went further and charged the knights of each hundred with reporting those suspected of serious crimes to the itinerant judges he had appointed. Thus, by the end of the twelfth century, knights had made the transition from hired swords to seigneurs and stalwarts of local justice. There was a clear hierarchy. A small group of titled magnates stood at the pinnacle, followed by lesser magnates, their retainers (the 'superior' knighthood) and county knights. Nevertheless, knights now formed a subset of the English aristocracy.

William's training reflects this transition. Most youths, whatever their background, played at being knights, fashioning swords and spears from branches. There was even a game known as *chevalers* that involved taking two plantain stalks and hitting them against each other, the winner being the boy who knocked the head off his rival's stalk. But attaining true knighthood entailed serving a long military apprenticeship.

When William turned 7 – the age at which medieval people reckoned infancy ended – he was sent away to serve as a page, possibly in the household of his feudal overlord, Earl Ranulf III. Leaving home could be a traumatic experience. Orderic Vitalis described how his father sent him from Shropshire at the age of 10 to become a monk at the Abbey of St Évroul. He departed, 'a weeping child', never to see his beloved father again. Perhaps William also shed silent tears for his dead father and absent mother in the privacy of the dark.

Wherever he was sent, William was taught the social skills expected of a page, including how to wait at table, carve the meat and present his master with a goblet of wine on bended knee. He also learned how to ride, groom a horse and wield a blade, using a wooden sword to practise with his fellow pages. By the time he was 14 he was proficient in fencing, falconry, horsemanship and hunting. At that point he was made a squire and began the gruelling exercise regime required to make him strong enough to fight in chain mail. Cased in armour, he ran long distances, turned somersaults and rehearsed vaulting into the saddle without touching the stirrups. He also trained with the sword, spear and bow and practised at the quintain, where many an inexperienced young squire was unseated to howls of laughter.

However, a squire's training didn't finish in the tiltyard. He was also apprenticed to a particular knight and tasked with tending his horses, arms and armour. William spent long hours kicking his master's chain mail around in a barrel of sand and vinegar to scour between the links, and polishing and oiling the helmet before storing it. On top of that he had to study strategy, support his master in tournaments and hone his understanding of etiquette.

The culmination of all this hard work was the ceremony at which he graduated to knighthood at about the age of 21. In its simplest form, initiation entailed being 'girded' or 'belted' with a sword. The lord who was conferring the honour strapped a sword and scabbard around the candidate's waist, drew the sword and dubbed him with a gentle tap on the neck or shoulder. But the ritual had become more elaborate and more overtly religious under the influence of the Church. William was probably expected to take a purifying bath and hold a night-long vigil in the castle chapel.

Most dubbings were held on important feast days and relatives often attended the ceremony. Sadly for William, Alice didn't live to see her son knighted. By 1230, Hugh de Brexes had married Maud Venables, the widowed sister of William Venables, baron of Kinderton – as evidenced by a grant of lands in Pickmere to Maud's nephew.[2] But William seems to have enjoyed a warm relationship with his stepfather and half-brother Hugh. Step-parents were regarded with suspicion; a meagre portion of bread was known as a 'stepmother's slice' and tales of wicked step-parents abounded. Yet a number of deeds show that William stayed in touch with his stepfamily.[3] So maybe Hugh and his son went to see William knighted and joined him at the lavish banquet that took place afterwards.

William had already endorsed all the endowments his father had made to Dieulacres Abbey in a formal deed of confirmation. Hugh de

Brexes had witnessed the document – partly, perhaps, because William was still a minor at the time. Soon after reaching his majority, William dealt with another pressing piece of business. Sir Geoffrey de Dutton had been anxiously seeking a promise that William would let the Duttons carry on subletting Warburton. On 16 August 1233, William authorised the continuation of the arrangement Hugh Boydell had reached with Adam de Dutton. He and his stepfather also witnessed a grant by Robert de Pulford, lord of Pulford. And when John le Scot confirmed his predecessors' gifts to St Werburgh's Abbey, after inheriting the earldom of Chester from his uncle Ranulf in November 1232, William was among those who attested the deed.[4]

For the most part, though, he was busy soldiering. In an underpopulated county on a vulnerable border there was always plenty to do, despite the fact that Cheshire was enjoying a period of unprecedented peace. The county remained calm when a small group of barons led by Richard Marshal, earl of Pembroke, rebelled against Henry III's heavyhanded attempts to exert his authority. Under the malign influence of Peter des Roches, bishop of Winchester and the king's former tutor, Henry had misappropriated various estates and given them to the bishop's cronies – following, it seemed, in the footsteps of his father, the notorious John. In late 1233, Marshal rose up in protest, but the majority of magnates stayed neutral. And when Marshal died in April 1234, the revolt fizzled out.

Relations between Cheshire and Gwynedd, the most bellicose of the old Welsh princedoms, had also been unusually cordial for some years. Llywelyn ap Iorweth, better known as Llywelyn the Great, ruled the whole of Gwynedd. In 1205, he had married John's illegitimate daughter Joan, a union that enhanced his status as well as giving him a powerful link with the English court. However, Llywelyn had his sights on a much grander goal: he wanted to create a 'principality' of Wales, in which he alone paid homage to the king of England, while all the other native rulers paid homage to him. In 1211, John forcibly curbed him, but by 1217 Llywelyn had created a federation of native Welsh lords and controlled southern Powys and Montgomery. Then, in 1218, he negotiated a truce with Earl Ranulf III, cementing the deal with the marriage of his daughter Helen to John le Scot in 1222.

The harmony between Cheshire and Gwynedd lasted even when Llywelyn backed Marshal in his revolt against Henry III and when John le Scot died unexpectedly in June 1237, allegedly poisoned by Helen.

But when Llywelyn himself died in 1240, Gwynedd was plunged into chaos. Llywelyn had decided that Dafydd, his son by his wife Joan, should be his heir. This meant overturning the Welsh laws of inheritance, which placed legitimate and illegitimate sons on an equal footing, and cutting out his illegitimate eldest boy, Gruffudd. By 1237, Gruffudd had taken up arms against his father, so Llywelyn – now paralysed and unable to oppose his son – asked for Henry's protection.

Henry was happy to accept Dafydd as Llywelyn's heir, provided that all the Welsh rulers paid homage to him directly. Dafydd agreed to these terms and, when Llywelyn died, he swore allegiance to the king. But Gruffudd refused to abandon his claim, so Dafydd tricked his half-brother into attending a peace council and imprisoned him. This was too much for Henry. When Gruffudd's wife, Senana, begged for his help, the king promised to secure Gruffudd's release and divide Gwynedd between the half-brothers in accordance with the 'custom of Wales'. In August 1241, he recruited the support of various native rulers and invaded the princedom. Faced with overwhelming odds, Dafydd caved in and freed Gruffudd. Then Henry changed his mind: he let Dafydd keep the whole of Gwynedd but insisted that the area between the Rivers Dee and Conwy (known as the Four Cantrefs) belonged to England. He annexed the castles of Deganwy and Dyserth to secure his grip on the region and shipped Gruffudd off to the Tower of London as a hostage for Dafydd's good behaviour.

North Wales in 1241 after Henry III's annexation of the Four Cantrefs

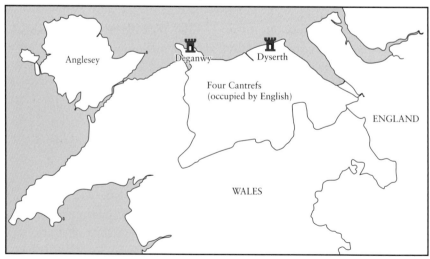

Dafydd felt deeply aggrieved. He resented the loss of the Four Cantrefs and, when Gruffudd died in March 1244, he was no longer constrained by Henry's implicit threat to partition north Wales. Gruffudd had tried to escape from the Tower one night, using an improvised rope of sheets, tapestries and tablecloths, but he was stout and the rope snapped under his weight, sending him plummeting to his death. Within weeks of hearing the news, Dafydd made overtures to the king of France and offered to become a papal vassal, thereby asserting his independence from Henry. He also adopted the title 'prince of Wales'. In early 1245, Dafydd stepped up his efforts and the king retaliated at last by launching an attack on Gwynedd from his base in Chester. The English army, led by Henry, reached Deganwy Castle at the end of August, but Dafydd had razed it to the ground before surrendering it in 1241. Sir William Boydell, who had been sent to check up on 'the munition of the castle' in June 1245, was one of the first English soldiers on the scene.[5]

Conditions at the ruined fortress were bleak as the English struggled to rebuild it. Forced to live in tents and clad only in lightweight summer clothing, William and his fellow soldiers were perpetually cold. They were also hungry because there was insufficient food. 'A farthing loaf now costs 5d,' one noble complained in a letter to a friend, which the thirteenth-century chronicler Matthew Paris later cited in his history of England. Moreover, the troops had to maintain a vigilant watch all the time for fear of the Welsh. On one occasion, the same noble reported, the Welsh captured a number of English knights, planning to imprison them. But when they learned that the English had slain some of their aristocrats they hanged the knights, chopped off their heads, 'tore their miserable corpses limb from limb and threw them into the water'. The English revenged themselves by decapitating nearly 100 Welshmen in a follow-up skirmish.

At last, in late October 1245, after completing the re-fortification of the castle, Henry made plans to withdraw to England. But before retreating he commanded his army to burn everything in sight. He even instructed the men to destroy the crops in the Marcher provinces and bordering parts of Cheshire to prevent the Welsh from stealing food. Homeless and starving, the wretched Welsh died in their thousands over the following winter. Dafydd's sudden death at his manor of Aber in February 1246 demoralised the survivors still further, ensuring that there would be no more trouble for some years.

In April 1247, Henry negotiated a settlement with Gruffudd's two eldest sons, Owain and Llywelyn, since Dafydd had no children. He let the brothers keep Gwynedd and pardoned them for all previous acts of war – on stringent terms. They were forced to cede the Four Cantrefs in perpetuity and required to provide military service, the first time such a condition had been imposed on the lords of Gwynedd. Henry also demanded that they pay him homage and that all the other Welsh lords did likewise. There was to be no independent Welsh state.

As a precautionary measure, Henry continued to maintain a strong military presence in the Four Cantrefs – and William carried on serving in a martial capacity. On 2 July 1250, he was one of four knights commanded to go personally to the castles of Deganwy and Dyserth, as well as the king's castles and manors in the county of Chester. They were to assess the state in which Sir John Grey, the outgoing justice of Chester, had left the castles, including how well each was 'munitioned with arms and other necessaries', and report back to Henry in writing. Just how significant a role William played in the defence of Cheshire is clear from the scutage (a tax on the holders of knights' fees) levied in 1253 to pay for knighting Henry's eldest son, Edward. Only five of the county's twenty-seven feudal lords held more than the 4½ knights' fees chalked up to Sir William Boydell.[6]

His military duties were only one aspect of William's responsibilities as a knight. He was also expected to play a part in the administration of law and local government, as the English legal system evolved. In Anglo-Saxon and early Norman times, justice was dispensed through a combination of local manorial courts and the king's court, which adjudicated on the most serious offences. The accused was tried by ordeal. Suspects might be forced to hold a red-hot iron bar or pluck a stone out of a cauldron of boiling water. If their hands started healing within three days, they were deemed innocent. Alternatively, they might be tied up and thrown into a pond. If they sank, they were again judged innocent, although the way in which they were tied – with right thumb to left toe and left thumb to right toe – made it very difficult not to float. Criminal and civil cases could also be settled through trial by combat, where the plaintiff and defendant or their appointed champions duelled, with victory determining innocence or the right to whatever property was in dispute.

William Rufus expressed scepticism about the effectiveness of trial by ordeal when fifty men accused of killing his deer were purportedly tried by fire and passed the test with unburnt hands. But this method of establishing guilt remained in regular use for the worst transgressions until Henry II made sweeping changes to the entire legal system to restore order after the civil war between Stephen and Matilda. At the Assizes of Clarendon in 1166, and Northampton in 1176, the king set up permanent professional courts in London and the counties, appointed travelling judges to investigate serious crimes and introduced the use of grand juries to report all such crimes committed in their own districts. He also established new procedures for resolving territorial conflicts, which were to be settled by calling on twelve reputable local men to assess all evidence provided on oath.

Manorial courts continued to deal with minor feudal infractions, but control of the criminal courts and the resolution of disagreements over land now lay with the crown. However, it took many more people to implement the new 'common law' and by the middle of the thirteenth century a growing number of knights were stepping into the breach. They served as jurors in the county courts, sat on local commissions and filled numerous new offices – acting as coroners, constables, bailiffs, escheators (the local officials responsible for upholding the king's feudal rights), keepers of the peace and tax collectors.

William was among this new army of part-time administrators. In 1249, he represented the barons and community of Chester in a dispute with a local prior and relayed their complaints to the king. In 1253, he participated in a major trial over the benefice of Sandbach Church. In 1260, he was one of the jurors in a case concerning the legal rights of grantees of land. And, in 1268, he oversaw a final concord (a form of property conveyance resembling a lawsuit) in which William Venables gave half of the village of Astbury to St Werburgh's Abbey.[7] As one of the *buzones* (or 'big shots') whose word counted in court, he was also frequently called on to witness deeds for other manorial lords.

In addition to his civic duties, William had his own estates to manage. He still held property in Chester, some of which he rented out to the monks of Rocester Abbey in Staffordshire. The rural economy was also expanding. Domesday Cheshire had largely consisted of isolated farms and scattered hamlets, separated by open fields, pasture, woods and extensive areas of waste. But the climate had improved in the years around the Conquest, with long, warm summers and moderate winters. As farming became more productive and the population of England grew, more land was turned over to husbandry to meet the rising demand for food. By the mid-thirteenth century, numerous manorial lords were enclosing common ground and cultivating it, or allowing their tenants to do so. William was no exception: in about 1240-50, he gave one of his longstanding tenants permission to clear, plough and sow a piece of moorland near Grappenhall and enclose the land with a hedge. His cousin John (Richard Boydell's son), who had settled in Lymm, witnessed the deed.[8]

William also donated generously to several religious institutions, as befitted a knight. In 1244-45, he gave Dieulacres Abbey a meadow next to Chester Hospital and the land for a right of way near Balderton. On 9 August 1250, he conferred two further plots in Balderton and Dodleston on the abbey, together with a right of way across his lands. And sometime between 1249 and 1253, he granted the monks of Stanlaw Abbey, a tiny Cistercian monastery situated in the Wirral Peninsula, the right to free passage across the river at Latchford.[9]

However, William's responsibilities consumed a considerable amount of time and money. In the scutage of 1253, for example, he contributed £9 towards the cost of the splendid ceremony in which Alfonso, king of Castile, knighted Henry III's eldest son.[10] Henry had been negotiating Edward's marriage to Alfonso's half-sister Eleanor. The king of Castile had struck a hard bargain, insisting that Edward be given lands worth £10,000 a year and that he himself dub the young prince.

William's hefty contribution was enough to secure him a prominent role in the celebrations when Edward and his new wife came to Chester on 17 July 1256, the day on which the prince turned 17. In 1237, when John le Scot died without any children, the king had purchased the earldom for himself. He had granted the 'lordship' of Chester to his son in 1254, and the prince was visiting the city for the first time. Blond, broad-chested and a strapping 6ft 2in tall, Edward cut an imposing figure – standing head and shoulders above the county's leading churchmen and laity as he progressed through streets lined with cheering townsfolk. He and Eleanor stayed three days, during which he received the homage and fealty of all Cheshire's nobles. William must have been among the knights who knelt before the prince, placed their hands in his and solemnly swore their fidelity.

But William now had a son of his own to provide for. In about 1254, he had married a spirited young woman called Amy. This may have been a second marriage, since he was now in his mid-forties. If so, his first marriage had not produced an heir. William and Amy's eldest son, John, was born on 2 February 1256.[11] They had three more children over the next few years – two sons, William and Hugh, and a daughter, Maud.

The number of men prepared to carry the military and civil burden of knighthood was also shrinking rapidly, placing a disproportionate share of the load on the shoulders of those who remained. In the early 1200s, there were about 4,500 knights in England. By the early 1300s, there were as few as 1,250. Most of the decline occurred within the course of a single generation; between 1215 and 1230 at least a third, and possibly as many as half, of the families that had previously provided the country's knights abandoned their knightly status.

The cost of the increasingly elaborate chivalric trappings required to become a knight was one deterrent. Knights were now required to complete an extensive training programme and go through an expensive initiation ceremony. Sometimes, a lord helped to foot the bill. The Tower of London Close Rolls show, for example, that in 1204 King John spent £33 on 'three scarlet robes, three green robes, two brocades, one mattress and other things necessary to make a knight'. However, not everybody could count on such support. Knights were also expected to provide their own equipment. According to one early twelfth-century treatise, a contemporary warrior needed a horse, bridle, saddle, spurs, hauberk, helmet, shield, lance and sword. Yet a good warhorse could easily cost £10 – ten times as much as a carthorse – and the best destriers went for far more. Only the higher echelons of society could afford such an outlay.

It wasn't just the price of military equipment that put many men off becoming knights; it was the lifestyle that discouraged those with modest incomes. Building a fine home, and dressing and dining well, could soon empty a man's pockets. Moated residences were one sign of status, but digging even a small moat involved moving about 3,000 cubic yards of earth. Most minor manorial lords couldn't command enough tenant labour to perform such a task, so they needed to hire workmen for wages. And many of the administrative duties that came with knighthood were unprofitable.

There were, of course, various illegal ways of supplementing one's income – and William wasn't above using them. In September 1260, when the Lord Edward was making one of his periodic visits to Cheshire,

William and his cousin Hamo de Massey were summoned to Shotwick to answer for certain offences. William had allegedly stolen some of the prince's cattle, while Massey had been harassing the poor.[12] But pilfering a few royal cows was hardly enough to pay for the expenses associated with knighthood.

In 1224, Henry III was sufficiently worried by the situation to start using legal force. He ordered the county sheriffs to distrain every adult layman who held a knight's fee to serve as a knight. When this failed to produce the desired numbers, he expanded the criteria to cover all men with lands worth £20 or more. In the 1230s, he also began selling respites, which proved an effective way of topping up the royal coffers. But the pressure was mounting: between 1240 and 1260, the king issued eight orders to identify those who were eligible for knighthood and make them perform their duties or pay to commute their obligations.

In the distraint of 1256, Henry cast the net as wide as possible. He was desperate to raise troops both to go on crusade and to put his second son, Edmund, on the throne of Sicily. Pope Innocent IV had offered Henry the kingdom, on Edmund's behalf, in December 1253. But he made it clear that a major military effort would be required to oust the incumbent ruler. Henry had neither the money nor the manpower to prosecute the campaign, so he dithered.

Innocent was prepared to offer a modest amount of financial assistance. However, when he died in December 1254, his successor took a much harder line. Alexander IV insisted that, far from getting aid, the king would have to pay the pope £90,000. Moreover, if Henry didn't hand over the cash and send his army to Sicily by Michaelmas 1256, the pope would be free to withdraw the offer, excommunicate the king and place England under an interdict. Horrified by this threat, Henry jumped into action. Whereas he had previously commanded that all men with land worth £20 or more should be distrained, he now reduced the threshold to £15, although the order was restricted to those who held their estates by military tenure.

In the event, Henry's plans came to nothing, but only after he had extracted a substantial amount of coin from many a middling landowner. In 1256, he granted respites to at least 370 men for half a mark of gold apiece. One of the people caught in his web was Ralph Boydell. On 7 January 1257, the sheriff of Lincoln was instructed to value Ralph's lands to see whether he should become a knight.[13] Quite where Ralph fits within the Boydell family isn't clear but, irrespective of his lineage, he illustrates the change in attitudes towards knighthood. By the mid-thirteenth century a much more selective form of knighthood had replaced the all-encompassing variety of earlier years. William and Ralph Boydell came at the end of this transformation and stood on opposite sides of the fence. Where William had readily become a knight, Ralph was reluctant to be 'girded'.

Cheshire was soon to need every chevalier it could muster. The royal officials who administered the Four Cantrefs, which Henry III had commandeered in 1241, were greedy and insensitive. Sir Alan de la Zouche was one of the worst offenders. He taxed the miserable inhabitants so heavily that horse-drawn carts were needed to transport the money down to the royal exchequer in London. The lot of the Welsh got no better when Henry granted the Four Cantrefs to his son Edward, together with the lordship of Chester. The young prince's servants carried on extorting as much cash as possible.

In 1256, Llywelyn ap Gruffudd – proud, ruthless and as martially gifted as his grandfather, Llywelyn the Great – decided to liberate Wales from this tyranny. Llywelyn had already seized his elder brother Owain's share of Gwynedd. At the Battle of Bryn Derwin in June 1255, he captured Owain and his younger brother Dafydd and imprisoned them. Seventeen months later, in November 1256, he set Dafydd free in return for his help in recovering the Four Cantrefs. Then he took Meirionnydd and raided the lands to the south, reaching as far as Pembroke.

The princes of Gwynedd

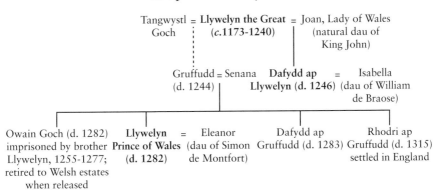

The king, still dallying with the idea of invading Sicily, took his time responding. Finally, in the summer of 1257, he came to Chester. He would take Llywelyn's stronghold in Anglesey, he blustered, and keep the island for the crown. In mid-August, he set out for Wales 'with no small army', as the *Annales Cestrienses* dryly notes. William Boydell, now in his late forties and a seasoned campaigner, must have been among the knights who rode with him. In late August 1257, the English reached Deganwy Castle and re-provisioned it, but Henry lacked the willpower to proceed with an assault on Anglesey. On 8 September, he started withdrawing his troops and, by mid-October, he was back at Westminster. Llywelyn didn't need a second chance. By 1258, he had seized southern Powys and proclaimed himself prince of Wales.

This was the dream that had inspired Llywelyn the Great. However, like his grandfather before him, Llywelyn soon discovered that claiming the title was much easier than converting it into reality. Many of the other native rulers were as unenthusiastic about paying homage to Gwynedd's overlord as Henry III was about letting them do so. Llywelyn trod carefully at first, but by the autumn of 1263 he had captured the castles of Deganwy and Dyserth, the last English outposts in the Four Cantrefs. That winter he also forced the lord of southern Powys to pay him fealty. Nonetheless, he still faced serious obstacles. His brother Dafydd had switched to Henry's side the previous Easter and the English government adamantly refused to recognise his title. So Llywelyn decided to support Simon de Montfort, earl of Leicester, who was leading yet another baronial rebellion.

The king's repeated calls for money and dissatisfaction with his methods of government had caused widespread discontent. In 1258, he had narrowly staved off disaster when he requested a tax to meet Pope Alexander IV's financial demands during the Sicilian affair. A group of armoured magnates led by the earl of Norfolk marched into the great hall at Westminster Palace. They left their swords at the door as a gesture of respect, but there was no mistaking their mood. A tremulous Henry agreed to cede governmental control to a special council of twenty-four men, half of them to be chosen by him and half by the barons. The members of the council included Simon de Montfort, the king's brother-in-law and one of his fiercest critics.

Simon de Montfort was a difficult person: clever, charismatic and a skilled military commander, yet arrogant, uncompromising and xenophobic. Ironically, he faulted Henry for promoting foreigners, even though he was a foreigner himself. In short, he had some sterling qualities, but he was most certainly *not* the right man to manage a quarrelsome bunch of barons, many of them motivated by self-interest rather than a genuine desire for reform. When the façade of baronial unity started crumbling in 1260, de Montfort was unable to plaster over the cracks.

Henry, for once, proved wily. His treasury replenished by a cash injection from Louis IX of France – provided in exchange for a promise to abandon any claim to Normandy and to hold Aquitaine as Louis's vassal – the king installed himself in the Tower of London and started hiring mercenaries. Then, in June 1261, he published a papal bull from Alexander IV quashing all the council's reforms. This move sparked stiff resistance in the shires, where the council had decreed that all sheriffs should be major county knights. However, Henry declared that the reforms had been ploys to increase the power of the barons and by the end of the year he had managed to win over most of his opponents. De Montfort alone refused to accept the king's backpedalling and withdrew to France in disgust.

Henry's triumph was brief. In April 1263, de Montfort returned to England. The wayward Prince Edward had befriended a gang of rowdy young knights from the Welsh Marches, but by 1261 he was nearly bankrupt. Seizing the opportunity to curb her headstrong son, the queen persuaded him to put aside his companions and surrender some of his castles in return for a bigger income. The prince's former associates promptly invited de Montfort back, hoping that a political upheaval would restore their flagging fortunes. By July, de Montfort had forced the king out of his refuge in the Tower of London and reinstated the reforms.

Yet de Montfort's coup proved equally short-lived. In August 1263, Edward bribed his friends back to his camp. Two months later, Henry managed to escape from Westminster and make his way to Windsor, where the royalist forces were gathering, and the realm split apart. Eventually, in a last-ditch attempt to preserve peace, both sides agreed to refer their quarrel to Louis IX. Louis's verdict, delivered in January 1264, was entirely predictable. As an anointed king himself, he was never likely to sanction any restrictions on royal authority. Condemning the council's reforms as illegal, Louis restored Henry to his full powers.

When de Montfort and his adherents refused to accept this ruling, the country was plunged into civil war.

Cheshire remained loyal to the king. When the earl of Derby attacked Worcester in February 1264, after siding with de Montfort, the county came to Prince Edward's aid. On 2 March, a royalist army led by William de la Zouche, justice of Chester, and Llywelyn's brother, Dafydd ap Gruffudd, took the city of Stafford and seized Chartley Castle. Sir William Boydell probably hauled his ageing body into the saddle and went with them. Immediately after returning to Chester, de la Zouche also set about bolstering the city's defences, fearing that the dissident barons or the Welsh might besiege it. In late March 1264, the townsfolk began building a protective trench around the northern part of the city.

Barely seven weeks later, their precautions proved irrelevant. On 14 May, de Montfort and his supporters inflicted a crushing defeat on the royalists at the Battle of Lewes, capturing the king, his brother, Richard of Cornwall, and Prince Edward. Early in November, de Montfort compelled the king to grant him Edward's lands, including the earldom of Chester. On 4 January 1265, all the citizens, 'nobles and freeholders' of the county – Sir William Boydell among them – grudgingly paid homage to de Montfort's eldest son, Henry, who was acting on his father's behalf. The next day, when Henry de Montfort met Llywelyn at Hawarden, the two men exchanged the 'kiss of peace', temporarily halting the war that had dragged on between England and Wales since 1256. Before leaving Chester, Henry also dismissed the incumbent justice, appointing the abrasive Luke de Taney in his stead.

Simon de Montfort was riding high again, yet the seeds of his destruction were already germinating. Many of his fellow magnates resented his fame and growing power. When Gilbert de Clare, the redheaded, hot-tempered earl of Gloucester, defected to the royalist camp and Edward escaped from captivity in May 1265, de Montfort's position was catastrophically weakened. The prince had been kept under close watch at Hereford but was permitted to receive visitors. On 28 May, he went riding with a small group of knights, one of whom was Clare's younger brother, Thomas. Robert of Gloucester's metrical history of England tells us what happened next. Following a bold plan carefully worked out with Thomas beforehand, Edward tried all the horses in turn, including those of the guards, and rode all but one to exhaustion. Then he jumped on the only fresh horse, dug in his spurs and galloped off, shouting 'Lordings, I bid you good day. Greet my father, the king, well and tell him that I hope to see him soon and release him from custody.'

After making his getaway, the prince rode to Ludlow, where he met up with Gilbert de Clare and other magnates rallied to his banner. On 30 May, the Marcher lord James Audley and Urian de St Pierre, baron of Malpas, seized Beeston Castle in Edward's name. Then they advanced on Chester, where they unsuccessfully besieged Luke de Taney and his soldiers in the castle for ten weeks. Sir William Boydell – whose first cousin, Sir Thomas de Dutton, was closely connected to Urian through the double marriage of his son Hugh to Urian's daughter Joan, and his daughter Katherine to Urian's son John – was almost certainly involved in orchestrating the siege.

Meanwhile, Edward and his allies took Worcester and destroyed the bridges across the River Severn, leaving de Montfort trapped on the western side and unable to join the troops his sons had mustered. On 3 August 1265, acting on intelligence received from a transvestite female spy called Margoth, the prince surprised de Montfort's younger son at Kenilworth – forcing him to rise from his bed and row naked across the moat to take refuge in the castle. The following day, Edward finally came face to face with de Montfort at Evesham. The prince cunningly ordered that the banners captured at Kenilworth should be carried in front of his army, so that his troops would be mistaken for rebel reinforcements. Then he led the attack on de Montfort's depleted force. What ensued was sheer carnage. The Welsh infantry, whom Llywelyn had sent to de Montfort's aid, fled, as de Montfort, his son Henry and many of the knights who fought with them were mown down. Edward was pitiless in victory: Simon de Montfort's head and genitals were chopped off, his genitals stuffed in his mouth and the severed head sent in triumph to the wife of the baron who had delivered the killing blow.

On hearing of de Montfort's death, Luke de Taney hastily surrendered Chester Castle to the prince. But it took another two years to restore peace in England and the Welsh remained a threat. Then, in July 1267, the political situation changed dramatically. Edward wanted to go on crusade and the English government was – as usual – desperately short of money. So Llywelyn made the king an offer he couldn't refuse. He promised to pay Henry 25,000 marks, provided that the king recognised him as prince of all Wales. The Treaty of Montgomery was concluded that

September. Llywelyn had at last succeeded in creating his principality and the people of Cheshire could breathe easy.

With the termination of hostilities, Sir William Boydell gratefully hung up his spurs and turned his attention to more personal concerns. His cousin Thomas had just been appointed sheriff of Cheshire, and it was probably at this point that William used his family connections to provide for his daughter, Maud. Various records indicate that Thomas had married Philippa de Standon, who was related to Robert de Standon, lord of Standon in Staffordshire. Robert had a young son and heir, Vivian, so William proposed that he marry Maud. Robert agreed. He granted Vivian 'five marks worth of land and ten marks worth of rents in the vill of Fenton Vivien', together with a meadow and 30s from the revenues of a mill in the village. If Vivian married Maud, Robert stipulated, she was 'to have her dower out of the land and rents'.[14] The wedding went ahead, forging a bond between the two families that would last nearly 150 years.

Thomas died in the spring of 1272, leaving William saddened, since he had been on good terms with his cousin. The two men had jointly attested a number of deeds, as well as using their influence to further each other's interests. But Thomas's death was soon overshadowed by another. On the evening of Wednesday, 16 November 1272, the king succumbed to the illness that had dogged him for the past two years. The naïve, somewhat hamfisted Henry was 65 years old and had reigned for fifty-six years, clinging to his crown despite everything. His funeral took place at Westminster Abbey the next Sunday. It was a majestic event, attended by all the country's leading magnates. The king's body, clothed in robes of red samite decorated with gold embroidery and precious stones, was borne from the palace on an open bier and reverently entombed in the abbey. Indeed, the chronicler Thomas Wykes caustically remarked, Henry 'shone more splendidly in death than he did in life'.

Henry's son and heir was on a ship bound for Italy at the time. Edward had set off for the Holy Land in August 1270 and Robert de Standon was among the knights who accompanied him. The Staffordshire Forest Pleas show that Robert had fallen foul of Henry after stealing venison from one of the royal forests. He had also sided with de Montfort in the baronial war. So he presumably hoped that taking the cross would restore him to the king's good graces. But whereas Robert was back in

England by the autumn of 1272 – when the Fine Rolls record that he paid half a mark to initiate a court case – the prince remained overseas. Edward was recovering from wounds sustained during an attempt to assassinate him and news of his father's death only reached him when he arrived in Sicily in January 1273. Even then, however, he didn't hurry home. He made a leisurely circuit of Italy and France, lasting a full eighteen months, before landing at Dover on 2 August 1274. Seventeen days later, Edward was crowned at Westminster Abbey, having spent the night quietly reflecting on his new responsibilities in the bedchamber where his father had passed away almost two years earlier.

William and his fellow Cheshire knights must have greeted the coronation of a new monarch with relief. Edward's four-year absence had left England rudderless, particularly during the regency government that had been put in place after Henry III's death. The magnates who stayed in England had seized every opportunity to usurp more power and some of them had begun feuding with each other for local ascendancy. Murders and robberies were on the rise, the courts were swamped and many people feared another outbreak of civil war. William, who was only a few years younger than Henry III, had no desire to assume a heavier judicial load when his own life was drawing to its close.

He, too, was dead by late 1276. With Henry's acquisition of the earldom of Chester, the former earls' feudal tenants had become tenants-in-chief – and when a tenant-in-chief died, a local enquiry was held to ascertain what rights were due to the crown. On 6 February 1277, Cheshire's ruling elite assembled to conduct William's inquisition post mortem. The twelve jurors reported that William was responsible for 'doing service of one knight's fee to the king at Chester in time of war', while his tenants did 'service at his castle of Dodleston' for another 3½ fees. William also held part of a wood from Sir Henry de Lacy, constable of Chester, for which he gave Lacy a pair of spurs or 4d a year. The heir to his estates was his son John, who had turned 21 just four days previously.[15]

John had done his father proud. William was buried in a fine tomb at St Wilfrid's Church in Grappenhall, where he had built a new family home. Situated on a sandstone spur 23 miles north-east of the Welsh border, Grappenhall was far more secure than Dodleston, which lay perilously close to the frontier with Wales. William had done his duty by his king, but he had chosen one of his safest and most pleasant manors in which to put down roots. His stone effigy has survived serious damage and enthusiastic 'restoration' by a local mason. Yet, despite all the abuse to which it has been subjected, it remains a beautiful piece of work. It portrays a recumbent knight clad in chain mail, with three pierced mullets etched on his breastplate – the gold stars on a horizontal blue band against a silver field that William took for his coat of arms – and a shield lying by his left shoulder. His right hand rests on the hilt of his sword, as if he is just about to draw the blade from its scabbard. His legs are crossed and his feet rest on the flanks of his dog (a symbol of faithfulness). John had chosen to represent his father in full martial array as a mark of his rank and virility.

7

One Welshman's Head

Shrewsbury town centre was packed with people. Public executions were popular events and a large crowd of onlookers had gathered to enjoy the spectacle. Some of the men were carrying children on their shoulders and one enterprising hawker was doing a roaring trade in meat pies. The mob surged forward, folk elbowing each other for a better view when the horse dragging the prince towards the High Cross crested the hill. The armed guards surrounding the scaffold quickly lowered their pikes.

John watched grimly as the ropes binding Dafydd to the hurdle were unloosed and the prince was hauled to his feet. Blood dribbled from a gash on his cheek, where a stone had caught him, and oozed out of the torn flesh on his back, dripping onto his filthy loincloth. The executioner's assistant tied Dafydd's hands behind his back and guided him up the ladder to the platform where the gallows stood, a black T silhouetted against the pale October sky. The executioner was waiting by the foot of the second ladder propped against the gibbet. Wisps of smoke drifted up from a brazier of red-hot coals filled with metal implements.

The noise from the crowd subsided as a trumpet sounded and a royal official strode to the edge of the platform, clutching a slip of parchment: 'Greetings from Edward, by the grace of God, king of England, lord of Ireland and duke of Aquitaine.' The official cleared his throat. 'After due trial and examination by the authority of the said Edward, David son of Griffin has been judged guilty of treason, murder and sacrilege. Sentence: to be dragged through the streets of Shrewsbury at the horse's tail for sedition, hanged for murder, disembowelled while breathing for having committed his crimes during the week of Christ's passion, and quartered; thereafter, the parts of the said David's body to be dispatched to the four corners of England because he plotted to kill the king in

91

various parts of the realm.'[1] Glancing at the prince, he muttered, 'May God have mercy on your soul.'

The official nodded to the executioner, who placed the noose around Dafydd's neck. The prince stared straight ahead, ignoring the mob, while the priest who had walked beside him as he was drawn through Shrewsbury intoned the Lord's Prayer. Once the priest had finished, the executioner pushed Dafydd up the second ladder. The prince wobbled, unable to balance properly with his hands secured behind him, but the executioner's assistant steadied him. As soon as he reached the top rung, the assistant shoved him off the ladder. Dafydd's legs thrashed, his eyes bulged, his chest heaved and his tongue stuck out of his mouth. More than a minute passed before he stopped jerking and, at a sign from the executioner, the assistant cut him down. He crumpled to the ground, gasping.

A few moments later four pikemen pinned the prince down and the executioner pulled a knife out of the coals, its metal blade glowing a dull orange. Dafydd uttered a single, muffled cry as the executioner sliced him open, searing his innards. Then the executioner stooped, tugged out his entrails and tossed them into the brazier. The sickening reek of burnt flesh reached John's nostrils as the still conscious prince flopped on the ground like a gutted fish. The crowd had fallen quiet. Time stretched out, swelling into the silence, until the executioner's axe slashed down, whetted edge arcing through the air to sever Dafydd's neck in a spray of blood.

Dafydd ap Gruffudd was a man of mercurial loyalties. In 1255, he had taken his eldest brother Owain's part against his middle brother, Llywelyn. And, in 1263, he had deserted the Welsh cause to join Henry III. Llywelyn had forgiven him on both occasions and even rewarded him with lands in the newly reconquered Four Cantrefs. But, in 1274, Dafydd went too far to be pardoned when he hatched a plot to murder Llywelyn. That November, after the conspiracy was uncovered, he fled to England, where Edward I sheltered him, presumably reasoning that he might prove a valuable political tool. The king behaved generously towards Dafydd, granting him the manor of Frodsham. He also gave Dafydd the wardship of John Boydell's estates – and thus the right to the profit from the lands until John attained his majority.[2]

Dafydd treated John with indifference, if not outright contempt. An heir could only inherit his paternal lands after a lengthy formal process that included a hearing to establish the date of his father's death, the nature of his tenure and the feudal service he owed. But when William Boydell's inquisition post mortem was conducted in February 1277, the prince failed to put in an appearance. On 12 April, Guncelin de Badlesmere, the justice of Chester, was ordered to invite him to a second inquisition. However, when another enquiry took place on 13 May, there was still no sign of Dafydd. The frustrated justice wrote to the chancellor, stating that he had 'caused the said David to be summoned daily, but he was unwilling to listen'. Eventually, the king intervened. On 22 August, while he was at Basingwerk overseeing the construction of Flint Castle, Edward ordered Badlesmere to let John take possession of his lands, since John was of full age and had already paid him homage.[3]

John had good reason to feel angry at the prince's cavalier behaviour. Dafydd's failure to attend William's inquisition was not just insulting; it had blocked John from claiming his patrimony for five months. Moreover, the delay couldn't have come at a worse time. A huge tree-felling programme was underway on the land adjoining John's estates in preparation for another war with Wales and John worried that his own rights would be infringed.

In September 1275, Edward had travelled to Chester to receive Llywelyn's homage. Instead of turning up for the meeting, Llywelyn sent a letter stating that he considered it unsafe to enter England, where his enemies – Dafydd, in particular – had been given asylum. The king waited in Chester for a week before giving up and returning south 'in a rage'. Llywelyn ignored two further writs to present himself at Westminster. So Edward, who possessed all the military nous his father lacked, was now planning a full-scale invasion of Wales to curb its insubordinate prince.

In November 1276, he appointed William Beauchamp, earl of Warwick, as captain of his army in Cheshire and Lancashire. The following spring, Beauchamp started clearing a path through the forest from Chester to the River Conwy. The woodcutters he hired began by widening the pass at Pulford, but the area to be cleared extended into the ancient forest of Swerdewood, which straddled the boundaries between Hawarden, Dodleston and Bretton. In April 1277, Beauchamp wrote to Edward, informing him that the woodcutters were working as hard as they could and that he was selling the timber for the best possible price. John wanted to ensure that the workmen didn't stray onto his own property; even an inferior oak tree could fetch 1s 8d, while a good one might go for several shillings. Yet, as long as his lands were still under Dafydd's control, there was little he could do to stop any incursions.

Soon, however, John was also caught up in the preparations for the war. In the summer of 1277, England's southern earls and their military retinues assembled at Worcester, in response to an order issued the previous November. Most of the cavalry, led by Edward himself, rode up to Chester to join the nobles who were responsible for guarding the north. On 15 July, when the king entered the city, Chester was buzzing with activity. A fleet of eighteen ships carrying about 700 seamen had sailed from the Cinque Ports and lay at rest in the harbour, while another seventeen vessels chartered by royal agents jostled for space in the Dee estuary. Roughly 3,000 foot soldiers had also come from other parts of the country – attracted by the prospect of earning 2d a day (or twice that in the case of the crossbowmen) – and more were trickling in all the time. A week later, Edward and his 15,000-strong army left Chester and crossed the border into Wales. John Boydell, honouring his feudal obligation to fight for his overlord, was one of the knights riding in the king's entourage.

Over the next two months Edward moved carefully. He paused to build two new castles at Flint and Rhuddlan and carried on the vast road-clearing programme Beauchamp had begun, as he pressed deeper into the Four Cantrefs. At the end of August 1277, he and his army reached Deganwy, where the castle his father had built stood in ruins. But by this point the campaign was faltering. The number of infantry had halved – some of the soldiers had been killed during the advance, while many more had deserted – and supplies were running short. Edward's invasion seemed destined to founder like every previous attempt on north Wales.

The king's solution was typically bold. The isle of Anglesey, north-west of Gwynedd, contained the best arable land in Wales and its granaries were crammed with corn after the harvest. So, in early September, Edward had 2,000 soldiers shipped across the narrow strip of water separating Anglesey from the Welsh mainland to capture the island and steal the grain. In one fell swoop he had restocked his army and stripped Llywelyn of the means to feed his own people during the winter months. Faced with starvation, Llywelyn had to submit. On 9 November 1277, he surrendered the territory he had gained in the 1260s and promised to provide war reparations of £50,000. Edward also insisted that the native Welsh rulers should henceforth pay fealty to him, not to Llywelyn, although he let the prince keep his royal title.

Cheshire's knights received a special commendation for their role in the campaign. Earlier in the year, Edward had levied a nationwide scutage at the usual rate of 40s per knight's fee to help finance the invasion. The returns for Cheshire were endorsed with a note that the men of the county had fulfilled their dues 'and more than that at the king's request', by fighting for longer than the forty days dictated by feudal custom.[4]

An uneasy peace prevailed between Wales and England for the next five years. Llywelyn was subjected to various petty slights: the royal officials in Chester impounded his horses and honey, while those in Aberystwyth imprisoned his huntsmen. His right to invoke Welsh law in Welsh lands was also challenged in a protracted legal dispute with Gruffudd ap Gwenwynwyn, lord of southern Powys. Nevertheless, he kept up the payments he had promised to make and behaved deferentially towards Edward. In October 1278, the king relented sufficiently to let him marry Simon de Montfort's daughter Eleanor, to whom he had earlier been engaged. This was a major concession, since Eleanor was Edward's cousin. With his wife's aid, Llywelyn slowly, painstakingly set about rebuilding his power base and, by 1281, he had recovered much of his political status, though not his lost lands.

The king was far too canny to drop his guard, even when Llywelyn proved compliant. He continued clearing the dense forests that still covered much of Cheshire and building a network of roads so that his soldiers could traverse the area more easily. When a flood swept away the bridge over the river at Chester on 3 February 1280, Edward also levied a toll on the citizens to replace it – deeming the bridge too vital for military purposes to be discarded. Yet he made no attempt to topple the prince. In the end it was neither Edward nor Llywelyn, but Dafydd, who brought everything crashing down.

Dafydd was disillusioned and angry. He had fought for Edward in 1277, believing that he would be rewarded with a share of Gwynedd as his rightful patrimony. When Llywelyn surrendered and the invasion of north Wales came to a halt, this was no longer on the cards. Dafydd received a far smaller prize than he had expected: two of the Four Cantrefs, together with the lordship of Hope in Flintshire, where he started erecting a castle. Then, in the autumn of 1281, the king dismissed Badlesmere as justice of Chester and replaced him with Sir Reginald Grey, a man convinced of the inferiority of all things Welsh. Grey routinely harassed Dafydd, stealing the timber from his lands and wrongly accusing him of harbouring fugitives. Worse still, the Marcher baron William Venables challenged Dafydd's title to Hope in Chester county court. Dafydd attended the first hearing in the great hall at Chester Castle (where the court met) 'out of reverence to the king' and wrote to Edward afterwards, asking him to make Venables drop the case. But when the court sat again in December 1281, the king merely sent orders that the plea be adjourned until the next session.

Pushed beyond the limits of his endurance, Dafydd launched a desperate bid to cast off the English yoke. On the night of 21 March 1282, which also happened to be the eve of Palm Sunday, he attacked Hawarden Castle with a band of armed men, slaughtered most of the garrison and carried off the constable, Roger de Clifford, one of Edward's oldest friends. A number of other Welsh nobles joined him, striking at various English castles in the vicinity of Hawarden in what was obviously a coordinated uprising. Llywelyn was left in a terrible position. Torn between the desire to see Wales liberated, recognition that the chances of success were slim and fear that his brother might unseat him as prince of Wales, he reluctantly declared war on England on behalf of all the Welsh.

It took three days for news of the first attacks to reach Edward. But though he was shocked by Dafydd's treachery, he reacted fast. In early April 1282, he started mustering his forces and purchasing supplies, with orders for food flying around the country. He also instructed the sailors of the Cinque Ports to ready their ships, planning to use the same two-pronged strategy – a joint attack by land and sea – that had worked so well before. Towards the end of May, the king rode north to Chester, intending to lead a large force out of the city into Wales. First, however, he had to tackle the resistance in the Four Cantrefs. In early June, as Edward was supervising the preparations for his push along the Welsh coast, Sir Reginald Grey directed the first inland strike. Backed by 7,000 foot soldiers, many of them archers, Grey made swift progress. On 16 June, he captured Dafydd's stronghold at Hope.

Dafydd had retreated after demolishing the castle and blocking the well with stones. Grey immediately commissioned more than 1,000 workmen to rebuild it. This was an enormous undertaking; 'every gallon of water, every load of stone, every balk of timber, every sack of charcoal, every barrel of lime, every piece of iron and steel brought from Chester, every length of rope, every pick and shovel and mason's

The key castles in the northernmost part of Wales in 1282

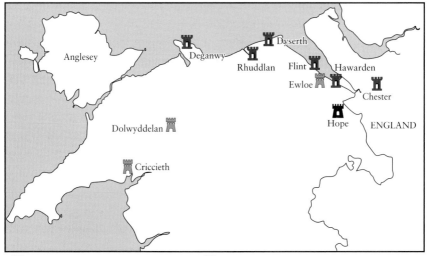

Castles under Anglo-Norman control   Castles controlled by Llywelyn ap Gruffudd

Castle built by Dafydd ap Gruffudd

axe, the canvas, the parchment, the nails, all had to be hauled by man or beast' up a steep hill. The men worked feverishly, under constant threat from the Welsh – and, in August 1282, they were able to send proof of their success to the king in the form of two barrels of water.[5]

While the work was going on, Grey used the castle as a base from which to harry the Welsh resistance. Sir John Boydell and his younger brother William were among the soldiers under his command. Between 16 June and 1 August 1282, John was paid 3s a day for the services of himself, his squire and his armoured horse. William soon joined him, leading a band of fifty archers. Between 22 June and 6 September, William earned 1s a day for his efforts. On 3 September, he and his two foremen also received a royal bounty of 12d 'for bringing in one Welshman's head'.[6]

John was in Chester when his brother rode into camp brandishing his grisly prize. On 1 September 1282, he was sitting in the draughty great hall at the castle as William de Tabley and Godfrey Esmerillon, Reginald Grey's chief clerk, engaged in a battle of words. Tabley claimed that Esmerillon had coerced him into handing over his house and lands in Knutsford Booth by imprisoning him in Chester Castle for two months. Esmerillon counter-claimed that Tabley had given him the property of his own accord. When the jury found in Tabley's favour, Esmerillon appealed against the decision. Remarkably, given that he was in the middle of conducting a war, the king himself got involved. Further probing at Edward's instigation revealed that Tabley had been gaoled because he was being prosecuted for another offence and that he had struck a deal to get Esmerillon's help in securing a release. But once bail was lifted and he was freed from prison, he had reneged on the agreement. The court decided that Esmerillon should be given the property and damages – evidence of the rather dubious fashion in which justice could sometimes work in the thirteenth century.[7]

As soon as the case was over, John sped back to the front. But rather than returning to Hope he probably hurried to Dodleston Castle, which lay just 7 miles north-east of Hope and had come under heavy fire from the Welsh. The danger the garrison faced is clear from a lawsuit in which John accused one of his tenants, William Lancelyn, of defaulting on his duty to provide an armed horseman for fifteen days to guard the 'fortlet' and erect a palisade. Lancelyn was dead by December 1286, when the case finally came to court. However, the jury concluded that his son had fulfilled the family's feudal responsibilities by serving as one of the king's constables and couldn't be blamed for failing to build the palisade because no Englishman would approach on account of the attacks of the Welshmen.[8]

The war was indeed progressing poorly, despite Edward's extensive preparations. In June 1282, the Welsh had ambushed part of the English army in the Tywi Valley, near Llandeilo, and though William de Valence, earl of Pembroke, had penetrated as far as Aberystwyth, he was unable to hold the town. Still, the king was not to be stopped. He advanced from Chester to the castle he had built at Rhuddlan in 1277 and pressed on with his plans to launch a coastal attack from Anglesey. By late September 1282, some 200 carpenters, working flat out, had constructed a bridge of boats across to the mainland, opening up Snowdonia. But the Welsh fought back. On 6 November, they succeeded in driving a group of English cavalry off the bridge of boats into the sea. Sixteen knights drowned – including Luke de Taney, the commander whose mailed fist had so oppressed the inhabitants of Chester while the city was under Simon de Montfort's control.

A month later, however, the tide turned dramatically in Edward's favour. In early December 1282, Llywelyn led his army into central

Wales, leaving his brother Dafydd in charge of Snowdonia. On 11 December, he arrived at Builth to find the full might of the Marcher lords awaiting him. Battle was struck at a place called Cilmeri, on high ground near Builth, and the Welsh army was wiped out. Llywelyn, who had somehow become separated from most of his men, was cut down as he fled through the woods. His head was lopped off and sent to the king, who had it displayed on a spike at the Tower of London, crowned with ivy in mockery of Llywelyn's princely ambitions.

While the English exulted, heaping scorn on the dead prince, the Welsh were desolate. Llywelyn was the 'jewel of his contemporaries, the flower of the kings of the past, the model of those of the future, the leader, the glory, the law, the light of the people', one Welsh bard lamented. Dafydd was no substitute for the warrior who had steered his people with courage and dignity for more than thirty years. Assuming his brother's royal title and the lands he had so long coveted, he immediately sued for peace – a plea that Edward, not surprisingly, ignored. In January 1283, the English took Dolwyddelan Castle in the heart of Snowdonia, where Llywelyn had been born, and in March 1283 they invaded Gwynedd itself. Dafydd fled into the mountains, but on 21 June he was finally captured by 'men of his own tongue', hiding in a bog. The betrayer had been betrayed.

The wounds Dafydd had incurred in the struggle were roughly tended and he was brought to the king at Rhuddlan. From there he was taken under armed guard, first to Chester and then to Shrewsbury, to face trial for high treason. Edward's anger at his perfidy infuses the wording of the writ in which he summoned eleven earls, two knights from each shire and two representatives from each of twenty-one cities, including Chester, to attend the prince's trial. He recalled how Dafydd had been 'received as an exile, nourished as an orphan and endowed with lands, and cherished with clothing under his [the king's] protection'.[9]

On 30 September 1283, the prince was found guilty of treason, murder and sacrilege and condemned to 'a miserable death'. He was to be drawn, hanged, disembowelled and dismembered for his crimes. Only one man of high birth – Sir William de Marisco, who had turned to piracy after being outlawed for murdering a royal messenger – had previously been subjected to such an end, and never before had the evisceration been performed while the culprit was still alive. The king had exacted a terrible revenge. The sentence was carried out on 3 October, after which Dafydd's head was transported to the Tower of London, where it was exhibited on a spike next to the head of his elder brother. Meanwhile, the citizens of York and Winchester squabbled for possession of his right shoulder and the citizens of Lincoln refused to accept any part of his corpse.

Dafydd's wife, Elizabeth de Ferrers, daughter of the fifth earl of Derby, had stood by her husband to the last. She watched, heartbroken, as her two sons by Dafydd were imprisoned at Bristol Castle, while their daughters and Llywelyn's only child, a baby girl named Gwenllian, were banished to the cloister. Within a decade of coming to the throne, Edward I had extinguished Llywelyn's family line and all hope of creating a united Welsh polity. By 1284, he had mopped up the last remnants of resistance, conquering princedoms unvanquished by any previous English monarch. Thereafter, apart from occasional outbreaks of unrest – the most serious being a rebellion led by Llywelyn's distant relative Madog ap Llywelyn in 1294 – the king had little difficulty in controlling his Welsh subjects.

Sir John Boydell had both general and personal cause for rejoicing. As the war with the Welsh drew to its sorry conclusion, his wife Margaret gave birth to their first child, a boy whom he named William. Margaret was at least a decade younger than her husband and probably a member of the Frodsham family, which held lands in Frodsham, a small market town some 10 miles south-west of Grappenhall.[10] Three more sons – John, Robert and Hugh – and a daughter called Matilda followed in swift succession.

Only one thing marred Sir John's contentment. The king had given the newly rebuilt Hope Castle to his wife Eleanor in February 1283. The castle was destroyed in an accidental fire just six months afterwards. In the interim, though, Robert Bures, the queen's bailiff, had seized part of John's moorland on the outskirts of Dodleston. John wasn't about to accept the theft lying down. On 1 April 1283, he and his tenants drove out the men Bures had installed. Bures promptly wrote to Eleanor, begging her to intercede and 'command Sir John to retire from these outrages'. John's claim that the moor belonged to him fell on deaf ears.[11]

But Bures had form. When the queen died in November 1290, an enquiry into the administration of her lands uncovered numerous complaints about his conduct and John renewed his claim. He charged Bures with depriving him of the rights belonging to his manor of Dodleston eight years earlier, adding that he had never been able to secure recompense for the trespass. Hugh de Cressingham, Eleanor's former steward, alleged that the king had granted the moor to Dafydd ap Gruffudd and that it had reverted to Edward by dint of Dafydd's treason. After that, he said, the king had given it to his wife. In 1291, justice finally prevailed; John recovered the moor and damages of £20. Then, point made, he tactfully remitted the money 'for the queen's soul'.[12]

In fact, John wasn't above misappropriating other people's assets himself. In December 1286, when his quarrel with the Lancelyns reached court, William Lancelyn junior accused John of stealing his cattle. John insisted that he had distrained the animals in lieu of the military service he was owed and dragged his feet over paying the fine he incurred on losing the case. Eventually, on 11 March 1287, he and his men were pardoned, after giving 'satisfaction in another way'. But eighteen months later he was back in the dock for the same offence. In October 1288, Roger Straket sued John for taking his cattle, while Alan de Rixton levelled similar charges against John's mother, Amy, and his brother Hugh. Amy and Hugh ignored the summons but were forced to attend court on 30 November to answer a further allegation of assaulting Rixton at Warburton, in which John was also implicated. The case was still crawling through the system in June 1289 when Rixton sued Amy for trespass.[13]

John fell foul of the law yet again in August 1289, when he and his mother – erroneously described by a careless scribe as his wife Anne – were involved in a dispute with David de Barton over some wasteland in Latchford. But the two men soon patched up their differences; several years afterwards they both attested a grant by Richard de Pulford to his kinsman Robert, rector of Coddington.[14] William de Brexes (probably the son of John's half-uncle Hugh), who also attested the grant, may have helped to broker a peace. Brexes knew the Bartons well and had witnessed several deeds with David's father, Patrick.

For the most part, however, John obeyed the law, as well as helping to uphold it in his role as a knight. In 1284, he sat on a case in which Simon, abbot of St Werburgh's Abbey, reached a settlement with Ranulf le Roter over the repair and maintenance of Fulford Bridge on the high road from Chester to Ince. In 1289, he also participated in the inquisition post mortem for John de St Pierre, who had married his cousin Katherine de Dutton, as well as mediating in a dispute between Abbot Simon and the citizens of Chester over the siting of the annual summer fair.[15]

Two fairs now took place in the city each year. The one held at the Feast of St John the Baptist was under the strict control of the abbey, which erected booths in the open space outside the abbey gate, let the booths for hire and levied a fee on every transaction. But in most towns the inhabitants had the right to hold fairs themselves, so Chester's citizens had clashed with the abbot. In 1289, the conflict was settled by negotiation; Abbot Simon agreed to let the townsfolk erect their own booths at a distance from the abbey gate and charge traders for using the stalls, in exchange for an annual payment of 40s 8d.

Apart from helping to administer justice through the courts, John was actively engaged in managing his own estates. He rented a house in Chester to Ranulf le Roter for one 'pair of white gloves' a year.[16] He also rented the manor of Dodleston to Dieulacres Abbey, probably with a proviso that the buildings were to be rebuilt at the abbey's expense, if they were destroyed by fire during a war with Wales.[17] And he leased four bovates of land in Dutton to his cousin, Hugh de Dutton. In 1295, John was forced to appeal to the justice, Sir Reginald Grey, when Hugh died and the escheator overzealously seized his entire estate. John received a far more favourable hearing than Grey's Welsh petitioners had ever enjoyed – but then he was English and moved in the same circles as Grey. On 7 May 1295, John's rights were restored after the court ruled that Hugh de Dutton held the land from him in return for providing two foot soldiers to guard Dodleston Castle for 2½ days in wartime.[18]

Shortly before Michaelmas 1296, John also gave his youngest brother, Hugh, a helping hand. William Boydell, who had served at Hope Castle with him, was already well provided for; he and his wife Emma held the manors of Hulme Walfield and Wardle from Hugh de Pulford, lord of the manor of Pulford. But Hugh Boydell had nothing. So John granted him 'a piece of land and wood [called Middlehurst] lying between Grappenhall and Thelwall'.[19]

Hugh had loyally supported John in a dispute with Richard Roulesham, the parson of Grappenhall, in 1293. He was also close to his mother, who may well have urged John to give him some territory of his own. Amy was growing feeble and probably wanted to see all her sons settled before she met her end. She was dead by February 1297, after appointing Hugh as her executor. However, Hugh rapidly found himself stuck in a legal dispute with John and Margaret de Ringstead, who claimed that they had lent Amy 21 marks. Hugh argued that there was no written record of the loan and that he had already distributed all of his mother's goods. In fact, he still had 8s from his mother's estate, which the court decreed that he should pay the Ringsteads. But Hugh refused to part with the money.[20]

John kept out of the quarrel, although his sympathies almost certainly lay with his brother. The previous year he had proved equally slow to answer to John de Warwick, one of the two sheriffs of Chester, for a debt incurred by Adam de Tabley. John had stood surety for the debt but ignored Warwick's repeated attempts to bring him to court. It was only when an order to distrain his lands and chattels was issued – more than nine months after Warwick had initiated legal proceedings – that John finally put in an appearance. The court instructed him to honour his pledge and pay up. Not unreasonably in the circumstances: in July 1296, while Warwick was still struggling to recover his cash, John had purchased two bovates of land in Handley for £3. He could clearly find coin for the things he wanted.[21]

In 1297, John also witnessed a deed in which Robert de Pulford formally confirmed a grant his great-grandfather had made to Dieulacres Abbey. But the era of lavish religious endowments was now over. John himself had made only two modest donations soon after coming into his inheritance.[22] And under the 1279 Statute of Mortmain, Edward I had banned further gifts of land to the Church without his consent. Feudal estates were subject to various tolls and military obligations. They were taxed when a landholder died and his property passed to his adult heir, or placed in wardship when the heir was a minor, in which case the wardship of the lands could be sold or given to a retainer. Lands held by a religious body, which never died and was never under age, didn't pay these levies. Nor did they revert to the feudal overlord, if there was no heir – or to the crown, if the landholder was convicted of treason. So the king had intervened to prevent more territory from passing to the Church and thus preserve the income and military service it provided.

Many men may have welcomed the new law. The medieval real estate market was complex and the monetary value of freehold land is difficult to determine. However, the trend towards higher rents shows that the price of land was climbing as England's population continued to expand. Conversely, the opportunities for earning territory through military service were declining, although they hadn't completely vanished. Edward I had certainly carved up conquered Welsh princedoms among his followers, but it was only the most important commanders who now received such spoils. Ordinary soldiers could expect nothing more than their wages – and the occasional shilling for an enemy 'scalp'. So lesser men needed to husband their resources. When they disposed of land, it was increasingly to take care of sons and siblings or to secure a material rather than spiritual gain. And when they bought land, they had to pay a premium for it. In the currency of the times, one luckless Welshman's head fetched barely half an acre of good Cheshire earth.

8

Blade and Trade

John stared miserably through the iron grille in his prison cell. From his chamber high above the entrance to Chester Castle, in one of the two drum towers forming part of the new gatehouse that Edward I had commissioned in 1292, he had a clear view of the outer bailey, with the well in the centre and the great hall, chapel and offices to the left. Fortunately, John could afford one of the better rooms in the county gaol. It was crude and cramped, but at least it had a window. He'd also paid for a bed, two meals a day and a charcoal brazier to stave off the damp that permeated the stonework. The cold was already beginning to bite, even though it wasn't yet December, and John felt the chill deep in his bones.

When he wasn't fretting about his situation, he was bored and frustrated. He was allowed to leave his cell to attend Mass and pursue his legal case. His wife also visited regularly, bringing candles, coals and food to supplement the meagre rations the gaolers provided. His cousins Peter and Roger had come to pledge their support too, and the constable of the castle had been very decent; he'd listened patiently as John protested his innocence. But time hung heavily on John's hands.

He could hear the king's two Welsh hostages talking in their soft, singsong language. They were playing dice again, one of the few things a prisoner could do to relieve the tedium. John had never really liked gaming; he preferred to spend his days on horseback, riding around his estates and talking to his tenants, when he wasn't serving in military campaigns or sitting on the jurors' bench at the county court. Now here he was, confined in Chester Castle like a criminal. It was so unfair, he thought bitterly. He'd trusted William Doncaster. He'd welcomed the merchant into his family. And, God knew, he'd honoured every single promise he'd made the knave. Yet Doncaster had played him for a fool.

In the first decade of the fourteenth century, real estate was still the primary sign of wealth in England, but it was no longer the sole path to prosperity. The country was gradually becoming more commercialised, as its share of the European wool trade increased and demand for a wider choice of goods and services rose. The wool trade was at its peak and 45,000 sacks of raw wool – the output of more than ten million sheep – were exported every year. Vessels groaning under the weight of wool, broadcloth, hangings, tin, lead and Welsh cloth sailed to the continent, returning with a growing array of exotic foreign goods, including figs, raisins, leather, dyes and honey from the Mediterranean.

Greater intra-national and international trade brought greater urbanisation. By 1300, between 15 and 20 per cent of the English populace lived in towns, although the vast majority of these municipalities were small settlements with fewer than 2,000 inhabitants. Only London, with an estimated population of 60-80,000, was large enough to count as a proper city by European standards. A robust transport network had also developed to cope with the increase in long-distance trade, with five main roads linking London to the rest of the realm. As the scholar Wendy Childs notes, the king's highways 'teemed with herbalists, jugglers, messengers, pedlars, wandering workmen, peasants, preachers, friars, pardoners, pilgrims and the like', not to mention the brigands who preyed on unwary travellers.

Chester was at the forefront of these advances. It had long been a major locus of trade with Ireland, but its importance as a financial and administrative base had expanded dramatically during Edward I's wars with the Welsh. Earlier campaigns had failed for lack of food and effective communications. Edward was determined not to make the same mistakes. In 1277 and 1282, the city served as one of the three military command centres from which he launched his attacks. Thousands of soldiers marched to their meeting point at Chester, while victuals, equipment, weapons and workmen flowed into the city to support the war effort.

Chester fulfilled the same function in 1294, when Madog ap Llywelyn led his last-gasp attempt to overthrow Edward's rule, and it continued to serve as a supply hub, albeit on a smaller scale, when the king eventually turned his attention to Scotland. In 1300, Edward implicitly recognised the city's contribution to the defence of the nation by granting it two substantial privileges. The mayor and sheriffs were, uniquely, allowed to hold the pleas of the crown (that is, to adjudicate on all criminal proceedings in the county). Chester was also added to the select list of towns with permission to operate an exchange for the purposes of trading bills, merchandise and currency.

The citizens were duly appreciative. In June 1301, Edward visited Chester to see the county's great and good pay homage to his 17-year-old son, Edward of Caernarfon. The king had granted his son the earldom of Chester and declared him prince of Wales in the spring of 1301 – resuscitating the title Llywelyn ap Gruffudd had once borne so proudly, in what was apparently an attempt to pacify the Welsh. The city authorities, eagerly anticipating the visit, commissioned major work on the castle, including two great chambers and three gardens, 'because the coming of the Lord the Prince to Chester was hoped for'.

These weren't the only changes taking place in the city. Its role as a vital military base and supply centre had created a new class of wealthy master craftsmen and merchants with whom the county's martial elite, Sir John Boydell among them, increasingly mingled. One such self-made man was 'Richard the Engineer'. In 1277, when Edward was looking for someone to build Flint Castle, he hired Richard. The young master mason clearly impressed the king. Richard subsequently supervised the erection or restoration of many of the fortresses Edward built to secure his dominion over the Welsh and, by 1300, he had become the king's master-of-works, a post he retained until his death in 1315.

Richard was handsomely rewarded for his expertise. In 1284, he purchased a twelve-year monopoly on the mills and fishery of the Dee, for which he paid the huge sum of £200 a year. He also owned a magnificent home in one of Chester's prime locations. His meteoric ascent was reinforced in 1294, when – as the Eaton Charters show – his daughter Agnes married Richard de Pulford, lord of the manor of Eaton, who could trace his pedigree back to the Conquest and epitomised 'old money'.

Richard the Engineer was friendly with other members of Chester's new urban gentry, including Hugh Brickhill and William Doncaster, the 'king's merchant'. Brickhill traded in wine and served as the city's mayor nine times between 1289 and 1313. By the late 1280s or early 1290s, he and his wife Mary were leasing large slabs of land from Roger de Monte Alto, who held a prominent position in Cheshire society as hereditary steward of Chester. John, who was acquainted with Brickhill and had once borrowed money from him, witnessed at least two of these contracts. On 21 April 1299, he and Brickhill also attested an agreement between Sir Hugh Venables and Richard the Engineer and his wife Agnes. A few years later, John witnessed another transaction in which Brickhill bought some land in Flintshire.[1]

Hugh Brickhill had amassed a considerable fortune. William Doncaster had, if anything, done even better. Doncaster was the third in a line of successful entrepreneurs of the same name. His father and grandfather owned several commercial properties in the centre of Chester and routinely witnessed legal documents for the city's bigwigs. Doncaster rapidly expanded on this foundation. He began his career by provisioning the royal army and the English garrisons in Wales but soon had a finger in every pie. One of his ships, the *Mariota*, carried wheat, oats and other supplies from Ireland to north Wales on a regular basis in the 1290s. Doncaster also traded in iron, lead, wool and wine and stocked the king's cellars on many an occasion. In June 1304, for example, Edward instructed his treasurer to pay the merchant £147 6s for wine his butler had bought for the royal household.

Doncaster invested the profits from his business shrewdly. He owned some of the most desirable real estate in Chester, including a mansion in Watergate Street, a number of shops and undercrofts in the city centre and a bakehouse in Eastgate Street. In December 1299, he also made the first of many land purchases in Flint, Rhuddlan and Anglesey. And, by 1307, he held the manor of Mostyn in Flintshire. But Doncaster wasn't just a local wheeler-dealer; he was a figure of national importance with considerable influence at court. In 1301, when he complained to the king that the duke of Brabant had stolen some of his goods and money in Antwerp, Edward personally intervened to order the restitution of his wares. And when the young Edward of Caernarfon wanted to help one of the men who had been in his service, it was Doncaster to whom he turned for assistance.

In short, William Doncaster was a useful man to know – and Sir John Boydell knew him well. On 29 September 1294, Doncaster leased some land in Dodleston, Balderton and Rudfield from Dieulacres Abbey. Much of it was territory John's father had given the monks. Five years later, the abbot of Dieulacres also let the manor of Dodleston to Doncaster for forty-five years, an arrangement that made Doncaster John's subtenant. Moreover, John often came into Chester. Cheshire was routinely called on to supply pork and bacon for the king's armies and John was one of many local landholders who capitalised on the opportunities this presented: in 1302-03, for example, the chamberlains' accounts show that he sold '20 bacons' for 30s.[2] So he probably dined at Doncaster's sumptuous townhouse on a number of occasions.

Their business dealings weren't all that united the two men. Doncaster and his wife Felicia had several unmarried daughters – one of whom, Nichola, was much the same age as John's eldest son, William. Reasoning that trade might bring the wealth the blade could no longer win, John set about arranging a match. The negotiations proceeded smoothly and the wedding took place in the first half of 1303, but then things went horribly wrong.[3]

John had borrowed £7 10s from Doncaster in March 1301 and repaid the money at the end of three months, as agreed.[4] In late 1302 or early 1303, he borrowed another 1,000 marks. This was a debt of a totally different magnitude; 1,000 marks amounted to the annual landed income of an earl. John may have decided to go into business on his own account. Alternatively, perhaps, he wanted to build a grand new house or was simply living beyond his means. In any case, he promised to reimburse Doncaster before 18 September 1305.[5]

Indebtedness was a ubiquitous feature of life in Chester, as in all medieval towns. Inhabitants at every level of society bought goods on credit. The city's traders and craftsmen allowed their regular customers to pay late, while many townspeople routinely extended credit to their relatives, neighbours and friends. Most of these debts were small and brief in duration, ranging from 6d for bread to 10d for three months' rent of a chamber. They were also informal and undocumented, although the debtor might be required to find a pledge who would stand surety for him and assume liability for the debt, if he defaulted. Commercial debts between traders, by contrast, were often backed by written instruments. The 1285 Statute of Merchants enabled creditors to register debts in certain towns and cities. If a debtor failed to pay on the due date, the creditor could have him incarcerated and get a writ for the seizure and sale of his lands or chattels, up to the value of the sum that was owed.

Chester was one of the places where mercantile debts could be registered. Creditor and debtor would both go to the city exchequer, where the debtor would formally swear to repay the debt in front of the mayor, and the 'recognizance' would be recorded in the Mayors' Books. But even debts of this sort rarely exceeded £50. John was borrowing more than thirteen times that amount and Doncaster naturally wanted to safeguard his own interests. So he and John visited the exchequer, where John duly bound himself to repay the money in front of Alexander Hurrell, that year's mayor.

However, soon after William and Nichola married, John and Doncaster entered into a covenant revising the terms of the loan. John undertook not to dispose of any of the property he and his wife held in Latchford, apart from a piece of meadow land and a farthing of annual rent that he planned to give his youngest sons, Robert and Hugh. He also promised that, when he and Margaret died, they would leave all their estates in Latchford to William. John had probably already arranged the marriage of his only daughter, Matilda, to Robert de Millington, who held the nearby manor of Millington.[6] And like most manorial lords, John had always intended to leave the bulk of his landed wealth to his eldest son.

In return, Doncaster swore to forgive part of John's debt: he would accept 800 marks and wipe out the remaining 200. These terms only applied if William and Nichola had a child. If they had no offspring, John agreed that he would give Doncaster and his heirs the manor of Handley, together with a house and two parcels of lands in Dodleston and an income of 10s a year for eight years, payable from the rent he received for leasing out certain lands in Kinnerton. Provided that John kept his side of the bargain, Doncaster would still write off the 200 marks and annul the recognizance.

The new contract was signed and sealed and John seems to have repaid 800 of the 1,000 marks he had borrowed. So the merchant's next move came like a bolt out of the blue. In the autumn of 1305, Doncaster had John arrested and imprisoned in the county court gaol at Chester Castle for debt. He had taken his copy of the original recognizance to the constable of the castle, invoked his rights under the Statute of Merchants and demanded that the constable detain John for non-payment, even though John – as he vigorously protested – had fulfilled all the terms of their agreement. Furious at this impugnment of his honour and bewildered by Doncaster's behaviour, John retaliated by counter-claiming for unjust imprisonment and breach of covenant.

Fortunately, John had kept a copy of the paperwork himself and was able to produce it at the preliminary hearing on 18 September 1305. He presumably made a favourable impression because the court authorities decided to release him from custody, if he could find a dozen men to stand surety for him at the next sitting. John's relatives and fellow manorial lords – indignant, perhaps, at the way Doncaster had treated one of their number – promptly rallied to his side. On 7 December, twelve local gentry trooped into court and stood bail for him. After three months in prison, John was free to go home.

Chester Castle with the new prison by the northern gate

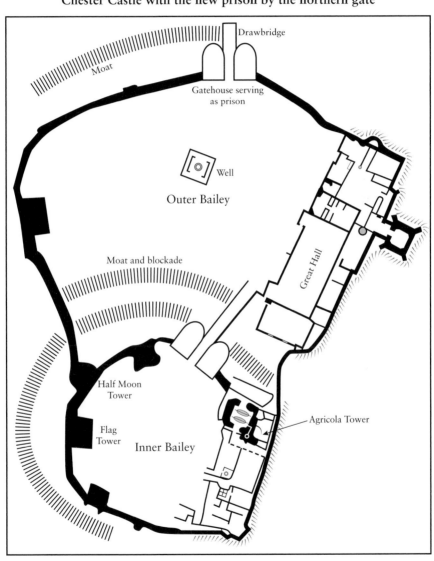

Source: Adapted from B.C.A. Windle, *Chester: A Historical and Topographical Account of the City* (1904), p. 100.

The case wasn't over, but John was only too glad to leave his cell; even for high-ranking inmates facing civil charges, prison was an unpleasant experience. Most county gaols were located within castles. Ordinary prisoners were kept in small wooden huts or cages in the castle yard, while more eminent prisoners were held in the gatehouse or one of the turrets. Some effort was also made to separate petty offenders from serious criminals. Whereas debtors and minor trespassers might be lodged in tower rooms high above the ground, major felons were confined in crowded underground dungeons. Nevertheless, although wealthy prisoners could pay for 'gentle keeping', such as better lodgings, food, fuel and bedding, the period of waiting in gaol before trial was expensive and stressful. Poorer prisoners fared far worse and charitable gifts were often all that stopped them from starving to death.

On 11 January 1306, John and Doncaster finally reached a compromise. John insisted that he had 'faithfully' adhered to the provisions of the covenant but agreed to withdraw his claim for damages and costs incurred as a result of being unjustly detained in the county gaol, while Doncaster agreed to drop his case. The recognizance and indenture would continue to apply, with certain modifications, including the addition of a clause to the effect that John wouldn't lease his lands and tenements to anyone for a term of more than fifteen years.

The lawsuit was resolved, but it had torn the two families apart. The situation must have been especially distressing for William and Nichola. Married off like the commodities in which Doncaster normally traded, they had then been forced to watch as their fathers fought over money. It was hardly a recipe for marital harmony. The case also exposed the gulf between the merchant class and local gentry. Where Doncaster socialised with Chester's mayors and business moguls, John mixed with knights and manorial lords. Only one of the twelve men who stood bail for him – John de Warwick, the former city sheriff – moved in the circles Doncaster inhabited. At least nine of the others belonged to John's extensive network of landowning friends and relatives. They may have had their differences; indeed, in the summer of 1302, John and his cousin Sir Peter de Dutton had squabbled over some property in Warburton.[7] Yet the two were quickly reconciled and Peter was first in line to bail John out. Blade and trade might intermarry, but when it came to the crunch blood and lineage outweighed lucre.

No sooner had he been released from prison than John resumed his normal responsibilities. The day after being granted bail he was back in court as one of the jurors in a case of abduction involving some of the very same gentry who had supported him in his quarrel with Doncaster. Medieval men sometimes resorted to stealing prospective brides to enrich themselves. In such cases, the kidnapper might rape the victim to consummate the nuptials or to shame her into consenting to the marriage. William de Dutton, the unscrupulous younger brother of Sir Hugh de Dutton, stood accused of bride-theft. He had broken into Hamo de Massey's manor at Dunham Massey with an armed posse of more than forty friends and abducted Massey's ward, a young heiress called Matilda de Stockport. The terrified girl had been dragged out of her bedchamber at dawn, stripped of everything save her chemise, thrown over the saddle of a horse and carried off to be forcibly wedded to William. Roger de Cheadle and William Venables, who had provided pledges for John, were both incriminated; the one had assented to the plan, while the other had sheltered the miscreants.[8]

Yet even though John was now back on the jurors' bench, he and his family were still mired in legal battles. While the common law had brought justice within reach of many more people, it had also spawned a litigious society with individuals from almost every walk of life prepared to sue at the slightest provocation. By 1275, the problem had become so acute that an act was passed forbidding maintenance (the funding of an unrelated litigant's case) and champerty (the provision of help for a litigant in return for part of the lands or money in dispute, if the action succeeded). Parliament also prohibited vexatious litigation and banned lawyers from manipulating the trial process.

William and Nichola Boydell had settled in Handley. By April 1306, they were embroiled in a row with Patrick de Golborne, who claimed that their bailiffs had detained two of his cows. The bailiffs replied that Golborne and his wife Mabel were in breach of their tenurial obligations. Golborne had abused his grazing rights by keeping more pigs than the terms of his tenancy permitted and regularly letting the animals stray into William and Nichola's woods to feed on the acorns and beechnuts there. He had also neglected to give the couple his third best pig, in accordance with the custom of the manor, and failed to attend the manorial court that Easter, as required. The case was eventually decided in William and Nichola's favour; Golborne, it seems, had been pushing his luck. In September 1306, John and Margaret also sued Henry de Lacy, the ageing earl of Lincoln, to recover a house in Latchford. But though both legal tussles were irritating, neither was as serious as the action Doncaster had brought against John and relations between the pair remained frosty.[9]

The arrival of a grandchild produced something of a thaw. In late 1307 or early 1308, Nichola gave birth to a boy, whom she and her husband named William, a diplomatic choice that recalled the child's maternal grandfather as well as his father. Shortly afterwards John borrowed £3 from Doncaster.[10] The two men were clearly on reasonably cordial terms again. There was little point in continuing to harbour a grudge when they had a grandson in common, a grandson who would carry on the family line when John was long dead and buried – a fact of which he was increasingly mindful.

At 52, John was old and his health was deteriorating. His joints were stiff of a morning and old injuries throbbed when he was tired. His physical frailties weren't the only reminder that the clock was ticking. The king's death on 7 July 1307 had reinforced his awareness of the passing decades. Edward's demise in one of the more remote parts of his realm – the village of Burgh by Sands near Carlisle – remained a closely guarded secret for almost two weeks because the government feared that the news would give heart to the Scots, with whom Edward had been warring on and off since 1296. But when word eventually spread, his subjects grieved. The same strong hand had rested on the national tiller for nearly thirty-five years. John probably felt the change keenly. He had been a young squire in 1274, when the king was crowned at Westminster Abbey after returning from the Holy Land, and could barely remember life under another monarch.

Moreover, Edward of Caernarfon had made a most inauspicious start to his reign. He was young, tall and prepossessing, as his father had been. 'God had endowed him with gifts of every virtue and had made him equal to or indeed more excellent than other kings', the anonymous author of the *Vita Edwardi Secundi* remarked. But as his true colours emerged, the nation that had welcomed him with open arms was rapidly becoming disenchanted. The new monarch's first royal act was to recall his friend Piers Gaveston from exile in Gascony and make him earl of Cornwall, a move that outraged many of the magnates. Gaveston was the son of a minor Gascon knight and this was a title previously granted only to senior members of the royal family.

Edward's bond with Gaveston had already set tongues wagging and even, perhaps, accounted for the young Gascon's expulsion.

Edward I had banished him for unspecified reasons in February 1307, but contemporary pundits speculated that the prince's 'inordinate affection' for Gaveston was the real cause. Gaveston's wicked sense of humour fanned the flames of hatred even higher. He had disparaging nicknames for all his court rivals; the earl of Lincoln was 'Bust-Belly' and the earl of Warwick 'the Black Dog of Arden', while Thomas of Lancaster, the king's first cousin, was 'Ham actor' – a tag that mortally offended Lancaster, a quick-tempered man with a keen sense of his own importance.

Edward II – weak and infatuated – simply ignored his critics. Spurred on by Gaveston, he dismissed some of his father's ministers, replacing them with men of his own choosing. He began by having Walter Langton, his father's treasurer, arrested and cast into gaol for administrative abuses and appointing Walter Reynolds, bishop of Worcester, in Langton's stead. Reynolds was the son of a baker and had formerly been controller of the prince's wardrobe. Selected, apparently, because he was Gaveston's friend and skilled at organising the theatrical productions Edward adored, Reynolds was completely unfit for high office.

In November 1307, the king conferred yet another honour on Gaveston with the gift in marriage of his niece, Margaret de Clare, sister of the earl of Gloucester. And when Edward and his bride, Isabella, the 12-year-old daughter of Philip IV of France, were crowned in a joint coronation at Westminster Abbey on 25 February 1308, Gaveston played a key role in the ceremony. Clothed in pearl-encrusted robes of purple – the colour normally reserved for royalty – Gaveston 'more resembled the god Mars than an ordinary mortal'. He outshone the magnates clad in their traditional gold cloth and eclipsed the king himself.

What incensed the barons and shocked spectators even more, however, was that Gaveston bore the crown of Edward the Confessor into the abbey, a privilege that should have gone to the highest noble in the realm. And at the badly organised banquet that followed the coronation, the king chose to sit next to his favourite rather than his queen, angering her two uncles so much that they left early for France. As a result, the *Annales Paulini* states, 'A rumour spread around all the land that the king loved this artful and malevolent man more than his wife, that most elegant lady and beautiful of women.'

The world was truly topsy-turvy, if a young *arriviste* like Piers Gaveston could upstage the country's greatest nobles. And the rot, as far as Sir John Boydell was concerned, was rapidly spreading north. In early 1308, John Bakester of Warrington and his wife Beatrix set fire to some of John's tenements near the bridge over the Mersey at Warrington – motivated, perhaps, by resentment at having to pay the tolls John levied for crossing the river. The Bakesters were outlawed, while the townships of Latchford, Grappenhall, Thelwall and Appleton were fined for failing to catch them within forty days, as required by the Statute of Winchester passed in 1285.[11] But the crime was incontestable proof that the times were out of joint. Arson was rare, and the danger from accidental fires so grave that those who deliberately started fires were regarded with particular abhorrence.

Alarmed by the terrible state into which the country seemed to be sinking under an intemperate whippersnapper of a monarch and conscious of his own impending mortality, John granted the hermit friars of the order of St Augustine at Warrington 'free passage through the vill of Latchford for their wains'. He was making the gift, he explained, 'for the health of my body and the safety of my soul, that of my wife Margaret and those of my heirs and parents'. In return, he asked only that every brother celebrate Mass on the anniversary of the day on which he died.[12]

That day was fast approaching. John was still alive on 8 October 1308, when he participated in an enquiry to ascertain whether Sir Reginald Grey's son had the right to pasture his livestock in Delamere Forest. But he died very shortly afterwards. A writ for his inquisition post mortem was issued on 27 November, and the inquisition itself was conducted on 2 July 1309. John had expired holding the manors of Dodleston and Grappenhall and two bovates of land in Latchford from the king. He had also leased a plot of land called the Middlehurst, in Grappenhall, from the earl of Lincoln for an annual payment of 4d. These properties, the jurors determined, were to go to his 26-year-old son, William.[13]

In fact, Edward II had already permitted William to take possession of his estates. On 26 December 1308, while the king was staying at Windsor Castle, he ordered the escheator of Cheshire to deliver the lands to William, since William had paid homage for them.[14] But Edward's celerity in granting William his inheritance came at a price; within weeks of taking possession of the family holdings William was wending his way abroad on royal service.

9

On the King's Business

Dusk was falling on Avignon as the two barges the diplomatic mission had hired rounded the bend and pulled under the great stone bridge spanning the Rhône. The river gleamed bright against the edges of the land, a dappled silver grey shot with molten gold where the sun spilled into the water. On the western bank, where the light was concentrated, a few buildings stood silhoutted against a bruised-purple backdrop. On the eastern bank the quayside was shrouded in gloom. The slope above was dotted with terracotta roofs, just discernible in the fading blue sky. There were two worlds, William mused: one well-lit and clearly defined; the other dark, covert, full of shadows and whispers.

The bells were pealing for vespers by the time both boats were moored at the wooden jetty. It would soon be pitch-black and they had a lot to unload. Bishop Reynolds had brought eight chests bursting with clothes, coverlets and drapes, and a coffer full of altar ornaments and service books. Then there was the iron strongbox containing the gold, silver and jewels the king had sent to smoothe the negotiations, which had to be guarded around the clock. Add all the baggage belonging to Reynolds' clerics and the earls of Richmond and Pembroke, and they would need at least two dozen packhorses to carry their goods.

William summoned some of the men standing around on the quayside to help the servants unload everything, while Peter Ingelard went off to find horses or mules. Eventually, animals laden and torches lit, they were ready to enter the city. Avignon seemed small and sleepy after London – an odd place in which to house the papacy, William thought, as he led his party through the streets, careful to avoid the runnels oozing down the middle. The bishop and his fellow emissaries would stay at the Dominican convent where the pope had set up residence, but the armed escort would have to find an inn. William suppressed a yawn. They had set off well before dawn and it would be midnight before he saw a bed. He hoped it wouldn't be as flea-ridden as the last one.

In March 1309, Clement V moved the heart of Christendom from Rome to Avignon, a prosperous little city on the banks of the River Rhône. Italy's warring aristocratic families had reduced Rome to a state of anarchy. Philip the Fair, king of France, had also been known to resort to violence when popes proved troublesome. Six years earlier, his soldiers had kidnapped Clement's predecessor, Boniface VIII, and probably subjected him to a severe beating. The hapless Boniface had died a month later, leaving the papacy in turmoil. Avignon belonged to the princes of Naples, so it fell outside Philip's control. But it still lay within easy reach of much of western Europe, thanks to an extensive network of roads and waterways. Above all, it was peaceful – the perfect refuge for an ailing pontiff weary of wandering around the continent. Since his election in June 1305, Clement had travelled some 3,000 miles, trekking over unpaved roads and muddy tracks regardless of the season.

As soon as the pope arrived in Avignon, Edward II sent his first important mission to the papal court. Led by Walter Reynolds, bishop of Worcester, John of Brittany, earl of Richmond, and Aymer de Valence, earl of Pembroke, its main purpose was to nullify the threat of excommunication hanging over Piers Gaveston's head. United in their loathing of the king's favourite, almost all of the magnates had risen up against Gaveston, binding themselves 'by a mutual oath never to cease from what they had begun until Piers had left the land of England'.[1] Edward stubbornly refused to banish his friend. But in May 1308, with the country teetering on the brink of civil war, he was forced to give in. That June, he sent Gaveston to Ireland as its lord lieutenant. The pugnacious Robert Winchelsea, archbishop of Canterbury, swore to excommunicate Gaveston if he didn't leave the country by 25 June – four days before Gaveston and his wife actually sailed for Dublin.

With Gaveston gone, the barons ceased their opposition to the king. However, Edward was determined to bring his friend back. He waited for the dust to settle before organising a diplomatic embassy to the pope. On 4 March 1309, Reynolds and the small band of clerics he had chosen to accompany him to Avignon were granted letters of protection from legal disputes while they went 'beyond seas on the king's service'. William Boydell was one of five men ordered to serve as the bishop's guard. They, too, were to have judicial protection while they escorted Reynolds abroad.[2]

The timing wasn't particularly convenient as far as William was concerned. His father had died a few months previously, leaving him locked in a battle with his cousin Robert over two houses and two bovates of land in Latchford. Robert insisted that Sir John had given them to his brother Hugh and that they now belonged to him as Hugh's son and heir, disregarding the fact that John had initiated legal proceedings against Hugh's widow, Alice, to recover the property. William had also promised to pay the Doncasters £60 a year for the duration of his mother-in-law Felicia's life. And his father-in-law's business – in which he had recently invested via a joint recognizance for 400 marks to the keeper of the privy seal – had suffered a setback, when the ship Doncaster hired to carry wool from Ipswich to Flushing for the Flemish market was driven ashore by a storm. 'Certain malefactors of Zeeland' had seized wool and other goods worth 500 marks. Although the count of Hainault had helped Doncaster's agents recover part of the cargo, he had ignored repeated requests for restitution of the remaining chattels or compensation. In March 1309, the exasperated merchant asked for the king's aid in securing justice.[3]

William wasn't in serious financial difficulties. He had, after all, just inherited the bulk of the Boydell estates. In May 1307, he had also received permission to hold a weekly market and annual fair in Handley, together with a grant to hunt game on his demesne lands.[4] Under medieval law all game belonged to the king, but exemptions could be given and the warrening of rabbits was very profitable. Dietary patterns were changing, with greater demand for meat, so the flesh and fur could be sold for good money. Still, William had a lot on his mind as he rode down from Cheshire to meet Reynolds.

The bishop's party set out from Worcester on 23 March 1309 – a date chosen, perhaps, for its auspicious connotations. It was Palm Sunday, the feast commemorating Christ's triumphal entry into Jerusalem. On the first leg of the expedition the convoy travelled down to Westminster to join the earls of Richmond and Pembroke and their men. Then, once everybody had assembled, they made their way to London by river, and from London to Dover via Rochester and Canterbury, a journey that took the best part of a day. At Dover, they probably chartered a ship to carry them to Wissant, near Calais, which was the most popular Channel crossing. This took another full day.

Landing at Wissant on the evening of the second day out from London, the embassy stayed overnight at a local inn before beginning the

William Boydell's journey to Avignon in 1309

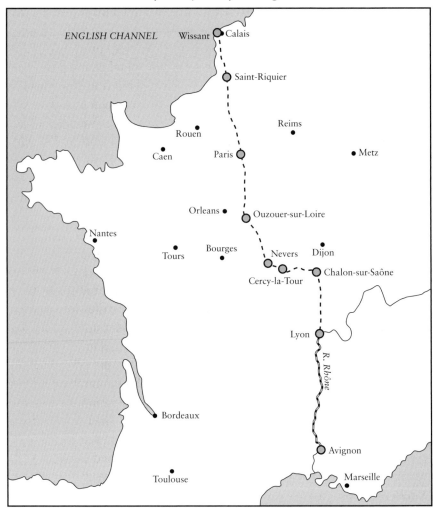

long slog to Provence. The king's messengers regularly visited Avignon, so in all likelihood Reynolds and his party followed the same route, riding south to Lyon via Paris, Dourdan, Ouzouer-sur-Loire, Nevers and Chalon-sur-Saône, a distance of nearly 500 miles. At Lyon, tired and saddle-sore, they had a good supper and rested for the night before hiring a couple of barges to carry them down the Rhône to Avignon, reaching their destination just as the light was fading.

The king's messengers could travel from Westminster to Avignon in eight days. The delegates, burdened as they were with baggage, probably took at least twice as long. Royal envoys needed to cut an impressive figure, so the bishop's party may not have arrived in Avignon until mid-April. But by 25 April, when Clement issued a papal bull blocking Winchelsea's threat to excommunicate Gaveston, Reynolds had achieved his primary goal. On 5 May, under the vigilant eye of William and his armed guards, Reynolds delivered money and valuables worth 30,000 florins (the equivalent of about £2.4 million in today's terms) to the Dominican convent where the pope was residing, as a mark of Edward II's gratitude. Two weeks later, Clement issued another bull directing the bishops of Lincoln and London to resume collecting the papal tithe, three-quarters of which was to be paid to the king. The mission had been a resounding success.

Their business concluded, the delegates set off on the return journey towards the end of May. Meanwhile, Edward was joyfully reunited with his favourite at Chester – the one and only occasion on which he visited the city during his reign. On 27 June 1309, when Gaveston sailed back from Dublin, the king was awaiting him on the dock. He greeted Gaveston like 'a friend returning from a long pilgrimage' and restored all the lands Gaveston had been forced to surrender before his exile. Edward had made a number of political concessions to secure Gaveston's recall, but he hadn't even waited for parliament to meet before rushing north.

By 22 July 1309, Bishop Reynolds was back in his old rectory at Sawbridgeworth in Hertfordshire. William still had to complete the last part of his journey to Cheshire, but by the end of the month he was also home. As he rode into Handley he feasted his eyes on the lush green countryside so unlike the terraced olive groves of Provence. The air was fresh with the tang of summer grass and newly turned earth, a scent infinitely sweeter than the acrid wood fires of Avignon or the stink of London's excrement-filled streets.

Much had happened in William's absence. His father's inquisition post mortem had been conducted. His mother had also found a new partner. William Gerard was lord of half of the manor of Kingsley, near Frodsham, and already knew the Boydells. In 1285, he had served as a squire to William's third cousin, Sir Hugh de Dutton, who had been so pleased with his service that he promised to give Gerard 'one squire's robe' every Chistmas for the rest of his life. Gerard had subsequently leased the manor of Nether Bradley in a deed witnessed by Sir John Boydell. He had wasted no time courting Margaret and the couple were married by 30 December 1309, when William sued them for a debt of £3 12s. Three months later they, in turn, sued William, his cousin Robert and Robert's widowed mother, Alice, to recover Margaret's dower.[5]

While William was away, Henry de Lacy, earl of Lincoln, and his henchman had also seized one of his horses. In October 1309, William sued Lacy, but before he could get very far with the case he was summoned down to Westminster again. The heirs of feudal tenants were required to pay their overlord 'relief' before taking possession of their inheritance and Magna Carta had set the level at £5 per knight's fee. William held 4½ knights' fees and therefore owed the king £22 10s. In January 1310, Edward ordered the justice of Chester to distrain William's lands and chattels and ensure that he came down to London in person that April to pay the tax into the exchequer.[6]

William was probably knighted at much the same time. Edward I had revived distraint for knighthood in 1277 at the start of his Welsh wars. In 1292, he set the threshold for compulsory knighthood at £40 a year and it had remained there ever since. Edward II cared little for chivalry but was ready to use the same tactics to raise the troops he needed – or to top up the royal treasury with fines from those who wanted to escape their obligations.

William had certainly been scrubbed and dubbed by the time he resolved his quarrel with his cousin, soon after returning from London. Robert was still pressing his claim to the two tenements in Latchford. The case had been put on hold while William was overseas, but he clearly had no desire for another family feud. In a conciliatory gesture he confirmed that Robert could keep the land in Middlehurst which John had earlier granted Hugh. Robert could also collect wood for repairing his house and fences and burning a hearthfire. Two years afterwards, William gave Robert another piece of ground on the road from Middlehurst to Warrington and some land lying between Grappenhall and Lymm, possibly to compensate for the loss of his portion of Margaret's dower, which Robert and his mother had refused to surrender. William's brother-in-law, Robert Doncaster, the newly appointed parson of Grappenhall, witnessed the deed. Encouraged by William and Nichola, the prior of Norton had presented Doncaster to the living on 10 February 1311.[7]

William was far less inclined to settle with Lacy, whose attorney – much to his annoyance – was trying to clear the earl on a technicality. William, he argued, had alleged that his horse was taken on the Friday after the Feast of St John the Baptist. Yet there were two such feasts: the feast of St John's nativity on 24 June and the feast of his decollation (or beheading) on 29 August. Since William had failed to specify which one he meant, his suit was defective. William's response was terse. The earl had unlawfully seized his property and he had provided more than enough evidence of that fact; days and years weren't words normally used in such pleas. Judgment was deferred, but Lacy was a powerful opponent. When he ignored a writ to come to court in September 1310, the king sent orders not to 'put him in default' for failing to show up. The earl had escaped all censure.[8]

If William resented Edward's interference, there was nothing he could do about it. Nor could he object when the king's eye fell on the Boydells again eleven months later. Edward had learned of Margaret's second marriage and wasn't best pleased. In August 1311, he commanded the escheator of Cheshire to seize her dower because she had married Gerard without his permission. Although the widows of tenants-in-chief could no longer be forcibly remarried, they were still required to obtain royal consent before entering into another union. Margaret, determined to control her own fate, had flouted the rule and now had to pay a fine to get back into Edward's good books.[9]

In fact, William had just fallen foul of the law himself. Towards the end of 1311, the people of Salford lodged a suit complaining that a group of men led by Sir Hamo de Massey, baron of Dunham Massey, 'came and chased large numbers of their livestock into Cheshire'. William and his kinsman Geoffrey de Warburton were among the accused. Writs of trespass were duly issued summoning all the culprits for trial in Lancashire, the county in which the crime had been committed.[10] However, it was notoriously difficult to bring Cheshire men to court in neighbouring counties, as Massey was aware. In 1296, he had petitioned against a summons before the King's Bench in Lancashire, claiming that the people of Cheshire had always been answerable to the justice of Chester alone and couldn't be tried anywhere else.

The offenders apparently got off scot-free. Only six months later, William was to be found sitting on a commission to establish who owned Rudheath, a large tract of wasteland in the middle of Cheshire. Traditionally, the locals had enjoyed the right to 'assart' – or enclose and cultivate – pieces of the heath and to pasture their beasts there. But under the Anglo-Norman earls of Chester, Rudheath had been designated a 'secular sanctuary', where fugitives could seek protection from the earls in exchange for serving them. Further assarting of Rudheath was banned without a licence. This was a source of great irritation, since the populace was still growing; assarting was an obvious way of feeding more people and profiting from the expansion. A number of neighbouring religious houses and manorial lords, including the Vernons of Shipbrook and Grosvenors of Allostock, therefore ignored the ban.

By 1309, much of Rudheath had been illegally enclosed, so the justice of Chester decided to reclaim it. He had the boundaries of the heath measured and recorded. Then, in July 1310, he issued orders to seize the lands the Vernons and Grosvenors had assarted. Both families protested and an inquisition was set up to investigate. In April 1312, William and his co-jurors concluded that Rudheath didn't belong to the king, as earl of Chester; the manorial landholders with territory adjoining the heath were the 'lords of the soil'.[11]

Fortunately for William, his role in an enquiry that upheld the rights of Cheshire's landed elite over those of the crown didn't harm his standing with the king. On 22 August 1312, Edward granted William and his heirs free warren – the right to hunt game and keep rabbits – in all their demesne lands in Dodleston, Grappenhall and Latchford, just as William already enjoyed in Handley.[12] But by that point the king had far graver matters on his mind.

The barons deeply resented his repeated attempts to extort money and the way he continued to lavish favours on Piers Gaveston, depriving them of the royal patronage they believed was their due. Edward had learned nothing from his earlier tussle with England's magnates and was still showering privileges on his friend. In 1310, the barons banded together with the leading clergy and forced the king to agree to the appointment of a committee of twenty-one 'ordainers' to draw up detailed proposals for reform. The Ordinances of 1311 curbed Edward's administrative powers and included specific clauses against 'evil' or 'deceptive' counsellors, a clear dig at Gaveston.

The king was determined to maintain his royal authority and protect his friend. His opponents – led by his cousin Thomas, earl of Lancaster – were equally determined that Gaveston had to go and they prevailed. In 1311, Gaveston was exiled again. He sneaked back into the country after the birth of his daughter at the end of the year. However, all Edward's attempts to arrange for his permanent return failed. In early 1312, a warrant was issued for Gaveston's arrest and that May he surrendered to the earls of Pembroke and Surrey.

Gaveston might still have been safe, were it not for the earl of Warwick. As Pembroke and Surrey were bringing their prisoner south, Warwick ambushed them and carried Gaveston off to his castle. There, Gaveston was subjected to a mock trial and beheaded in front of the earls of Lancaster, Hereford and Arundel. Just three years after William had joined Reynolds on his arduous journey to Avignon to bring Gaveston back from exile, the king's favourite was dead. Word of his execution spread rapidly through the country via a vicious little ditty celebrating Lancaster's role in taming 'the pestiferous one'. But Edward was devastated by the loss of his beloved Piers; from then on, he regarded Lancaster as his mortal enemy.

The king's revenge would have to wait. Scotland – under the leadership of the recently crowned Robert Bruce – presented a more immediate problem. In 1286, Alexander III, the last in a long line of Scoto-Norman monarchs, died while attempting to cross the Firth of Forth late at night to visit his new bride. Alexander's three children by his first wife, Margaret, one of the daughters of Henry III of England, were all dead and he had remarried in the hope of fathering another royal clutch. On 18 March 1286, he spent the evening feasting at Edinburgh Castle before setting off on horseback for Fife, dismissing all advice to delay the journey. But as he rode across the beach at Kinghorn in the dark, he became separated from his guides. The next morning his body was found on the beach, where he had fallen from his horse and broken his neck. Liquor and lust had proved a fatal cocktail.

Alexander's sole heir was a granddaughter, Margaret – the child of his eldest daughter and her husband, Eric II of Norway. But Margaret was only 3 years old, so the Scots established a committee of guardians to govern the country on her behalf. After negotiating with the Norwegians, they also secured a promise that Margaret would come to Scotland when she was older. And Edward I, spotting a chance to unite the two kingdoms, proposed that she wed his son Edward. However, this scheme collapsed when Margaret died in October 1290, without once having set foot in Scotland.

Two Scottish nobles, Robert Bruce and John Balliol, emerged as candidates for the vacant throne. In 1292, Balliol was crowned king, but he proved incapable of imposing order on the country. Three years later, the Scots – led by Bruce's son, another Robert – rebelled against his rule. In 1296, they created a council of twelve prominent Scotsmen and formed an alliance with France, under which both parties pledged to support each other against their common foe, England. Over the next decade, a bloody struggle took place, as various Scottish contenders vied for the top seat and Edward I tried to subdue his fractious northern neighbours. But, by 1306, Bruce was the clear winner. He was crowned Robert I of Scotland on 25 March, six weeks after murdering his last remaining rival, 'Red' Comyn, before the high altar of the Greyfriars church at Dumfries.

Edward II had half-heartedly continued to prosecute the war with Scotland but lacked his father's military skills and imperial ambitions. When Bruce started raiding England, he was unable to deliver an effective martial riposte. In November 1311, he decided to explore other avenues and sent William Lamberton, bishop of St Andrews, on a diplomatic mission to Scotland. William Boydell's brother John was one of the ten 'king's yeomen' appointed to guard Lamberton on his journey. John had served in the previous year's Scottish campaign, when he was hired by Bishop Reynolds to provide part of the military service the diocese of Worcester was required to supply. Now he was to escort Lamberton north. Riding alongside him would be Peter Ingelard and William Drawespere, both of whom had accompanied William Boydell on the embassy to Avignon.[13]

Lamberton certainly needed guarding, albeit for different reasons from those Edward had in mind. He had actively campaigned for the Scottish nationalist cause and diverted vast sums of money from his diocese to help finance Scotland's war against the English. He had even played a role in Bruce's coronation in 1306, for which Edward I had him clapped in irons and imprisoned in Winchester Castle. Only his status as a man of the cloth had saved him from execution. In May 1308, Edward II freed Lamberton, although the bishop was required to pay a ransom of 6,000 marks and remain in the diocese of Durham. Thereafter, Lamberton acted as the king's envoy on various occasions, but he secretly remained loyal to Bruce.

Not that Bruce had any intention of settling with the English, when the war was going his way. In early 1314, he captured the castles of Roxburgh and Edinburgh, while his brother Edmund besieged Stirling. Edward had no option but to fight. Mustering an army of 2,500 cavalry and 15,000 foot soldiers, he marched into Scotland. At the Battle of

Bannockburn on 24 June 1314, Bruce inflicted a catastrophic defeat on the king's forces, cutting his cavalry to shreds. Edward himself barely escaped with his life. Blame followed shame, with accusations of cowardice and incompetence swirling through the air as the king and his barons denounced each other for England's humiliation.

A terrible famine shortly afterwards compounded the nation's misery. Unusually wet conditions produced a poor harvest in 1314. The next year the weather was even worse. Torrential rain caused much of the seed grain that had been planted to rot before it could germinate. Country folk foraged for what they could, gathering edible roots, plants and nuts to supplement their depleted stores, but the summer of 1316 was equally wet and cold. By the spring of 1317, starving families were forced to slaughter their livestock and eat the seed grain they normally put aside to grow the next year's crops. The poorest consumed cats, dogs and other 'unclean things' and there were horrific rumours of people stealing children to eat. The suffering continued even after the weather improved in 1317; without seed grain to plant or draught horses and oxen to till the ground, there could be no quick recovery.

Cheshire fared as badly as the rest of England. In 1316, harvesting at the manor of Frodsham dragged on for five weeks, as the fieldworkers desperately tried to glean every precious ear of corn from the sodden ground. And with grain prices rocketing, Sir William Trussell of Warmingham had to pay the princely sum of £30 6s 8d for wheat. Sir William Boydell was one of three people who stood surety for the debt, but he was doing better than most. His father-in-law, commercially astute as ever, had entered the long-distance trade in corn, rye and barley and seems to have included William in at least one of his deals. Doncaster had entered into a bond with the earldom of Chester, to which William was also a party. No reason is provided, but it was the earldom that had supplied Trussell with grain.[14]

An abundant harvest in 1318 marked the end of the most serious phase of the famine. But yet another disaster now occurred. There had been a widespread sheep murrain – a general term for various livestock diseases – in 1317. At Easter 1319, a new epidemic affecting cattle and oxen began to work its way up the country. A mediocre harvest in 1320 and another appalling harvest in 1321 also pushed up grain prices again. It was not until 1322 that conditions finally returned to normal, with better harvests.

The cumulative effect of this cruel combination of crises was shattering. Between 1315 and 1322, as much as 15 per cent of England's population perished. The bodies of paupers who had starved to death littered the streets of large towns and cities, leaving a foul odour because the gravediggers couldn't bury them fast enough. The rural populace managed marginally better. But many of the neediest smallholders survived only by selling their parcels of land to more prosperous neighbours, so that they could raise money to buy ever dearer food. And in areas where the soil was especially poor entire villages were vacated.

The Boydells were cushioned by their wealth. Yet even William was feeling the pinch – one reason, perhaps, why he chose to go soldiering in Scotland in 1319. There is nothing to show whether he or any of his brothers participated in the Battle of Bannockburn in June 1314, although his near neighbour Robert de Pulford was one of the many English knights who fell on the field. However, Cheshire still retained the distinctive system of government that was a feature of its palatine status and military service was still defined in terms of wars in Wales. Earl Ranulf III had explicitly exempted Cheshire knights from serving 'beyond the Lyme' (or eastern edge of the county) except of their own free will and at the earl's expense. Edward I had confirmed these rights in March 1300. So William wasn't obliged to serve in Scotland, although he was well aware of the need to defend England's borders.

Buoyed by their success at Bannockburn, the Scots had made repeated forays deep into northern England. Edward – still at loggerheads with Lancaster – had largely disregarded them. But when the Scots captured the vital port of Berwick-upon-Tweed in April 1318, it was clear that this situation couldn't continue. In July 1319, temporarily putting aside their differences, the king and his cousin marched north to retake the port. They lingered in Newcastle for a month, despite the fact that the campaign had already been delayed by two months, arriving at Berwick on 7 September. William was one of the many knights who went with them. On 4 August 1319, he was granted letters of protection to go to Scotland 'in the company of Thomas, earl of Lancaster'.[15]

The English launched a heavy assault on Berwick by land and sea and nearly scaled the walls on the first day of the offensive. But the inhabitants rapidly 'regained their courage and defended themselves with spirit', managing to destroy the siege engines the English had brought to mine the town walls. Recognising that he lacked the strength to attack Edward's forces directly, Bruce also organised a diversionary raid into Yorkshire, where he had discovered that Queen Isabella was staying. His plan to abduct the queen was foiled when a Scottish scout was caught and confessed the plot to William Melton, archbishop of York; Isabella was packed off to Nottingham for safety and Melton hastily cobbled together an army of townsfolk to take on the enemy. But on 20 September 1319 the Scots won a second decisive victory at Myton, 12 miles north of York, killing some 4,000 Englishmen and driving another 1,000 into the River Swale, where they drowned.

When news of the defeat reached the king and his commanders at Berwick, they quarrelled bitterly. While Edward and his southern advisers wanted to divide their troops in order both to attack the Scots still remaining in Yorkshire and to continue the siege, the northern lords under Thomas of Lancaster wanted to return to England to protect their lands. Lancaster refused to stay, forcing the king to abandon the siege. The campaign had been a disaster. And as soon as Edward disbanded his army the Scots struck again. In November 1319, they raided Cumberland and Westmorland, burning the crops and carrying off both men and cattle. Edward was compelled to seek a truce, to which Bruce agreed shortly before Christmas.

William returned to Handley, probably relieved to escape the friction between the king and his cousin, as each blamed the other for the debacle. Once he was home, he witnessed a deed with William de Mobberley, the new county sheriff, and Sir Robert de Holland, who was serving a third stint as justice of Chester.[16] William was closely acquainted with Holland; his cousin, Hugh de Dutton, had married Holland's sister Joan some years previously. But Holland was a difficult man to like. He had risen from the ranks of the Lancashire gentry to become the earl of Lancaster's chief household official. His swift ascent, grasping ways and blatant abuse of power had made him deeply unpopular.

Moreover, the tensions that William had, perhaps, hoped to avoid when he went home were now permeating the whole of England. Relations between Edward and Lancaster had deteriorated still further after their abortive attack on Berwick. Some of the king's advisers even whispered that the earl had taken £40,000 from Robert Bruce to aid his cause secretly, by mounting a half-hearted siege and betraying the queen's whereabouts to the Scots. In fact, there was no evidence whatever of foul play on the earl's part; it was probably a disaffected knight called Edmund Darel who had given away the queen's location. But Edward was only too ready to listen to such allegations. According to the *Vita Edwardi Secundi*, he is said to have muttered darkly: 'When this wretched business is over, we will turn our hands to other matters. For I have not yet forgotten the wrong that was once done to my brother Piers.' The king had never forgiven Lancaster for his part in Gaveston's execution.

Nor had he changed his own ways, for once again it was Edward's favourites who helped to foment the conflict between the king and his cousin. After Gaveston's death Edward had turned to two men – Hugh Despenser and his son Hugh – for support. Hugh the Elder was the son of a Marcher lord who had died fighting alongside Simon de Montfort at Evesham, but he himself had served Edward I faithfully. By 1305, he was also close to the prince of Wales and, when Edward II was crowned, he became one of the king's chief counsellors. Hugh the Younger's relationship with Edward was more chequered. Initially, Edward neither liked nor trusted him. But when Hugh was appointed royal chamberlain in 1318, he rapidly won the king over – so much so, indeed, that rumours of Edward's homosexuality resurfaced. Hugh the Younger was much the king's age and court gossip suggested that he and Edward were lovers. The gossip was probably unfounded, given that Hugh and his wife Eleanor had nine children. Nevertheless, the Despensers were universally detested.

By the autumn of 1320, Hugh the Younger was firmly entrenched at Edward's side. Various commentators, including Geoffrey le Baker and the anonymous authors of the *Chronicle of Lanercost* and the *Brut*, complained that Hugh 'had bewitched the king's mind'. He was Edward's 'right eye' and 'kept so to the king's chamber that no man might speak with the king' without paying a bribe. The besotted Edward would listen only to Hugh and his father. History, it seemed, was repeating itself. But Hugh was a far more malevolent figure than his predecessor. Gaveston had been a foreigner of modest birth who exerted his influence indirectly, rather than trying to wield power in his own name. Hugh was related by blood or marriage to all the most important people in the realm and thoroughly versed in court politics. He behaved like 'a second king, or worse, the ruler of the king', Geoffrey le Baker grumbled.

In 1321, infuriated by the Despensers' machinations, the earls of Lancaster and Hereford led a coalition of northern magnates and Marcher lords in an attempt to drive the Despensers into exile – and, by 1322, Edward was openly at war with his barons. That March, his army crossed the River Trent at Walton, outflanking Lancaster's foot soldiers, whom the earl had placed at Burton to defend the bridge. Deserted by Sir Robert de Holland, on whom he had been relying to provide reinforcements, and vastly outnumbered, Lancaster and his fellow barons fled to Yorkshire, traversing the River Dove with such haste that the earl's war chest, stuffed with more than 1,500 silver pieces, fell into the water.

Lancaster and his allies got as far as Boroughbridge, where they were cut off by Sir Andrew de Harclay, a veteran of the Scottish wars, who had hurried south with a large contingent of men from Cumberland and Westmorland. The earl tried to win Harclay over, bemoaning the way in which the Despensers had misled the king with 'false counsel' and begging him to help 'destroy the venom of England'. When that failed, he had no choice but to fight. Harclay's troops held the bridge over the River Ure and the nearby ford, the only two places where the river could be crossed. And with the royal army following hard on their heels, Lancaster's troops risked being attacked from the rear.

The ensuing battle was vicious. Hereford was killed as he led an attack on the bridge by foot, when a pikeman hiding underneath the wooden planking thrust his spear between the timbers and pierced the earl in the rectum. Lancaster was captured the following day as he mounted an assault on the ford. He was stripped of his armour and forced to don the uniform his household squires wore, a calculated insult to a man of high birth. Then he was taken to the castle he had built at Pontefract, tried before the king and convicted of treason by a rigged jury that included the Despensers. On 22 March 1322, six days after being defeated at Boroughbridge, the earl was led from his prison cell to a hillock outside the castle on a bony old nag, and beheaded in front of a jeering crowd. Thomas of Lancaster had suffered the same fate he had visited on Piers Gaveston and the king had at last gained his vengeance.

As the earl was being carried by boat to Pontefract Castle, under the watchful eyes of Harclay's armed guards, the Boydells and their friends were entering his heartlands. On 14 February 1322, the king had ordered Sir Oliver Ingham, the newly appointed keeper of Cheshire, to raise a force of 100 foot soldiers. William and his brothers had joined Ingham. They had ridden to Walton in Edward's army and clashed with Lancaster's followers at Burton. Then, at the king's command, they had swung north-west to pursue the rebels fleeing towards the River Mersey. Now they were ready to cause mayhem.[17]

10

Floating in Blood

William gazed blearily at his brother as Hugh raised his brimming goblet. 'To the king, God save his Grace,' Hugh slurred. Hugh was completely cup-shotten. Actually, they all were. The butts of wine they'd taken from the cellar at John Radcliffe's house had been welcome after a long day in the saddle. Mid-March nights in Lancashire were cold enough to freeze a man's balls off, so they'd broken into Radcliffe's home for shelter. That Bordeaux had been a lucky find; it was good stuff, not your typical rotgut. Radcliffe would be furious when he discovered it was gone – assuming he kept his head, since he'd backed the wrong man.

Cheshire's leading gentry had turned out in full force to support Edward II in his battle with Thomas of Lancaster. When Oliver Ingham came recruiting, William Boydell and his three siblings – John, Robert and Hugh – had all volunteered. So had various members of the Massey and Warburton families, as well as the Fitton brothers, the Carringtons, Cheadles and Baguleys. They'd hurried down to Burton, only to see Lancaster's army turn tail. Then they'd ridden back to Runcorn and crossed the Mersey into Lancashire, leaving all the boats on the other side of the river to prevent the rebels from using them. After that, they'd started rounding up fugitives and confiscating their chattels.

The day's haul had been excellent, William reflected. They'd captured a number of rebels and carried off a lot of livestock, including a prize stallion. It was a pity about the old villein in Prestwich whose beard Robert had pulled. They hadn't meant to kill him; he'd simply collapsed at their feet in an apoplectic fit. But accidents happened in wartime and there was no point in weeping over spilled ale. It felt good to be doing proper men's work and then to sit eating, drinking and singing with his brothers-in-arms – especially when they could sit under a dry roof rather than leaking canvas.

On 15 March 1322, Sir Oliver Ingham and his retinue entered Lancashire with orders to sequester all the earl of Lancaster's possessions and round up his supporters, some 500 of whom were said to be marching from Wigan to Rochdale. The Cheshire levies, including the Boydell brothers, spent the next five days ranging the southern part of the county and harrassing the populace. In their zeal, they seized 'horses, mares, colts and fillies, oxen and cows, sheep, pigs and goats, to the value of 2,000 marks' from people who had never even been Lancaster's adherents. When the earl's rising was finally quashed, the victims lodged a formal complaint. They insisted that they had always been 'at peace and in friendship with the lord king' and demanded reparation for the animals Ingham's company had stolen.[1]

The county sheriff was instructed to bring the culprits to court to answer for their crimes. Then the king stepped in. On 6 November 1322, Edward wrote to the chief justice, ordering him to halt the trial. He explained that he had commanded a number of men to aid him 'in resisting and restraining the malice of the Earl of Lancaster' and his rebels. The accused were to be held accountable for genuine trespasses, but not for anything done 'to maintain their expedition'. Neither the Boydells nor most of the other men from Cheshire and Lancashire who had participated in the events of that March were on the list of names Edward provided. Some of them had joined Ingham's force for valid reasons and were subsequently pardoned. Others had spotted a chance to indulge in some pillaging and, perhaps, to settle old scores.[2]

Cheshire and Lancashire were commercially interdependent and there was a considerable degree of social intercourse between the gentry of the two counties. But the men of Cheshire regarded themselves as a cut above their neighbours. Their marginal position on the Anglo-Welsh border had helped to create a distinctive regional identity. Lucian – probably a monk at St Werburgh's Abbey – had written the *Liber Luciani* 'in praise of Chester' at the end of the twelfth century, in which he claimed that Cestrians differed from the rest of the English, being 'partly better [and] partly equal'. The role Cheshire had played in defeating the Welsh during Edward I's reign had done nothing to diminish that sense of superiority.

Moreover, Lancashire was in a parlous condition. It had suffered particularly badly during the famine of 1314-17. Political and territorial squabbles between some of the chief local families had added to the general level of distress. The earl of Lancaster had used force to pursue his private quarrels and the lesser gentry had copied his example, forming confederacies to support each other in their rivalries. Armed bands roamed the countryside, robbing and ill-treating traders, plundering and burning property. No man's person or possessions were safe in the lawless state that prevailed.

After Lancaster's execution, a number of these longstanding feuds flared up again and two of the Boydell brothers got involved. Robert and Hugh were friendly with Sir William Bradshaw of Haigh and Blackrod, who had been engaged in a prolonged dispute with the rapacious Robert de Holland. Bradshaw had helped to mastermind a revolt against Holland in 1315 and had fled the country when it failed. In the autumn of 1322, with Holland safely incarcerated at Kenilworth Castle, he returned from exile and resumed his vendetta. The first blood was shed in January 1323, when Bradshaw and some of his kin encountered Holland's cousin, Sir Richard de Holland of Cayley, in Warrington. In the ensuing altercation Sir Richard's squire was injured. Within days of the incident, various men – including Robert and Hugh – rallied to Bradshaw's cause. Assembling at Blackrod, they swore 'a mutual oath to live and die together and to support and maintain one another in every kind of suit'.[3]

Sir Richard de Holland was quick to respond. On 30 January 1323, he and his allies attempted to oust Bradshaw from the manor of Blackrod but were repelled with the loss of two retainers, who were slain in the fray. Several months later, Holland launched another attack on Bradshaw, while he was attending a service at Leyland Church, and killed one of his servants. The feud dragged on over the spring and summer, with men from both camps assaulting and robbing each other. The two ringleaders also rode through the county with their partisans, terrorising the inhabitants and interfering with the course of justice if the victims pressed charges. Robert and Hugh Boydell were among those who galloped alongside Bradshaw, 'molesting and murdering farmers at work in their fields'.[4]

At last, the king intervened again. On arriving in Lancashire, he ordered that the culprits be arrested. Bradshaw was tried at Wigan in October 1323, convicted, imprisoned and dispossessed of his lands until August 1324, when he was freed on bail of £200. Meanwhile, Holland went on the run. But, in January 1324, he was also convicted – and eventually pardoned in exchange for serving Edward in his wars. The chief architects of the chaos had received remarkably light sentences, as did their followers once they were apprehended. In late 1324, Robert and Hugh Boydell were each fined half a mark for their transgressions – a tiny sum, considering the trouble they had helped to cause.[5]

Sir William Boydell was preoccupied with family matters and had wisely refrained from participating in Bradshaw's vendetta. He and his wife had only two children, William and Margaret, but Nichola was now pregnant again. In 1323, she gave birth to another daughter, Joan. William was also in the midst of arranging his son's betrothal to Maud Vernon, probably the daughter of Sir Ralph Vernon of Hanwell, the eldest son of Ralph Vernon, baron of Shipbrook, who had died a few years earlier. Ralph's widow was one of the St Pierres, with whom the Boydells had long been on good terms.[6] And William's support for Ralph and his father during the court case over the assarting of Rudheath had cemented his friendship with the Vernons.

William simultaneously revised the plans he had made for securing his son's inheritance. In 1322, he had transferred Grappenhall to his brothers Robert and Hugh, and Robert's son (called Robert like his father), to hold in trust for William junior. But with Robert and Hugh marauding through Lancashire at Bradshaw's side, he had second thoughts. If they were detained and their possessions seized, Grappenhall might be forfeit as well. So William turned to his brother-in-law, Robert Doncaster, rector of Grappenhall and an altogether more peaceable man. On 10 January 1324, he granted Doncaster the manors of Dodleston and Grappenhall. Doncaster, in turn, granted William a life interest in the two manors, with a reversion to his 'heirs male' after his death. In 1325-26, William also gave his son and new daughter-in-law a house in Grappenhall.[7]

He had arranged one union to his satisfaction. Another was causing him considerable annoyance. His mother had been widowed again by 1316, when she sued her stepson for some dower land in Newton.[8] Soon afterwards Margaret embarked on a third marriage to Hugh de Standish, one of Sir Robert de Holland's former officials. Standish was the (probably illegitimate) son of Robert de Haydock, rector of Standish, and a social climber. He had acquired the manor of Heapey and some property in Standish. He had also exploited his link with the Hollands to advance himself by rather dubious means. In 1315, for example, when Henry de Duxbury was imprisoned for rising up against Holland, Standish had extorted a payment of 5 marks a year from Duxbury in return for securing his release.

William and Standish disliked each other intensely, although whether their animosity arose from clashing personalities or conflicting affiliations is unclear. In 1326, the two came to blows – and in the heat of the moment William killed Standish. The indomitable Margaret promptly sued Standish's son by his first wife, claiming that she was still entitled to part of her deceased husband's estate in Duxbury and Standish by way of dower.[9]

In the grand scheme of things, William's dispute with Standish – and its lethal outcome – was just one small instance of the disorder into which the whole of England was falling under Edward II. The king's dependence on the Despensers had alienated the vast majority of his subjects, high and low. In 1324, twenty-seven men from Coventry were even alleged to have hatched a scheme to kill Edward and Hugh the Younger by making wax images of them and sticking them with pins. According to their chief accuser – a convicted murderer who had turned king's witness to save his skin – the conspirators had hired a necromancer and obligingly provided him with 7lbs of wax for the task!

However, it wasn't the citizens of Coventry whom the king needed to fear: it was his wife Isabella, daughter of Philip the Fair. Raised in one of the world's greatest courts, Isabella was an intelligent woman who deeply resented coming second to Edward's male favourites. As relations between her husband and the barons worsened she gradually assumed a mediating role. But with her own rise to prominence, her loyalties were shifting. In 1325, Isabella and her son, the 12-year-old Prince Edward, went on a diplomatic mission to France. The queen refused to come back. In a dramatic speech before the entire French court, she swore that she would 'put on the robes of widowhood and mourning' until she was 'avenged of this Pharisee' – Hugh Despenser the Younger – who had wrecked her marriage.

On 1 December 1325, the king wrote to Isabella, ordering her to come home. The next day he penned the first of three letters to his son, begging Edward to return with or without his mother. But the time for reconciliation was past. By early 1326, Isabella had found comfort in the arms of the charismatic Roger Mortimer, one of the leading Marcher lords, and was plotting to overthrow her husband. She had also arranged the prince's betrothal to Philippa, the daughter of Count William of Hainault, to build military support for an invasion of England.

FLOATING IN BLOOD

By the autumn of 1326, Isabella and Mortimer were ready to act. On 24 September, they landed at Walton in Suffolk, with William of Hainault and a small army. His authority crumbling, the king tried vainly to muster a force to resist them and Mortimer swept west with ease. As the invaders moved on London, Edward panicked and fled. Accompanied by Hugh Despenser the Younger – and laden with the 60,000lbs of gold that remained in the royal treasury – he started making his way towards south Wales, with Mortimer and his troops in hot pursuit. But on 10 October, as he was entering Gloucester, he learned that his cousin Henry, earl of Lancaster (Thomas's younger brother), had thrown in his lot with the queen. Between them, Isabella and Mortimer had won over the baronial lords of the north and the Marches, destroying the king's hopes of any comeback.

On 26 October 1326, Mortimer took Bristol Castle, where Hugh Despenser the Elder had sought refuge. The very next day Despenser was given a mock trial at which he was denied the opportunity to defend himself, on the grounds that he and his son hadn't let Thomas of Lancaster speak at his own trial in March 1322. The verdict came as no surprise. Despenser was to be drawn for treason, hanged for robbery and decapitated for his crimes against the Church, after which his head was to be taken to Winchester, where he had been earl 'against law and reason'. The sentence was carried out immediately; Hugh the Elder was hanged still wearing his armour. His head was then cut off and sent to Winchester to be displayed on a spear there, while the rest of his body was chopped up and fed to the hounds.

As Hugh the Elder was swinging from the gallows, Edward and Hugh the Younger were hurrying to Chepstow, where they attempted to get a boat to Ireland. But even the wind was now against the king. Driven back to shore, he and Hugh desperately headed deeper into south Wales. On 16 November 1326, they were captured in the open countryside near Neath. Great cracks of thunder and bolts of lightning ripped through the sky, torrential rain flattened the coarse grass and ferocious gusts of wind tore at the king's cloak, as he and his few remaining followers were hunted down. Edward was transported to Kenilworth Castle, while Hugh the Younger was carried off to Hereford, 'tightly bound on the smallest, scrawniest, most wretched horse' his guards could find.

On 24 November, after a trial as perfunctory as the one his father had received, Hugh the Younger was dragged through Hereford with a crown of nettles on his head and biblical verses inscribed on his bare shoulders, while screaming women pelted him with refuse. Then he was hanged on a gibbet 50ft high, cut down and castrated because he was 'alleged to be a pervert and a sodomite – above all with the king'. Finally, his head was lopped off and his body quartered. Hugh had known that he could expect no mercy and had stopped eating or drinking in a fruitless attempt to commit suicide before he could be executed. But by one account he died bravely, enduring his punishment 'humbly and patiently'.

That Christmas, while Edward grieved for his friend, Isabella and Mortimer celebrated their victory at Wallingford in Oxfordshire and began arranging a transfer of power. At the start of January 1327, a parliament stage-managed by the queen and her lover declared Edward a tyrant, incapable of ruling the realm. Edward reluctantly agreed to abdicate and, on 21 January, Sir William Trussell – in his capacity as 'speaker' of the House of Commons – formally renounced England's allegiance to the king. On 1 February 1327, Prince Edward was crowned Edward III in a lavish ceremony at Westminster Abbey, where the greatest nobles in the land were decked out in cloth of gold, and lesser ranks in silk or bluett.

Four months later, on 29 May 1327, Edward III granted John and Hugh Boydell general pardons for unspecified offences on condition that they joined 'the expedition against the Scots'. Criminals were often pardoned in return for providing military service, even when they had committed the most heinous felonies. Almost everybody else on the list of men to be pardoned was guilty of homicide, so in all likelihood John and Hugh faced similar charges. William Boydell had to wait another five-and-a-half years for royal clemency. But he, too, was pardoned on 23 October 1332 – for killing Hugh de Standish 'in the time of the late king'.[10] Ironically, the delay had probably saved his life.

In 1323, the Scots and English had signed a truce intended to last thirteen years. However, when Edward II was deposed in favour of his son, Robert Bruce saw an opportunity to wrest official recognition of his title and Scotland's independence from the English. Mere hours after the young Edward III was crowned, a Scottish force surreptitiously forded the River Tweed in the dark, scaled the walls of Norham Castle, just across the border in Northumbria, and made an unsuccessful attempt to win the fortress by surprise. The English government, still in turmoil, was reluctant to do battle. So, after sending reinforcements north, it opened negotiations with the Scots. Nonetheless, relations between the two realms continued to deteriorate and, by April 1327, England was gearing up for war.

The king and his court travelled north to York, where a small body of Hainault mercenaries raised at Queen Isabella's request joined them in June. John and Hugh Boydell had probably arrived in York already and troops were pouring into the city from all over the country. But while the army was assembling, three Scottish war bands under the earls of Mar and Moray and Sir James Douglas – all formidable fighters – invaded northern England. When the English reached Durham, they could see the smoke from the villages the Scots had set on fire, although there was no sign of the Scots themselves. Riding on 'sturdy rounceys' (all-purpose horses) and unencumbered by baggage trains, they had perfected the art of raiding and retreating, living off the land and laying waste to everything they couldn't carry off.

As the invaders pressed south, the English gave chase. Three weeks later, when they returned to Durham, both men and horses were in a sorry state. They had toiled through the countryside, sleeping rough and going hungry after abandoning their supplies to travel light. Yet, despite all the hardships they had suffered, they had failed to come to grips with the Scots. When they finally caught up with Douglas and his war band, the raiders were based in an impregnable position on a hill protected by the River Wear, from which they refused to budge. The mortification of the English was complete when Douglas led a bold midnight foray into the heart of the English camp, during which the Scots cut the guy ropes to the king's tent and killed more than 300 men before quietly slipping away and heading home.

Edward III shed tears of vexation on discovering that the Scots had eluded him, but there was no hiding the fact that the Weardale campaign had been a total fiasco. The evidence (or, rather, lack of it) also implies that John and Hugh Boydell were among the casualties. There is no further reference to either brother in the records. They had presumably died – as they lived – by the sword.

The dispirited English made their way back to York, where they disbanded. However, the humiliation inflicted by the Scots had inflamed what was already a politically volatile situation. Queen Isabella had resisted all calls to have her husband executed, but the deposed monarch was a magnet for disaffected loyalists. His friends had made several attempts to rescue him from Kenilworth. So in April 1327, he was moved to Berkeley Castle, where he died the following September. Rumours soon spread that he had been suffocated on Mortimer's orders. A lurid story also began to circulate that he had been pinned down and pierced with a red-hot poker up the anus to avoid leaving any visible marks on his corpse. The story is probably untrue. Yet, as the playwright Christopher Marlowe wrote many years later, the throne on which Edward II sat had indeed ended up 'floating in blood'.

The former king was buried with all due pomp and circumstance at Gloucester Cathedral shortly before Christmas 1327 and then posthumously accused of everything from incompetence to the destruction of the Church and loss of England's foreign dominions. Meanwhile, Isabella and her lover became the country's *de facto* rulers. The queen soon proved even more profligate than her husband. Her links with Mortimer – a man as brilliant with words as he was with weapons – also frightened his baronial rivals, and the flamboyance with which the couple conducted their affair caused outrage. But it was two other issues that spurred the young Edward into action at last: the conciliatory policy Isabella and Mortimer had adopted towards the Scots after the bungled Weardale campaign; and the execution of Edward II's half-brother, Edmund of Woodstock, who had been ensnared in a plot to free his sibling after being told that he was still alive.

The teenaged monarch hadn't forgiven the man he believed responsible for the murder of his father. He was also tired of being a pawn and virtual prisoner. Edward had opposed the signing of a treaty with the Scots in May 1328 and the marriage of his little sister, Joan, to Robert Bruce's 4-year-old son, David, to seal the truce. He had made his feelings plain by refusing to attend the wedding, although poor Joan had even more cause for dismay when David stained the altar cloth because he was suffering from diarrhoea at the time. The execution of Edmund of Woodstock, engineered without Edward's knowledge, was the last straw. On 19 October 1330, just before his eighteenth birthday, he was staying at Nottingham Castle with his mother and her lover. That evening he retired to bed early, pretending to be sick. While Isabella, Mortimer and the bishop of Lincoln were closeted in the queen's chamber, discussing how to deal with a suspected plot to overthrow them, the king – or one of his allies – crept through the darkened corridors and unlocked the door leading to a secret underground passage into the castle. As midnight fell, his accomplices stole through the tunnel, made their way to Isabella's rooms, killed the guards and seized Mortimer.

Bound and gagged, Mortimer was conveyed to London, where a compliant parliament convicted him of murdering Edward II. On 29 November 1330, he was taken from the Tower to Tyburn, the capital's main place of execution, and ignominiously hanged like a common thief. Isabella's pleas to her son to spare her lover's life had fallen on deaf ears. The queen herself was stripped of her powers and sent to Castle Rising, a remote fortress in Norfolk, while the youthful king set about healing the schisms his father had created.

Sir William Boydell celebrated the return of law and order – and the pardon he doubtless believed he deserved for killing Hugh de Standish, when it came – by commissioning a new chantry at St Wilfrid's Church in Grappenhall. He hired some local workmen to build a single-bay chapel with a separate entrance at the south side of the church.[11] Then he rode into Chester, where the best glaziers in the region were based, to find a craftsman who could make him some fine stained glass windows.

Over the next few months, William went into Chester regularly to view the master craftsman's sketches drawn on the whitewashed table in the workshop and select a design. He eventually settled on eight panels depicting key biblical figures such as the Virgin Mary at the annunciation and St Peter holding the keys to heaven. Each panel would also feature William's heraldic arms, a gold *cross patonce* (with the ends terminating in three floriated points), coloured using the new process for producing yellow glass by painting it with silver nitrate and firing it an oven.[12] There was to be no mistaking the benefactor's identity.

Such work was expensive. When Master John of Chestre was designing some of the windows for St Stephen's chapel at Westminster Abbey in 1351, he commanded a wage of 7s a week. So, in January 1332, Sir William and his son borrowed £5 from Thomas Capenhurst, a chancery clerk and moneylender, to help defray the charges. At last, in early 1335, the chapel was complete. On 19 January, the entire family went to St John's Church in Chester, where William Boydell junior swore on the cross 'to find an honest chaplain' to celebrate daily Mass for the souls of his parents and those of 'all the faithful departed, in the chapel of Gropenhale' that his father had built.[13]

Supporting a parish priest to hold Mass every day was also quite costly because the family that benefited from the priest's ministrations had to foot the whole bill. The going rate was 5 or 6 marks a year. And there were instances where the families of the deceased, or the cleric concerned, tried to cut corners. One vicar was even accused of using the juice of berries rather than wine at communion. But William had ensured that his son could afford the outlay. In November 1334, he had granted William junior the right to the tolls from the passage across the River Mersey at Latchford.[14] Since this was still the only way to reach Warrington from the south bank of the river, without travelling some distance up or downstream, it remained a steady source of income.

With his afterlife provided for, Sir William returned his attention to earthly affairs. In 1336, he sued Robert Tuchet for the manor of Nether Whitley, which his great-grandmother Alice had received as her marriage portion when she wedded his namesake, the erstwhile clergyman. The Duttons had somehow recovered the manor and sold it to Thomas Tuchet. Sir William had already made one attempt to reclaim it in 1325-26, but neither effort was successful. Between 1339 and 1343, he also witnessed various deeds and made several minor grants. And, on 1 March 1344, he sold the wardship of William, son of Richard Hooton. Richard had held a small estate in Poulton Lancelyn before he died, so the guardianship of his son had passed to Sir William as his feudal overlord.[15]

This was to be Sir William's last public act. In early 1345, when the advowson of Grappenhall fell vacant and the prior of Norton Abbey nominated a new priest, it was 'William fitz William le Boydell' who disputed the prior's choice. He lost the case and the prior presented Roger Shipbrook to the living on 10 August 1345. William's father would probably have been furious, after spending so much money on a new chantry for the church, but Sir William was dead. In a final filial gesture, his son commissioned a glass panel depicting a knight and his lady kneeling in worship, with Sir William's coat of arms between them and an inscription underneath, begging passers-by to 'pray for Sir William Boydell and Nichola, his companion'.[16] The young hell-raiser who had raided Salford with his friends in 1311, whooping and cheering as they made off with their victims' cattle, had apparently turned into a law-abiding citizen, pious Christian and devoted family man. There was just one problem with this carefully cultivated image: Sir William had two families.

11

Illicit Amour

William watched as Sibyl sat on a chair on the other side of the hearth feeding their youngest son. Her hair was unbound and her robe undone, exposing one heavy breast, blue-veined and swollen with milk. The flames from the fire cast a flickering golden glow over her face as she bent over John, gently positioning the baby to latch onto her nipple more easily. She wasn't beautiful and yet William never tired of looking at her, admiring the arc of her eyebrows, the line of her nose, the mobility of her mouth and full, sensuous lips – even the little crow's feet, hidden in the firelight but becoming ever more pronounced in the harsher glare of the day. It was a face he loved, imperfections and all.

The room was quiet, save for the intermittent crackling of the logs and the small gulping sounds John made as he sucked and swallowed, sucked and swallowed, his chubby little body slowly relaxing and eyelids fluttering, until he eventually let go of Sibyl's nipple with a grunt, closed his eyes and fell fast asleep. Sibyl sat peacefully for a while, holding John in her lap, before she stood up to carry him into the bedchamber and tuck him in his cradle. When she returned, dress neatly pinned back in place, William reached out and pulled her onto his knee. As he caressed her flanks and felt the ripe curve of her bottom pressing into his groin, his penis stirred. He would have to leave before dawn to ride back to Grappenhall, where his wife would be waiting, silently reproachful. But he would not think of that now. Nor would he think of the quarrel that he knew would take place when Nichola learned that he planned to give his illegitimate son Richard the manor of Latchford.

The woman who had captured Sir William Boydell's heart was no peasant – the sort of girl whom many men from the upper classes regarded as 'fair game', whether or not she was willing. On the contrary, Sibyl de Pulford came from another prominent Cheshire family.

More noteworthy still is the fact that she returned William's love. While a man might stray, it was a very different matter for a woman from a respectable background to 'fornicate' without a ring on her finger.

Medieval audiences were mesmerised by Arthurian romances in which knights wooed married noblewomen with fair words and brave deeds, setting out on dangerous adventures and slaying monsters to prove their devotion. Stories of star-crossed couples such as Lancelot and Guinevere or Tristan and Isolde defied the social norms, pitting love against fealty, adultery against fidelity and ardour against order. But romantic literature bore little, if any, resemblance to reality.

Courtly love was love for its own sake, true love untainted by financial or dynastic concerns – and thus, by definition, extra-marital love, since marriage was an economic arrangement. In theory, it ennobled both lover and beloved: lover, because he was inspired to behave more gallantly, striving to charm his lady and preserve her honour at all costs; beloved, because she was the source of inspiration, not just a vehicle for conveying land or perpetuating a family line. The chivalric love affair followed a strict formula. Mute worship gave way to fervently voiced adoration, virtuous rejection and then renewed courtship, with oaths of eternal loyalty and acts of derring-do. Once the lady's heart was won and the secret love (rarely) consummated, numerous adventures took place, culminating in a tragic conclusion where the lovers were separated by death or other means.

The romantic genre originated in twelfth-century southern France, with the coming of the troubadours or wandering minstrels. Most French poetry was written to lionise great warriors; the troubadours broke with this tradition and sang of love. Their influence eventually spilled over into tournaments and jousts. Early tournaments were bloody events barely distinguishable from war, but over time tourneying evolved from a military exercise into an expression of chivalry. The tournament became a dazzling spectacle, marked by pageantry and feasting. A gaggle of nobles sitting in brightly coloured pavilions would watch knights challenge each other in mock battles, with the ribbons of the ladies for whom they fought tied to their lances. The presence of noblewomen was an important feature and, when the sport was ended, the singing and dancing continued long into the night.

Eleanor of Aquitaine, who was both a patron of the troubadours and a source of inspiration for many poets and writers, probably brought the culture of courtly love to England after marrying Henry II. It soon took hold. Edward I possessed copies of several romances and, in July 1284, he celebrated his victory over the Welsh by holding a sumptuous tournament called a 'Round Table'. The contestants assumed the personae of Arthurian knights, while the king took the part of Arthur, thereby associating himself with all the virtues of Camelot's famous sovereign. Edward's daughter-in-law, Queen Isabella, also owned at least ten romances, including a 'great book' about King Arthur's deeds, bound in white leather.

But courtly love was a literary artifice and those who forgot that did so at their peril. Isabella and Roger Mortimer were a case in point. In August 1329, Mortimer – whose family claimed to descend from Arthur – decided to hold his own Round Table at his stronghold in Wigmore. He played the part of his putative ancestor, to Isabella's Guinevere. The event, an extravagant affair attended by all the leading barons, proved a terrible mistake. Mortimer's costly jewellery drew envious glares, while his overt intimacy with the queen caused deep offence. How, his enemies asked, could an adulterous upstart without a drop of royal blood in his veins compare himself with Arthur, 'the most worthy lord of renown'.[1] Such hubris would surely be punished – as, of course, it was. Fifteen months later, Mortimer was swinging from a gibbet, while Isabella was locked up in a castle in Norfolk. They had succumbed to their own fantasy and paid the price for losing sight of the hard truth.

Infidelity was all very well in stories. Beyond the pages of books, it attracted censure, even when the wrongdoer was a powerful man. The Church and state attempted to control every aspect of people's lives, including their sexual conduct. Canon law laid down numerous regulations. Intercourse was forbidden on feast days, fast days and Sundays and when a woman was deemed 'unclean' (during menstruation, pregnancy, breast-feeding and for forty days after childbirth). The only acceptable form of coitus was heterosexual vaginal intercourse in the missionary position, at night, preferably with the participants partly clothed. And the sole purpose of intercourse was procreation. It was not to be used for pleasure; thus, all sex outside marriage was a sin.

In the eleventh and twelfth centuries, canonists devised a detailed list of penances for anybody who erred, based on fasting and sexual abstinence. They varied rather curiously in severity from a modern perspective. For instance, if a man fornicated with a servant or unmarried female, he was required to do penance for ten days. But if he engaged in dorsal intercourse (with the woman on top), he was required to do penance for a full three years – regardless of whether the woman concerned was his wife – because this was deemed contrary to nature, which prescribed that the man should take the dominant position.

By the middle of the thirteenth century, few handbooks written to guide priests in the confessional contained set penances; the confessor was generally left to use his own discretion. Still, this didn't mean that the Church had relaxed its attitude to illicit carnal relationships. When the Dominican friar John Bromyard penned a preacher's guide in the mid-fourteenth century, he graded different forms of lust in ascending order of enormity: from simple fornication (extra-marital relations between a single man and single woman) to the deflowering of a virgin, adultery, rape, sacrilege (intercourse with a nun), incest and sodomy.

Adultery came third in the hierarchy of sexual depravities and the Church taught that it was as grave a sin for a married man as it was for a married woman. In practice, however, female adulterers were often treated far more harshly than their male counterparts. They could be expelled from their homes, separated from their children and divested of their dowries, reducing them to penury. In many places, adulterous women also had their heads shaved and were paraded through the streets before booing bystanders.

A single woman who entered into a liaison with a married man usually incurred less opprobrium, unless she belonged to the upper classes or sat at the base of the social pyramid. If she was a member of the nobility or gentry, her virginity was important in making a good marriage. And if she came from the bottom of the heap, she was an easy target – especially for manorial stewards eager to swell their accounts. Some medieval English manors levied a fine called *leyrwite* (literally, a 'fine for lying down') on people who conducted extra-marital relationships. But it was typically the poorest bondswomen, as distinct from women of free birth or of no fixed abode, who were forced to hand over their hard-won coin.

Yet even a freewoman who formed a stable relationship with a wealthy married man might have a rough time of it. Although concubinage enabled someone from a poor family to better herself, it also left her vulnerable. She faced major drawbacks from which a wife was spared, including damage to her reputation, snubs from her neighbours and economic insecurity. By the fourteenth century, church courts had the power to order fathers to support their natural children, with paternity payments fixed at anything from 1d to 6d a week. But mistresses and the offspring they bore outside wedlock were viewed with disapproval.

In short, there was a huge gap between literature and the real world. In minstrels' songs, a knight might venerate his beloved and put her on a pedestal. He might honour and obey her and rejoice at receiving the smallest favours, exalted by the uplifting passion only a truly chivalrous man could sustain. In daily life, the Church spoke of sin and the state of legal sanctions – and theirs were by far the louder voices.

So what sort of woman was Sir William Boydell prepared to imperil his soul for, and why was she willing to put aside her own prospects of marriage to become his lover? The various deeds in which William gave Sibyl property show that she was the daughter of Kenrick de Pulford. Kenrick was born in about 1275, but his father – also called Kenrick – died while he was still a child. In 1281-82, his widowed mother, Margaret, sued Sir Hugh de Pulford, lord of Pulford, to recover her dower of one messuage, half a bovate and sixteen selions of land in Pulford. Kenrick remained in the area; in 1311, he was the grantee of a rent in Eccleston from Giles the Engineer, one of the sons of the highly successful builder Richard the Engineer. However, Kenrick was dead by 1 May 1340, when his widow Wernilla confirmed the grant in Eccleston to John de Belgreve, probably Giles's son.[2]

Sibyl's lineage beyond this point isn't certain because there were two families with the name of Pulford living in the area. One had forked in the late twelfth century: the older branch, descending from Sir Robert de Pulford, held the manor of Pulford, while the younger branch, descending from Richard de Pulford, held the manor of Eaton, which Richard's wife Sibyl had inherited. The other family was clearly Welsh in origin and far less affluent. It descended from Maradoc ap Gwion, who settled in Pulford in the early thirteenth century. Maradoc had witnessed several grants to Dieulacres Abbey between 1208 and 1228, as well as making his own modest endowment to the abbey.

Given that Kenrick is the anglicised version of the Welsh name Cynrig, it would be logical to assume that Sibyl came from the second of these two families. But she herself shared a first name with Sibyl de Pulford of Eaton and, when she had her own children baptised, she chose forenames that recurred repeatedly in the family that held the manors of Eaton and Pulford.

Besides, the lords of both manors had various dealings with Richard the Engineer and his sons, just as Sibyl's father, Kenrick, had done (and as Sir William Boydell was later to do). Indeed, Richard's great-grandson would eventually marry the heiress to the Pulford estate. Taken together, these slender threads suggest that Sibyl was a member of the Pulfords of Eaton and Pulford, rather than a descendant of Maradoc ap Gwion. But the particular offshoot from which she came was a junior one, for although her parents and grandparents weren't landless, neither were they wealthy.

It is easy to see how a young woman with ties to one of the more powerful families in the county, but no money of her own, might have fallen prey to a married man from the 'set' to which her richer kin belonged. Sibyl may initially have been flattered by Sir William's attentions – and perhaps she also saw a chance to secure some of the material comforts she coveted. Yet, if the relationship began as a fling on William's part, or as a cynical exchange of sexual favours for gain on Sibyl's, it soon blossomed into something far deeper.

By the early 1320s, the couple had three children and William was determined to ensure that they were properly provided for. On 1 January 1321, he gave Sibyl 16 houses, 60 acres of land, 60 acres of meadow and a rent of 14s 6d in Grappenhall, naming her sons Richard, Robert and John in the deed. Two years later, he went much further and granted 'Richard Boydell' an interest in the manor of Latchford. This was as public an avowal of Richard as it was possible to make. William had explicitly accorded him both the family name and a share of the family estates.[3]

Such open acknowledgement of Richard's paternity may have been too much for poor Nichola. In subsequent deeds, William referred more cautiously to his natural children as the 'sons of Sibyl, daughter of Kenrick de Pulford'. Nevertheless, he continued to heap gifts on his second family. By 1339, Sibyl had borne a fourth son, Thomas. William granted him a life interest in some tenements and several pieces of land in Kinnerton, with successive 'remainders' to his brothers Richard and Robert; in other words, if Thomas died, the assets were to pass to Richard and then Robert, in that order. William also granted Richard some property in Dodleston and Latchford, with remainders to Thomas and Robert – simultaneously extracting a written confirmation of this last grant from his legitimate son, William, who was obviously far from happy about the situation.[4]

By 1341, Sibyl had given birth to another two children – Matilda and Ellen – and the presents were coming thick and fast. That December, William pledged to pay Sibyl and her six offspring 10 marks apiece. A few months later, he conveyed the freehold of the manor of Latchford to Sibyl. He also drew up a deed stipulating that, when his grandson Ralph died, all the houses, lands and rents in Grappenhall in which Ralph held a life interest were to go to Sibyl for life, with successive remainders to her sons and their male heirs.[5] William had already granted Sibyl an interest in these estates in 1321, so he had presumably modified his plans in light of Ralph's birth (or marriage). But he was still prepared to put his illegitimate sons before any legitimate great-grandsons.

Over the course of twenty years, Sir William had showered his mistress and second family with gifts of money and land, much of which came from the manorial estates the Boydells had held since Osbern fitz Tezzo first acquired them. But, no matter how generous he was, William couldn't save his illegitimate offspring from the 'stain' of bastardy.

Children born outside wedlock were probably quite unusual in medieval England. In the sixteenth century, when the illegitimate birth rate can first be measured (after the introduction of parish registers to record baptisms, marriages and burials), it was never more than about 4.5 per cent. The incidence of illegitimacy seems to have been even lower among the landed elite of the Middle Ages. In her doctoral dissertation on 'Illegitimacy and English Landed Society c.1285-c.1500', Helen Matthews estimates that fewer than 2 per cent of landowners living in the thirteenth and fourteenth centuries fathered baseborn sons or daughters. Even allowing for significant under-reporting in the surviving records, she concludes, illegitimate births can hardly have been 'widespread amongst the gentry and nobility'. So Sir William's offspring by Sibyl belonged to a tiny minority.

The low rate of illegitimacy owed more to Christian ideas of morality than it did to effective birth control, although medieval women sometimes used contraceptives. Certain sympathetic churchmen even played a part in disseminating the knowledge they needed. While most clerics railed against contraception and abortion from the privileged heights of the pulpit, others were more understanding. Indeed, one remarkable pontiff may even have provided medical advice on such matters. The *Treasury of the Poor* – written in about 1270 and generally ascribed to the Peter of Spain who later became Pope John XXI – provides a number of prescriptions for preventing conception and 'provoking menstruation'.

However, medieval birth control was a decidedly hit-and-miss affair. Drinking potions made from rue or artemisia (also known as wormwood) was supposed to impede impregnation, for example. This at least had some basis in scientific fact.[6] Other, more dubious methods for avoiding pregnancy included carrying the roots of an astringent pear tree under one's clothes, jumping around immediately after intercourse and draping one's body with the testicles of a weasel wrapped in goose skin – a recommendation that may well have worked, if only because it destroyed all sexual desire.

When contraception failed, some women tried to terminate their pregnancies. A human foetus had certain rights under the common law, which equated abortion with murder. But the medieval definition of abortion was quite different from the modern one. A foetus wasn't thought to acquire a soul until it 'quickened' in about the fourth month of development. Thus, the Church viewed all attempts to induce a miscarriage before 'ensoulment' as contraception. It was only after this point that ending an unwanted pregnancy counted as murder.

Various medical texts provided recipes for abortion. The *Trotula* – a compendium of three twelfth-century texts on women's afflictions – included one such prescription, a poisonous draught concocted from a combination of herbs with proven abortive qualities and painkillers. But many remedies were completely useless and some were downright dangerous. They could cause foetal deformities without triggering a miscarriage or kill the mother as well as the baby. Medieval pharmacology was more art than science and it was only a really desperate female who resorted to such measures. In most instances, a single woman who fell pregnant ended up giving birth, unless nature intervened.

The popular view of illegitimate children was quite hostile. They were called 'bastards', a term first found in England soon after the Norman Conquest, when it was used to describe William the Conqueror. As the illegitimate son of Robert, duke of Normandy, William was a bastard himself. Other derogatory terms included 'horcop' (whore head) and 'leir-child' (child of the lair or lying), both denoting conception outside the marriage bed. And in law an illegitimate child was known as *filius nullius*, or nobody's son, for most purposes.

In practice, the treatment of the illegitimate was more nuanced and sometimes more broad-minded. Indeed, the very definition of illegitimacy was byzantine in its complexity. The common law distinguished between 'special bastardy', where the parents subsequently married each other, and 'general bastardy', where they did not. But the Church didn't recognise special bastardy as bastardy at all. Anyone born of parents who married each other, no matter when the wedding took place, was deemed legitimate – unless the child was the product of adultery. The Church also discriminated, in cases of general bastardy, between situations where the relationship between the parents was free from canonical impediment and those where it was not. Children born outside wedlock to parents who could marry without impediment were illegitimate but 'natural', while those who were born of a prohibited union, or whose parentage was unknown, were both illegitimate and 'unnatural'.

These distinctions had material implications, particularly when it came to inheritance. Whereas the common law precluded special bastards from inheriting their parents' property, canon law ruled that pre-nuptial bastardy didn't provide grounds for disinheriting them. But it was the secular courts that determined disputes involving inheritance, so a compromise was reached: the secular courts retained final jurisdiction over the ownership of land, while reserving the right to use the canonical definition of illegitimacy.

General bastards, by contrast, couldn't inherit under either common or canon law. But under canon law natural bastards *could* receive testamentary bequests from their parents and, if there were no legitimate children, a father could leave his entire estate to his illegitimate issue. Unnatural bastards, like William and Sibyl's brood, were more disadvantaged, since they could never be legitimised by the marriage of their parents. Under common and canon law alike, the offspring of such a liaison couldn't inherit by right or by written will. Bastards of every kind were also handicapped by the fact that they could only leave land to their direct heirs; if they had no children, their estates escheated to the feudal overlord.

However, there were two devices for skirting the common law: the enfeoffment to use and the entail. An enfeoffment to use was a form of trust where a donor granted property to one person for the use of another. An entail was a conditional grant. If the recipient died without issue, the property reverted to the donor or 'remained' to a specified third party;

the land couldn't be sold or willed to anyone else. Entailing an estate prevented a feckless heir from squandering his legacy and ensured that land granted to an illegitimate child stayed within the family, if his or her line failed. By the fourteenth century, both devices were a key part of the landed gentleman's toolkit for controlling the distribution of his estates after his death.

A man could also provide for his illegitimate offspring by giving them part of his land while he was still alive. And if he had sufficient influence, he could arrange for a bastard son to marry an heiress or wealthy widow – although this course was only available to those with powerful connections, such as kings and magnates, since an illegitimate son wasn't normally viewed as an ideal choice of husband for a woman who was rich in her own right.

Thus, there were various ways in which a prosperous man could ensure that his bastard children were financially secure, even when he had legitimate sons and daughters. Sir William Boydell had used every legal mechanism in the book. In addition to giving Sibyl and her offspring lands and money during his lifetime, he had entailed part of his estate so that it would pass to his second family after his death.

Yet bastards at every level of society still experienced discrimination. Illegitimate townsfolk might find it difficult to join a craftsmen's guild because the chief means of gaining admission was by inheritance as the son or daughter of a member. Similarly, they might struggle to get municipal privileges such as the right to trade and own property within the town. Bastards were also banned from a career in the Church unless they obtained a dispensation.

Such barriers could certainly be surmounted. William the Conqueror was a prime instance of just how far a talented bastard from the upper ranks could rise. Despite his questionable birth, he had managed to claim and rule Normandy, seize England and pass both to his descendants. Nevertheless, a bastard's success often depended on the goodwill of his legitimate blood relatives. The Conqueror was no exception; he had only been able to acquire his father's duchy because Robert recognised him as his heir. And that was the fly in the ointment. Family members who had nothing to lose by acknowledging their illegitimate kin might be willing to help them, but a legitimate heir whose interests were diametrically opposed to those of his bastard siblings might not feel so charitable.

There was little love lost between Sir William's two families and he had only himself to blame. He had lavished gifts on Sibyl and his six children by her; in some respects, indeed, he had favoured them over his children by his wife Nichola. His legitimate son and daughters were understandably outraged. Their father may have believed he was doing the right thing by the woman he loved; they saw a besotted old fool throwing away their patrimony.

When Sir William died in late 1344, his son William sprang into action. He sued Sibyl in the county court at Chester, asserting that his father had only possessed a 'fee tail' in the manor of Latchford. In other words, one of Sir William's ancestors had already entailed the manor, so he was legally barred from granting it to Sibyl and her 'bastard sons'; the property could only pass to the legitimate 'heirs of the body' of the original owner. William produced documentary evidence to support his claim and won his case.[7]

William also seems to have succeeded in stripping Sibyl and her sons of almost everything else they had received from his father. When an inquisition was conducted after his death, the jurors found that he held half of the manor of Grappenhall, while the rest belonged to his son Ralph. He also held the whole of the manors of Dodleston, Handley and Latchford, as well as extensive lands in Kinnerton, and was feudal overlord in all the other territories his ancestors had leased out in return for money or military service. William's grasp on the family estates was complete, with only one exception: 'five messuages, eight bovates of land and 26s 8d rent in Latchford, which William Boydell, chiveler, gave to Richard his son'.[8]

Sibyl's children had been sidelined and she herself had been publicly humiliated. Her relationship with Sir William had obviously long since ceased to be secret, but facing down sharp-tongued gossips was a far cry from being hauled up before a county court and officially branded a fallen woman. Sibyl's reputation was in shreds. Yet, by early 1351, it no longer mattered: she and her six children by Sir William Boydell were all dead.[9] The bubonic plague had snuffed out their lives, just as it had the lives of so many other people in England.

12

Cornered and Constrained

Chester was humming with activity as William Boydell made his way to the shire hall just outside the main gate to the castle. The city housed about 4,000 people and was still quite small, given its importance as a regional capital. But the streets were busy and William recognised several men by sight, although he couldn't name them. Castle Lane, the cobbled road leading to the shire hall, was always congested. The tailors plied their trade there, hoping to attract the gentlemen attending the exchequer and county court. A number of clothiers had set up stalls at the verges. Others wandered around, loudly touting their services. One persistent vendor even tried to grab William by the arm but backed off when William glared at him, hand hovering threateningly over the sheath of his dagger.

William had more important things than a new tunic on his mind. He'd ridden into Chester the previous day and dined with his cousin, William Doncaster, before staying the night at his townhouse. The real purpose of his visit wasn't social, however; he was in the city to represent the 16-year-old Prince Edward in yet another dispute over the ownership of Rudheath, the moor in central Cheshire to which the Vernons, Grosvenors and other local lords had laid claim in 1310. The prince's agents had declared that it formed part of his inheritance and were now pressing his title to the land. The county court only met about eight or nine times a year and sessions typically lasted only two days. There was often a backlog of business to be dealt with and the shire hall was usually packed with petitioners. But Sir William de Shareshull, second justice of the Court of Common Pleas, had come up from London to hear the case. So, when William entered the hall, it was even more crowded than normal.

The courtroom was a magnificent chamber, measuring some ninety feet by thirty, with a lofty timber ceiling. It had been designed to convey the full majesty of the law and could be quite intimidating. However, William knew it well. He'd sued – and been sued – in the county court on several occasions and had stood in for various acquaintances when they couldn't attend court themselves. The prince was by far the most illustrious person he'd ever represented, but he'd mentally rehearsed what he would say as he rode along the highway from Grappenhall to Chester and felt confident that he could make a good argument.

William watched as Shareshull swept into the hall, scarlet robe swishing, and sat down in the high-backed seat at one end of the chamber. Sir Peter de Gildesburgh, the prince's clerk, positioned himself at the table immediately in front of Shareshull, placing his quill and a roll of vellum at the ready. The babble was already dying down as the sheriff called the court to order. William waited patiently while the first few grievances were heard. Then it was his turn. Striding to the front of the court, he cleared his throat and prepared to present his case.

In the early medieval era, knighthood provided the main means of social advancement. By the middle of the fourteenth century this was no longer true. The growing power of parliament and increasing demand for legal remedies were jointly altering the constitution of the upper classes. The role of the House of Commons, in particular, had expanded considerably during Edward II's turbulent reign. It became a forum for trying lords of the realm and those charged with treason, a tool for curbing wilful monarchs, a venue for dealing with private petitions and the body that deliberated on royal demands for taxation. The social base from which the members of the Commons were drawn was broadening accordingly.

As the population swelled and competition for limited local resources intensified, the volume of litigation also continued to rise. Most of those who cultivated the soil for a living relied on the courts of the manors in which they resided. Although the manorial courts were principally concerned with protecting seigneurial rights, they handled a mounting number of private suits to settle debts and disputes over land. The Court of Common Pleas – which dealt with actions that didn't involve the crown – was kept increasingly busy, too. During the thirteenth century, the business of the Common Bench at Westminster multiplied almost thirty-fold and, by the 1330s, the court was hearing as many as 6,000 cases a year. Litigation was costly and time-consuming, but it conferred several advantages on those who could afford the expense. It was, for example, the most secure way of conveying land from vendor to purchaser through a final concord, recorded by the justices of the Bench.

Cheshire was not immune to these changes, despite the fact that its exceptional standing as a county palatine meant it wasn't represented in parliament; this would not come until 1542. Lacking capital and unable to increase rents and services for lands held by ancient custom, many knightly families turned to the control – and abuse – of office to maintain their incomes and status. They also formed intricate networks of interlinking affiliations to support each other, be it through the exercise of influence or force. In some respects, indeed, the opportunities to secure positions of authority and sway the course of justice were greater precisely because Cheshire functioned semi-independently and had more power than other counties. The county court had full jurisdiction over all criminal and civil proceedings, whereas most county courts couldn't deal with personal actions worth more than 40s or quarrels over land except those where the litigant had been denied a hearing in his feudal lord's manorial court.

So a working knowledge of the legal system and membership of an influential local network had arguably become more valuable than martial prowess and the English upper classes – in Cheshire as elsewhere – were evolving from a military elite into a more diverse 'squirearchy'. William, son of Sir William Boydell, typified this shift. His father, grandfather and great-grandfather had all been knighted. William was not. Yet he undoubtedly qualified for knighthood, since his estates generated an income of more than £40 a year.[1]

William had been consolidating his position even before his father died. In January 1342, he acquired four burgages in Frodsham from his aunt, Matilda de Camelsford, who had inherited three of the four from her mother Margaret, the widow of Sir John Boydell.[2] Two months later, William bought back 12 houses and 60 acres of land in Catterich, which Sir John had given his son Robert. William promised to pay Robert an annual stipend of £4 in exchange for the property.[3] And, in 1343, he was one of eleven men to enter into a bond for £213 6s 8d[4] – possibly a pledge for the good conduct of a friend who was about to assume office, this being another distinctive feature of Cheshire's administration. Officials weren't necessarily appointed for a specific period of time, as they were in other parts of England. They might be appointed 'for life', 'during pleasure' or 'during good behaviour'. In short, William had no monetary woes. He had, it seems, deliberately shunned knighthood, choosing to hone his grasp of the law rather than his skill with the sword.

He wasn't a trained advocate, although the English legal system was slowly becoming more professional. By the thirteenth century the law was so complex that ordinary people required aid when they were involved in litigation. Proceedings in the royal courts were also conducted in Norman French or in Latin. Most litigants therefore hired 'pleaders' conversant with legal procedures and the language of the courts to speak on their behalf. These men were the precursors of the modern lawyer. However, the development of the legal profession took far longer in the provinces than it did in London, where the higher courts were based.

Outside the capital, the old system still prevailed. Litigants had long been permitted to appoint 'attorneys' to represent them in court and manage their legal affairs, if they were too busy or too sick to attend court themselves. Attorneys were friends, relatives, stewards, bailiffs and the like and they generally knew no more about the law than the people they represented. Nevertheless, a few individuals were repeatedly employed as attorneys, probably because they had acquired a reputation for being successful. William was sufficiently competent to represent Edward, the Black Prince – Edward III's eldest son and heir, who held the earldom of Chester. On 16 December 1346, the prince rewarded William for the 'good service' he had provided at Chester county court in recovering certain lands in Rudheath by reducing the fine William had incurred for an unspecified offence by 20 marks.[5]

The Black Prince was the most powerful ally any Cheshire esquire could hope to have, but William could call on a sprawling web of influential local connections, too. He was related to the Duttons and Masseys of Dunham Massey through his great-great-grandmother Alice, and the Boydells had maintained a strong bond with their cousins down the generations. William was also related to the Vernons of Hanwell and Shipbrook through his wife Maud. So he had close links, forged through blood and marriage, with three of the leading county families.

The recognizances William entered into show that he was likewise on good terms with various other members of the Cheshire gentry. And he had recently secured an advantageous match for his son Ralph in Elizabeth, one of the two daughters of Peter and Ellen Legh of Betchton.[6] Since Peter and his wife had no sons, Elizabeth and her sister would inherit everything their parents owned. But Peter was also well connected. His father, John Legh of Booths, had purchased the manor of Knutsford Booth in the late 1290s and, demonstrating an unusual degree of entrepreneurial flair, had invested heavily in improving the estate to capitalise on the economic opportunities provided by an expanding population. Peter's eldest brother, another John, had built on their father's achievements. After an unsavoury youth spent running around with the Coterel Gang, a notorious bunch of thieves and murderers led by the son of a minor Derbyshire landowner, John had abandoned the criminal life. He now used guile rather than force to advance his interests and wielded considerable local clout.

Thus, by late 1346, William was flourishing. He had bought back the lands held by his uncle, Robert Boydell, demolished the claims of his father's mistress and recovered almost all of the property Sir William had given Sibyl and her children. He had provided for his son, with a marriage into one of the most ambitious families in the area. His legal knowhow had earned him the Black Prince's gratitude and he was a respected member of Cheshire's upper classes, his good name unblemished. Within months, his fortunes had been reversed. He had been indicted for killing William de Hyde and two of his retainers and cast into gaol.[7]

Hyde moved in the same circles as William. He was the youngest brother of Sir John de Hyde, lord of Norbury, and the nephew by marriage of John Legh of Booths. He himself was married to William's fourth cousin, Katherine de Dutton. Quite why Hyde and William quarrelled is unclear, but the majority of disputes among the landholding classes involved property and Hyde had been caught up in a rancorous territorial battle.

The case centred on the manor of Dunham Massey, which Katherine's grandfather, Sir Hamo de Massey, had sold to Sir Oliver Ingham – the same man who had led the raid on Lancashire in which William's father participated – in 1322. Massey had retained a life interest in the property but, when he died in 1334, Ingham took possession of the manor. On Ingham's death in January 1344, it passed to his daughter Joan, who had married Roger Lestrange, baron of Knockin. But no sooner was Ingham in his grave than Massey's heirs sued to recover his lands. The claimants included his eldest daughter, Cecilia, the widow of John Fitton of Bollin, and his seven grandchildren by his daughters Dionisia and Isabella.

The parties to the dispute over Dunham Massey

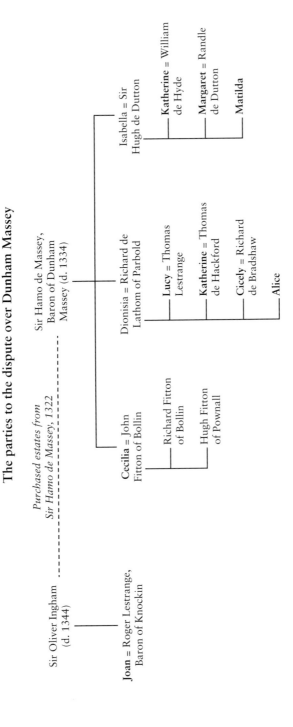

In July 1344, Hyde and Cecilia's son Richard entered into a recognizance with the escheator to prosecute the case on behalf of their womenfolk. Two months later, Hyde, Richard Fitton and Fitton's brother, Hugh, pledged another 50 marks to the Black Prince, probably for the same reason. William Boydell was one of the sureties – suggesting that, initially at least, he sympathised with Hyde and his fellow suitors.[8] But then the prince's representatives claimed part of Ingham's estate and Edward issued a writ to halt all proceedings while he was campaigning in Flanders. When the ban was lifted after the prince's return, Roger and Joan Lestrange immediately alleged that Massey's three daughters were bastards and therefore unable to inherit his lands. Cecilia and her nieces vigorously denied this smear and the county court ruled in their favour.

However, the dispute didn't end there. In late 1345, Henry de Grosmont, earl of Lancaster, acquired Dunham Massey from Massey's descendants. He kept a life interest in the manor for himself and settled the reversion on Lestrange and his heirs, in exchange for some lands in Lincolnshire. By this devious stratagem Lestrange had thus secured a much stronger title to the manor than the fragile claim he held through his wife Joan. Cecilia and five of her co-plaintiffs, together with their husbands, were parties to the two final concords in which Lancaster 'bought' Dunham Massey, although they had obviously been bullied into relinquishing it; a year later they were trying to raise a loan, to be repaid only if and when they recovered their lands. But Katherine and her spouse weren't named in either concord.

Whether Hyde had resisted Roger Lestrange of Knockin's attempts to intimidate him isn't certain. What we *do* know is that he and William clashed fiercely soon after the earl of Lancaster procured Massey's estates. William was in a difficult position. On the one hand, he counted the Duttons and Masseys – and, by extension, Hyde – among his kinsfolk and closest friends. On the other, Roger Lestrange was his brother-in-law's overlord. His sister Margaret had married Owain Voil of Hampton. There were actually two places with this name, but the *Black Prince's Register* shows that Owain's home lay in Hampton, Flintshire – now known as Welshampton – which formed part of the barony of Knockin.[9] William may well have feared that alienating Lestrange would bring the baron's wrath down on Owain's head.

So perhaps Hyde refused to drop his wife's claim and William proved less supportive than he had expected. At any rate, the two quarrelled and since most men carried daggers or staves an argument could easily escalate into lethal violence, as it did now. William was out riding with a couple of servants when he encountered Hyde and his retainers. During the angry exchange that ensued William lost control of his mount – or his temper – and Hyde or one of his followers was trampled to death, while the other two were killed in the mêlée.[10]

Such incidents were all too frequent; nearly a quarter of the cases in one study of 10,500 medieval felony charges concerned unlawful killings. Brawling was rife and poor medical care meant that relatively minor wounds might result in death from infection. The practice of granting pardons to hardened criminals in return for fighting for the crown had exacerbated the problem – so much so that, in 1347, the House of Commons petitioned Edward III to curtail it. Moreover, the inhabitants of Cheshire had a reputation for being especially belligerent. Under the Anglo-Norman earls of Chester the county had become an asylum where debtors and felons could remain on payment of a fine, and repeated conflicts with the Welsh had produced a bloody-minded people quick to draw their blades.

Most murder suspects came from the lower classes for the simple reason that the gentry could delegate their dirty work to their servants or retainers. And if a member of the upper classes *was* indicted for murder, he would normally be pardoned quite rapidly. But William had tangled with the wrong man. Hyde's eldest brother, John, was one of the Black Prince's 'bachelors' – the knights whom the prince usually retained in his service for life – and had connections every bit as influential as William's. Indeed, he had already been pulling strings to get his son Ralph pardoned for committing the very same crime of which William stood accused. When William was arrested and thrown into prison, Hyde and his family used their contacts to ensure that the wheels of justice ground as slowly as possible.

In the summer of 1347, William wrote to the earl of Lancaster, asking him to speak to the Black Prince on his behalf. He claimed that he had been acting in self-defence, yet he had been denied a trial. The earl was sympathetic to his plight. On 20 July 1347, the Black Prince commanded Sir Thomas de Ferrers, the justice of Chester, to release William and his two co-accused on bail until the next county court session or the next Michaelmas, if the case couldn't be heard before then. On 1 September, the prince sent fresh orders to Ferrers, telling him to try all three men at the next session, if he could do so without jeopardising the prince's rights or damaging the interests of the parties concerned. If this was impossible, the prince added, Ferrers was to let William and his fellow defendants out on bail.[11]

In the meantime, William's horse was declared a deodand (an animal or object that was forfeit to the crown because it had caused the death of a human being) and impounded. Under common law deodands had to be surrendered to the king or one of his agents, who sold them and put the money to pious uses. On 26 December 1347, the Black Prince instructed John de Burnham, the county chamberlain, to send William's steed to his stable master in London and promised to repay Burnham for the cost of keeping it. When the chamberlain submitted his annual accounts, he duly presented the bill for looking after one 'bay' horse.[12]

The loss of a prized mount was the least of William's worries, however. He still had to stand trial for slaying three men. In fourteenth-century England virtually all forms of homicide were punishable by hanging, except for those arising from the enforcement of the peace, excusable accidental killings, deaths inflicted in self-defence and instances where there were extenuating circumstances such as insanity or the youth of the offender. The legal authorities recognised that there was a difference between murder – which the great twelfth-century jurist Ranulf de Glanvill defined as slaying done secretly, out of sight of anyone save the perpetrator – and 'simple homicide' (essentially, every other form of killing). But indictments, accusations and appeals made no distinction between the two categories.

In practice, medieval jurors often discriminated between homicide with malice aforethought and slaughter 'unmotivated by contemplation of hatred', recognising that a blow delivered during a scuffle might be unintentionally fatal. If every man who was guilty of killing someone in hot blood were to be executed, this would have involved condemning friends, neighbours and people of generally good repute to the noose. However, the rules on self-defence were extremely rigid. The legal definition had been formulated to exclude all but acts of last resort and the test was objective. In other words, it wasn't enough for the jury to decide that a defendant had *believed* he could only save his life by slaying his opponent; the defendant was required to prove that there had, in fact, been no alternative. As a result, defendants desperate to escape the gibbet wove elaborate tales of being 'cornered and constrained' at every turn and many a jury clung doggedly to the defendant's version of events even when questioned by a sceptical bench.

Moreover, a verdict of self-defence didn't result in acquittal. The killer was 'remitted to the grace of the king', a formula that meant he had to obtain a royal pardon. Indeed, even convicted murderers might obtain clemency, although this was becoming more difficult – and much more expensive – as Edward III responded to parliamentary pressure to restrict the granting of pardons to the worst offenders in return for money or military service.

When William's case finally came to court, he must have told a plausible story. On 2 December 1348, he was pardoned for 'the death of William de Hyde and others', subject to paying a fine of £266 13s 4d. He promptly handed over the first £58 6s 8d. And just two months later, he was back in the crown's good graces. On 29 January 1349, Edward III wrote to the Black Prince, stating that he had ordered the earl of Huntingdon to transfer Halton Castle to the earl of Lancaster. The king warned his son not to molest or aggrieve Lancaster or his 'attorney', William Boydell, who had taken possession of the premises on the earl's behalf.[13] It was typical of the times that William could atone for his crime with coin. Nevertheless, the penalty he had incurred was much larger than his annual landed income. A moment of unbridled fury had left him with crushing debts.

The previous two years had been traumatic for William. His role in Hyde's death had jeopardised his longstanding ties with the Dutton and Massey families, kept him confined in prison for many months and cost him a great deal of money. He had at last secured his liberty and could set about rebuilding his life. Yet a far more momentous crisis was now looming – a crisis so terrible that it would completely dwarf his personal problems. For, even as William was clattering across the drawbridge and pounding on the wooden doors to Halton Castle, a 'great death of men' had England firmly in its grip.

13

Black Smoke

William's head clanged like a bell. His entire body ached and he felt unbearably hot. He thrashed from side to side, trying to find a comfortable position. At one point the door opened and Maud entered the chamber. She bent down, touched his forehead and said something. When he next looked up, Hyde was sitting on the edge of the bed, shattered ribs poking through his chest and the hideous gash on his face dripping blood. 'Forgive me,' William pleaded. 'It was an accident.' Hyde laughed, the slit in his cheek flexing like a second mouth.

William closed his eyes and sank into a troubled sleep. When he woke, hours had passed and a candle flickered in the gloom of the winter afternoon. He was burning up. Flames licked his throat, chest and abdomen, setting his torso ablaze with tongues of fire. They burn heretics, he thought, fear fluttering in the pit of his stomach. He knew he was a sinner, but he hadn't realised that he'd strayed so far from God's path. It was evening by the time he roused again. He watched the shadows on the ceiling dancing as the candle flared spasmodically in the draught from the window. There was something he needed to understand, something important, but it kept slipping away, sliding just out of reach.

Sometimes it was light, sometimes dark. In his delirium the hours merged into a single, endless night. The candle was guttering, sending a plume of smoke corkscrewing into the air. Grey tendrils drifted around him, hovering at the edges of his vision. Maud kept piling blankets on him. He tried to kick off the covers, teeth chattering as his fever rose higher and higher. He was a torch, a brand blazing at the centre of a pyre. He was the flame itself.

In May 1348, two ships left the English port of Bordeaux and started making their way home. Rather than crossing the Channel at its widest point, they sailed to the Channel Islands before heading north for England, a voyage of just over three weeks. The two ships docked in Melcombe Regis (now Weymouth) in Dorset in early June 1348. One of them was bound for Bristol and just pausing on its journey, but in the meantime both crews disembarked.

Among them were some Gascon sailors who had fallen ill during the Channel crossing and had to be carried ashore. When the sailors were stripped of their clothing, they were found to have strange black cysts about the size of a crabapple in the armpits and groin. The sick men suffered acute pain, with blood and pus oozing from the swellings and dark blotches forming on their skin. Nobody knew what was wrong with them, but within days of arriving they were dead. Almost immediately after they were buried the rest of the crew began showing similar symptoms and most soon followed their Gascon shipmates to the grave.

News of the mysterious malady was suppressed to avoid frightening people off coming into Melcombe to trade, but by mid-June several of the townsfolk were displaying signs of illness. On Monday, 23 June 1348, the disease claimed its first English casualty. As it spread, other symptoms appeared. Instead of developing a dark rash and hard red boils or buboes that turned black, some victims coughed, sweated profusely and spat blood. In both instances everything that issued from the body – breath, mucus, perspiration, urine and excrement – smelled foul. However, those with the respiratory form of the illness died even more quickly, within three days and sometimes as little as twenty-four hours of falling sick.

Word of the terrible epidemic travelled swiftly, transmitted by wandering entertainers and wayfaring preachers or passed on at markets and fairs. By the end of July 1348, the vast majority of the population had heard of the great 'mortality, pestilence and infection of the air' that had swept through mainland Europe and was now threatening England.

The disease was the plague and it came in three forms. The bubonic type, which caused buboes and internal bleeding, was communicated by contact with an infected person or through minor cuts and sores exposed to contaminated material, such as sheets, rags and clothing. As the bacteria spread from the lymph nodes, the victims' buboes and skin blackened and their bodies rotted from the inside. The more virulent pneumonic type was spread by inhaling plague bacteria. Bubonic plague might also turn into pneumonic plague if the bacteria reached the lungs, or septicaemic plague if the bacteria entered the bloodstream.

By mid-August 1348, the pestilence had reached Devon and Somerset and was firmly established in Bristol, where the second ship had docked. It killed indiscriminately, leaving not a single city, town or village untouched. Terrified friends and relatives sometimes fled, abandoning the sick to die alone, uncared for and unshriven. A number of frightened priests also deserted their parishioners, although most continued to visit the sick, hear their confessions and perform the last rites. But many of those who attempted to alleviate the suffering of their kinsfolk and neighbours died themselves and the toll was so great in some places that there were hardly enough people left to bury the dead.

As shocking stories of the devastation spread throughout the country, dire prophecies began to circulate. God was surely punishing mankind for his sins, although it was difficult to know precisely which transgressions had incurred his divine wrath. Various candidates were proposed, including the disgraceful behaviour of those who attended tournaments and the immodesty displayed by devotees of foreign fashions, with their indecently short, tight-fitting tunics. Alternatively, perhaps, the malign influence of the planets was to blame. In parts of mainland Europe the Jews (always convenient scapegoats) were also denounced for having allegedly poisoned the water in the wells. But they were the one group of people whom the English could not fault, since Edward I had expelled them from the realm in 1290.

Whatever the putative cause, the panic-stricken populace endeavoured to express its remorse. Some people undertook pilgrimages to Canterbury or to local shrines. Others fasted and mortified their flesh by wearing sackcloth, sleeping on stone and earth floors and going barefoot in all weathers. A few practised even more extreme forms of self-abasement, such as ritual flagellation. Naked save for cloths draped around their loins, they paraded through the streets, beating themselves bloody with thonged whips as they sang the Christian litany.

Still the plague continued its relentless progress. In late October or early November 1348, it reached London. On 1 January 1349, the king was forced to prorogue the forthcoming parliament at Westminster because 'the plague of deadly pestilence' was daily increasing in severity. Between February and mid-April, when the epidemic was at its height in the capital, more than 200 corpses were buried every day in the new burial ground next to Smithfield Market, in addition to all the bodies buried in the city's other churchyards. But with the churchyards overflowing, many bodies were simply cast into plague pits.

By early 1349, the pestilence was creeping north and by midsummer it had reached Chester. In August 1349, the heads of two of the largest religious houses succumbed and in the four months from June to September the archdeaconry had to replace thirty priests. Work on a new stone bridge over the River Dee simultaneously ground to a halt, the revenues from the mills and fishery nosedived and the eyre of the forest (a court held every three years to punish offenders against forest law) had to be cancelled for lack of justices.

William Boydell was accustomed to riding regularly into Chester, both for business and for pleasure. As the threat drew ever nearer he retreated to Grappenhall, where his wife and son were. Yet he couldn't ignore all his responsibilities; his demesne lands still had to be farmed, his tenants supervised, his animals fed and tended. And no place was safe. Even though the great woodlands that still covered much of the county formed a natural barrier, once the plague had penetrated Chester it swept rapidly through the countryside. The situation was especially grim in Goostrey, 16 miles south of Grappenhall, which only had a small chapel. The parishioners normally took their dead to be buried at the mother church in Sandbach 6 miles away. But transporting the decomposing bodies of plague victims there was a difficult and dangerous task, so corpses were simply dumped by the roadside and left to rot, accelerating the rate at which the pestilence spread.

There are no records showing precisely what happened to William and his family in the late autumn of 1349. Nevertheless, contemporary accounts and the many books that have been written about the Black Death, as it was later called, can help us reconstruct their final days.

Picture Maud on her knees in the chapel her father-in-law had built, begging God to spare her loved ones, as William prepared for the worst. He probably stocked up on holy water; drinking it was supposed to prevent the plague. Perhaps he also consulted an apothecary and bought an exorbitantly priced 'cure' containing filed horse hoof, crocus jovis (an amalgam of mercury and tin) and conserve of peony flowers. Then he ordered his servants to cover the windows of the manor house with waxed cloth and turn away any strangers. And on the increasingly rare occasions when he rode out to inspect his estates he wore a bag of crushed herbs over his nose to ward off poison in the air.

William had done all he could to protect his household, yet the plague marched inexorably closer. At first, he could hear the bells for the passing dead toll sonorously in the distance: nine strokes for a man, six for a woman and three for a child. But, one by one, the villages around Grappenhall were falling silent. The fields lay empty and unharvested, the only sign of life the smoke spiralling into the sky on the horizon, as the clothes and bedding of the victims were burned. William tried to hide his dread for the sake of his wife and son.

When the pestilence arrived at last, William was almost taken by surprise. He went to bed early one evening, feeling tired and listless but reassured by the absence of any swellings on his body. He woke up the next morning with a blinding headache and an odd tingling in his arms and legs. He forced himself to rise. However, as the hours passed, he felt increasingly hot and feverish. Eventually he returned to bed, where he lay tossing and turning, drenched in sweat. He was dimly aware of Maud bathing his face with cool water but failed to register her gasp as she stroked his neck, covertly checking for signs of disease. Maud was almost sure that she had detected a slight bump under one of his ears. Drawing down the sheet, she stared in horror at the small red nodule on her husband's groin.

As the hours passed, William's condition deteriorated. He had brief spells of lucidity, during which he was conscious of an excruciating pain like burning cinders in his throat, stomach and crotch. But most of the time he swung between violent raving and wearied prostration. The pustule on his inner thigh was now the size of a plum and dark purple. Smaller boils had also emerged in his armpits and on his ankles and a patch of blackened skin stained his abdomen. Neither the holy water nor the apothecary's potion had worked.

Maud struggled to master her terror and fatigue as she cared for her husband, wiping his face and body with wet cloths and spooning broth into his mouth to give him strength. But by the fourth day of William's illness the bubo on his groin was leaking a putrid black pus and Maud knew that he was dying. The servants had fled, so she sent Ralph to get the priest. When Ralph returned, he told her that Roger Shipbrook was too frightened to come.

Maud burst into tears, distraught that her husband would die unshriven. She knew that Shipbrook resented William for opposing his appointment to the benefice of Grappenhall, but how could the priest forsake the dying? It was his sacred duty to give the last rites, although, if truth be told, Shipbrook had always been a careerist cleric rather than a man with a genuine vocation. He had spent more time courting the bishop of Salisbury – for which he had just been rewarded with a canonry – than he had curing the souls of his parishioners.

When Maud calmed down, she cast around for ideas. She vaguely recalled being told that anyone – even a woman – could hear someone's confession in extremis, *but she worried that it wouldn't really count in God's eyes. Besides, William was now almost comatose. Still, she could pray for him. Returning to the bedchamber, she removed the crucifix hanging round her neck and gently placed it on her husband's chest. Then she sat by his side and started reciting a pater noster. She paused briefly, convulsed by a hacking cough, before pressing on to the end:* 'Libera nos a malo. *Deliver us from evil. Amen.'*

William lay quietly, his ribcage scarcely rising as Maud watched over him through the night, intermittently praying and dozing. Her fitful sleep was troubled by dreams of winged demons hovering over her husband's reclining form. Maud swatted them away with her Bible; she would not let them steal his soul. Dawn was breaking when William made a rattling sound, almost as if he was trying to clear his throat, and finally stopped breathing.

Maud washed her husband's corpse, forcing herself to overcome her repugnance as she swabbed the suppurating pustules and blackened skin. Then she wrapped the body in a clean sheet. Leaving the bedchamber, she walked numbly down the stairs to the hall, where Ralph sprawled fast asleep on the floor in front of the fireplace. She bent down to kiss her son's head; she would tell him of his father's death when he woke. First, she would rest a little. She sank into one of the wooden chairs by the hearth and closed her eyes. She had a pain in her side and her cough was getting worse. She tried to quell another spasm, covering her mouth to suppress the noise. When she took her hand away, there was blood on her palm.

Between the autumn of 1348 and the spring of 1350, the Black Death reached its zenith in the British Isles. The disease didn't vanish entirely afterwards, but it would never again cause such havoc. By the time it abated, a third of the inhabitants had died. In England alone there were some two million fatalities. 'We see death coming into our midst like black smoke,' the Welsh poet Ieuan Gethin later wrote, grieving for the son he had lost in another outbreak. 'Woe is me of the "shilling" in the armpit; it is seething, terrible, wherever it may come.'

The peasants suffered particularly heavily, weakened by successive famines earlier in the century, although the toll varied dramatically from one place to another. At Brightwell in Berkshire, a 'mere' 29 per cent of manorial tenants succumbed to the pestilence. At Oakington in Cambridgeshire, the mortality rate was a horrific 70 per cent. The nobility and gentry fared better because they could retreat to their country estates. Nevertheless, about 26 per cent of all tenants-in-chief died. The plague struck arbitrarily, respecting neither riches nor lineage. Some families were completely wiped out; few were left unscathed. Even the royal family was affected when Princess Joan perished in Bordeaux on her way to wed the Infante Pedro of Castile, leaving her parents 'desolated by the sting of this bitter grief'.

Cheshire was more sparsely populated than most of the country, so the number of casualties was lower than in other parts of England. Nevertheless, its losses were severe. In 1350, the bailiff of Drakelow reported that fifty-seven tenants had died of the pestilence and 'divers tenants' in Rudheath had been granted relief 'until the soil becomes better'. Another forty-seven tenants had died in Bucklow, while thirty-four were in arrears with their rent. The county chamberlain's accounts also contain frequent references to land that lay uncultivated, mute testimony to the men and women who were no longer alive to work the fields.

William Boydell, his wife Maud and their son Ralph were among the many victims. William died before the onset of winter 1349, when his inquisition post-mortem was conducted. The original document is now illegible, but an inspection and summary of the contents, produced in 1576, hints at the price the plague had exacted. The value of 120 acres of arable land in Kinnerton, which William farmed himself, had plunged from 2s to 8d an acre, 'owing to the pestilence'. Another 120 acres of land had fallen by the same amount, 'owing to the death [of] the tenants', while Dodleston was worth nothing at all.[1]

Ralph's inquisition post-mortem took place the following year, although he probably died at much the same time as his father and the delay arose because so many people had perished. On the day of his death Ralph held the manors of Dodleston, Handley, Latchford and Grappenhall, apart from certain lands and tenements in Grappenhall formerly belonging to his great-grandmother Margaret. He also owned a number of properties in Chester, some of which had possibly come from his grandmother Nichola. William had granted Ralph and his wife Elizabeth all these estates in a charter of dower and they were collectively worth £40.[2]

William's sister Margaret and her husband were dead as well: other likely casualties of the plague. Remarkably, however, their children, Hywel and Felicia, had survived, as had Ralph's wife, who may still have been living with her parents when the pestilence reached the Boydell household. Child brides often remained with their parents until they were old enough to engage in sexual relations with their husbands. Elizabeth subsequently sued for her dower and remarried. Meanwhile, the rest of the family estates were divided between William's younger sister, Joan, and his nephew.[3]

At the age of 26, Joan was old enough to take possession of her share of the lands immediately. Indeed, her husband, Sir John Danyers – who already held part of the manor of Lymm with William's distant cousin, John Boydell of Lymm – was only too eager to secure her inheritance. But Hywel was a minor. On 8 December 1349, the Black Prince ordered the escheator to sell Hywel's wardship and marriage, and raise 'as much as possible' from the sale for 'the mending and repair of [his] "halle" of Kenyngton and of the other houses within [his] manor'.[4] The prince was in the throes of renovating Kennington Palace, the London residence Edward III had given him in 1337, and needed all the money he could get.

The resolution of William's affairs took several more years, reflecting the disorder that prevailed once the plague had passed. In June 1353, the Black Prince complained that the escheator had still not responded to the writ he had sent to ascertain whether 'Maud, late the wife of William Boidel,' held any lands that should revert to himself, as earl of Chester. The prince wrote again on 5 September regarding the death of 'Ralph Boidel'. What he didn't know was that Sir John Danyers and his cronies had already cashed in on the situation. By 9 August 1350, Danyers had purchased Hywel's wardship for £80.[5] Death had visited William Boydell and his family 'like black smoke'. Now the vultures were circling over his lands.

14

An Unequal Contest

The first-floor chamber in the rectory was warm, with a blazing fire to stave off the bitter north wind, but Hywel was trembling as he tried to gather his thoughts. He'd approached Roger Shipbrook, the parson of Grappenhall, in desperation, and Shipbrook had advised him to petition the Black Prince. As earl of Chester the prince was the ultimate authority in the palatinate and could overrule the officials whom Hywel's uncle had bribed or intimidated into doing his bidding. However, Edward spent most of his time in London or overseas, waging war on the French. Indeed, he had yet to visit his earldom. So the only way of reaching him was by letter and that meant relying on Shipbrook.

Hywel could speak English, Welsh and French. He could also read all three languages and stumble through the book of Latin devotional prayers that was one of his most treasured possessions. But he couldn't write or sign his name. Priests learned how to wield a quill. The most successful merchants were likewise literate and numerate – and in some villages there might be one or two people with rudimentary writing skills attained by serving in the parish church or in a lord's domestic chaplaincy. In general, though, educated men in medieval society rarely learned to write; they perfected the art of Latin dictation and ratified documents with a seal or a cross.

Shipbrook was literate and Hywel knew that he disliked Sir John Danyers intensely. But could the priest be trusted? His reputation was decidedly tarnished. In March 1347, he had been appointed Cheshire's controller of pleas, receipts and issues to act as a check on the chamberlain's financial probity and administrative efficiency. Yet, two years later, he'd been caught embezzling and hauled up before the king to answer for his crimes. Would Shipbrook betray Hywel? And, if not, what price would he demand for his aid?

Shipbrook was sitting at the table, scratching notes with a stylus on a wooden writing tablet overlaid with coloured wax. He paused and peered up at Hywel as the young man paced nervously, waiting for him to carry on speaking. Hywel took a deep breath, ignoring his doubts. If he didn't do something, his uncle would simply continue to bully and exploit him – or even, perhaps, ensure that he met with a convenient 'accident'.

The barbarity of the Welsh was an established fact in the minds of most medieval Englishmen. The chronicler Thomas Wykes casually asserted that when Simon de Montfort led his followers into Wales in 1265, they had to live on milk and meat because the Welsh didn't know how to make bread. Others observed that the Welsh fought bravely but were utterly savage. And their moral failings were legion. In 1280, when John Peckham, archbishop of Canterbury, reviewed the Welsh legal canon, he concluded that much of it was 'contrary to reason . . . [and] in clear derogation of the laws of God'. The Welsh, the monk Matthew Paris noted disparagingly, were the 'dregs of the human race'.

Yet, in Cheshire at least, this hostility towards the Welsh was only half of the story. According to the conventional version of events, the county was an embattled frontier land continually threatened by a warlike neighbour covetous of its greater wealth. In practice, the situation was far more complex. When the Cheshire chronicler Ranulf Higden was composing his 'universal history' at St Werburgh's Abbey in the 1320s, he remarked that Chester was now a city the Welsh and English alike held in great esteem. Welsh settlers had moved into the area, drawn by the opportunities for trade, and marital ties had furthered the development of a distinctive Anglo-Welsh community. Moreover, some of the members of this community were socially influential, especially in south-western Cheshire.

Hywel ap Owain Voil was the product of one such Anglo-Welsh union. Margaret Boydell had married Owain Voil of Welshampton in about 1330. Owain's origins are shrouded in mystery, save for the fact that he owned a small estate in Flintshire, one of the four new counties Edward I had created from Llywelyn ap Gruffudd's former principality. But given Margaret's social standing, Owain probably came from a well-to-do Welsh family. Hywel had been raised in the expectation that he would inherit his father's lands. When his uncle William and cousin

Ralph died of the plague, he had also inherited half of their holdings and been catapulted into much greater prosperity. However, he was still a minor and Sir John Danyers – his uncle by marriage – was now abusing his position as Hywel's guardian.

Special arrangements were necessary when property passed to children. Where the land was held by military tenure, the deceased landholder's overlord was entitled to retain control of the estate and custody of the heir until the heir came of age – at 21 for a boy and, generally, on marriage for a girl (although the age of majority for girls was subject to dispute). Alternatively, the overlord could sell or assign wardship of the land, custody of the heir or both to a third party. The guardian had certain obligations. He was supposed to ensure that the deceased's debts were paid, that the heir was properly maintained and educated and that his or her lands were responsibly managed. Similarly, if a guardian arranged his ward's marriage, he was supposed to choose a spouse of at least equal social status. But any income left over from the heir's estate after discharging these duties became the guardian's property, as did the profit arising from the arrangement of the heir's nuptials.

Thus, wardships of land held by knight's fee offered plenty of opportunities for extortion. An unscrupulous guardian could keep his ward on short rations, clothe him shabbily and neglect his schooling. He could also put pressure on his ward to marry someone socially inferior; a child who was destined to inherit a valuable estate was a desirable match and many ambitious men were prepared to pay handsomely to secure the marriage of one of their offspring to a wealthy heir or heiress. In some cases, a guardian could even keep the ward's fortune within his family by marrying his ward off to one of his own children, although not all such marriages ran counter to the heir's interests, since guardians usually came from a similar social background to those of their wards.

Danyers had purchased Hywel's wardship from the Black Prince, William Boydell's feudal overlord, and betrothed the boy to Joan de Lymm. Joan was an eminently suitable bride. Her father, Peter, was the son and heir of the latest Gilbert de Lymm to hold half of the lordship of Lymm, while her mother, Emma, was the daughter of Alan Rixton, who owned lands in Lancashire. Equally pertinently, Joan was another vulnerable young orphan; her father, grandfather and only brother were all dead by about 1343.[1] She had inherited lands in Godley, Newton in Longdendale and Mottram, together with her sister Matilda – and the avaricious Danyers saw a golden opportunity to maximise the returns on the £80 he had paid for Hywel's wardship. Joan Boydell, whom he had married after the death of her first husband, Thomas de Sale, was too weak or too cowed to intercede on her nephew's behalf.[2]

Danyers held all the cards. Hywel was still in his teens, while Danyers was a seasoned soldier in his thirties with powerful contacts; his father, Sir Thomas Danyers of Bradbury, was a war hero. He had fought at the Battle of Crécy, where he retrieved the Black Prince's standard from the French and captured the *comte* de Tancarville – for which the prince had rewarded him with a generous annuity – and was now the county sheriff. Danyers took full advantage of the situation. Roger Shipbrook had already lodged a formal complaint about his conduct. In early 1352, Shipbrook wrote to the Black Prince with a litany of grievances. Danyers, he alleged, had pilfered his torches and timber to build a grandstand for the spectators at a tournament he was planning to hold in Warrington. He had also repeatedly harassed Shipbrook by borrowing his horses without permission and threatening to break the arms and legs of the servants Shipbrook had hired to harvest his crops, intimidating them so badly that they ran away. Then Danyers had broken into the rectory at Grappenhall and stolen the rest of Shipbrook's crops and, when the priest tried to sue him, he had seized Shipbrook's steed.

The prince had listened to Shipbrook. On 12 February 1352, Edward sent a sharply worded letter to Sir Thomas Ferrers, the justice of Chester, instructing him to order Danyers to 'redress the said oppressions and cease henceforth from such wrongs against Holy Church'. He didn't want to have to write again on the subject, he warned. If Danyers continued to persecute Shipbrook, he would have to 'answer for the perils that [might] ensue'.

Heartened by this sign that Shipbrook had Edward's ear, Hywel decided to enlist the priest's aid. In the summer of 1352, he asked Shipbrook to help him entail his share of the Boydell estates, so that it would be legally locked up and safe from Danyers' clutches. Hywel planned to grant the property to Shipbrook, who would then re-grant it to Hywel, his wife Joan and their heirs. Shipbrook agreed and, on 31 July 1352, the Black Prince ordered the escheator to review Hywel's application to alienate the land. But this was a protracted process and Hywel didn't know how long he would be able to withstand the duress his uncle was putting him under – assuming, of course, that he was still alive. If he died without leaving any children, his sister Felicia would inherit his estates.[3] She would then become Danyers' ward and Danyers might consider her more malleable.

Eventually, on Shipbrook's advice, Hywel approached the Black Prince directly. In early 1353, he sent a petition to the prince complaining that Sir John Danyers had been systematically milking his inheritance. Danyers, he said, had cut down the trees on his lands and sold the timber, demolished some of the houses and sold or given away others. Then, in collusion with his friends, he had arranged a fake enquiry to 'prove' that Hywel was of age and had forced him to hand over part of his estate. Danyers had also swindled the prince himself by lying about Hywel's age at William Boydell's inquisition post mortem and stacking the jury with relatives who condoned the lie. He had claimed that Hywel was 19, not 16, so that he could acquire Hywel's wardship at a cheaper price.[4]

These were grave charges. One of the few things a guardian could *not* do, theoretically at least, was misuse his ward's lands. The law was quite explicit on this point, as the jurist Henry de Bracton noted. A guardian was supposed to 'maintain the houses, parks, game preserves, ponds, mills' and everything else belonging to his ward's estate and restore it to the heir 'no less well stocked than he found it', when the youth came of age. If he breached the rules, he would be compelled to forfeit the wardship and make good the damage. However, Hywel wasn't just alleging that Danyers had despoiled his lands; he had also, shrewdly, appealed to the prince's self-interest. The value of a wardship depended upon the size of the inheritance and age of the ward. The younger the heir the more his wardship would fetch, because the guardian had a longer time in which to profit from his ward's lands. So, in pretending that Hywel was three years older than he actually was, Danyers had conned Edward out of a considerable amount of money.

The Black Prince was incensed. Danyers had been quick to petition him for the return of Dodleston Moor and the manor of Latchford, which he claimed – correctly – that the justice and escheator had wrongly withheld from his wife and nephew after William Boydell's inquisition post mortem. Danyers had also been given permission to delay paying his wife's share of the outstanding balance on William's fine for killing Hyde.[5] Yet, despite these concessions, he had harried Roger Shipbrook, dragged his feet over giving Ralph Boydell's young widow her dower and, if Hywel was right, had defrauded the prince himself.

Edward was notoriously extravagant. He spent large sums of cash on 'play' (probably dice), costly jewels and other finery and liked to give lavish presents to his friends. He was also in the midst of refurbishing Kennington Palace and needed money to fund his military campaigns. His main sources of income were the lands he held in Wales, Cornwall, Cheshire and Aquitaine and he was a harsh taskmaster when it came to raising cash from his tenants. But for all the skill with which his officials had managed to boost the revenues they extracted, the prince's finances were still embarrassed. And here, it seemed, was a deliberate attempt to evade payment of his dues.

The prince took a very dim view of that indeed. On 17 February 1353, he forwarded a copy of Hywel's petition to John de Burnham, the county chamberlain, and ordered him to look into the matter because, if what Hywel said was true, then 'very great profit might rightfully accrue to him [Edward]'. He added that since the justice had excused himself from the case, as one of the parties was staying with him, Burnham was to appoint two other men to hold an enquiry. The chamberlain was also to ensure that Danyers' father, the county sheriff, was not involved and that the jurors who participated in the enquiry were genuinely independent.[6]

Danyers was unapologetic. On 15 April 1353, the prince wrote to Thomas Young, the newly appointed escheator, stating that he had heard Hywel's lands had been taken out of wardship without going through the proper legal process and ordering Young to reclaim them. Young was also to conduct an inquisition to find out whether any 'waste' had been done to Hywel's lands and, if so, what sort of waste, who was responsible for it and how much damage Hywel had suffered. Three days later, the prince wrote to Young again, instructing him to 'seize the keeping of the lands and heir of Morgan de Mulleton', who had been one of William Boydell's military tenants in Handley and whose wardship therefore belonged to Hywel as heir to William's lands there.[7]

Thomas Young, who wasn't abreast of all the details, immediately repossessed William's entire estate. On 10 June 1353, the Black Prince had to issue further instructions clarifying what he meant. He explained that he had only intended Young to take Hywel's lands, not those belonging to Joan, who was of full age. So Young was to restore her half-share of the property to Joan and her husband. The prince also reminded

Young to ascertain from twelve people speaking under oath whether Hywel's lands had been laid waste and helpfully supplied a list of local men who would make suitable jurors. Among them were Hywel's great-uncle, Robert Boydell, and his distant cousin, John Boydell of Lymm.[8] At last Hywel could count on some friendly faces on a jury his uncle couldn't rig.

John Boydell had watched with growing concern as Danyers fleeced his nephew, although he had made no effort to intervene – partly, perhaps, because he was in a delicate position. He and Danyers shared lands in Lymm. He was also friendly with other members of the Danyers family and had witnessed a dubious arrangement in which Danyers' cousin married off his ward, Clemence Norreys, to his son William and then gave William all the land she had inherited.[9] It wasn't in John's interests to kick up a fuss. But when the charges Hywel had levelled against Danyers were investigated, John finally spoke up for his young kinsman.

Within months, the wardship of Hywel's lands was back in the hands of the Black Prince. Edward had been visiting Chester to investigate the behaviour of some of the county's 'great men', after receiving repeated complaints about their behaviour. On 14 September 1353, while he was staying in the city, he commanded the escheator to pay Hywel an annual income of 10 marks out of the profits from his estates for the rest of his minority. Fortuitously, Hywel's minority was nearly at an end; on 24 February 1354, the prince instructed Young to collect proof of Hywel's age because Hywel had notified him that he was now 21. But Hywel had already expressed his gratitude to John Boydell by granting him a squire's outfit and a rent of 20s a year for life.[10]

Meanwhile, the case against Danyers rumbled on. Three weeks before asking for evidence that Hywel had reached his majority, the prince ordered Young to find out just how much property Sir John Danyers and his wife had acquired without permission, where the property was held from him as earl of Chester. Edward wanted to know the full extent of 'the lands, rents and woods' the Danyers had obtained, what they were worth and – most importantly of all – how much damage might accrue to him and his heirs as a result of their actions.[11]

The escheator reported back to the prince. And, on 10 May 1354, the matter was resolved – to the prince's satisfaction, though hardly to

Hywel's. Danyers and his wife would be pardoned for acquiring half of the manor of Grappenhall without royal consent, provided that they paid a fine of 20 marks. They would have to pay Edward a further 70 marks for other violations, but they could keep everything they had taken from Hywel.[12]

The following day the prince wrote to Thomas Young, ordering him to let Hywel take possession of his lands because he had proved that he was of age.[13] The news must have come as bitter-sweet relief to Hywel. On the one hand, he finally had control of the estates he had inherited. On the other, those estates had been significantly depleted by the depredations of his guardian and there was nothing he could do to get redress. Danyers had lied, cheated and connived with his friends to subvert the law. But he was useful to the Black Prince and Edward was pragmatic. By May 1354, when the case was closed, the prince had made Danyers one of his household bachelors – those who formed the core of his military retinue. Hywel, young, inexperienced and lacking influential allies, had been completely outflanked.

While Hywel was locked in battle with his uncle, seismic shifts were taking place in England as a whole. The changes had begun before the onset of the plague, but the demise of a third of the population turned tremors into shockwaves. The Black Death had caused a catastrophic shortage of manpower and the dearth of people willing to work the soil had loosened the links between lords and villeins. Outsiders now held much of the land formerly occupied by families with long ties to the acres they farmed. Those who remained were aware of their improved bargaining position and wanted a better deal. In short, the peasants were getting uppity.

In June 1349, parliament enacted the Ordinance of Labourers. It was expressly aimed at workers who, 'seeing the necessity of lords and the scarcity of servants, will not serve unless they receive excessive wages'. But the malefactors refused to take the hint. So, in 1351, parliament passed a law to deal with people who disregarded the ordinance in the interests of their own 'ease and greed'. The Statute of Labourers set the maximum wage at the level it had been in 1346-47, restricted the movement of workers and decreed that any able-bodied individual who refused to work should be put in the stocks or sent to gaol.

The statute was predictably unpopular. It was also ineffective. Between 1340 and 1360, the daily wage for an agricultural worker rose from about 1¾d to 2⅓d in nominal terms. However, wages comprised only a small part of the remuneration farm labourers received; 'gifts' of cash and corn became increasingly common. The poet John Gower, who came from a Kentish gentry family, summed up the feelings of many a manorial lord. In the good old days villeins didn't expect 'to eat wheat bread', he grumbled. 'Their bread was made of beans and of other corn and their drink was water. Then cheese and milk were as a feast to them; rarely had they any other feast than this.' But now they were 'sluggish, scarce and grasping'. The peasant demanded 'things for his belly like a lord'. He even wanted to dress like his betters and had the audacity to desire such luxuries as a bed and a pillow.

In reality, the villeins still received a paltry share of the rewards for their toil – and their lot was improving far less than manorial accounts or medieval literature might suggest, because the prices of almost all basic goods were rising as well. Higher wages were only one element in the mix. Many feudal lords, lacking people to plough their demesne lands, turned to less labour-intensive activities, such as raising cattle and sheep. The result was rampant inflation. Between 1346 and 1355, the price of grains and barley malt soared by 31 per cent. Meat, fish and dairy products cost an extra 17 per cent, and fuel and textiles an extra 46 per cent.

Manorial lords and large landholders were able to cope with these inflationary pressures because they could profit from the higher prices their produce fetched, even though labour was more expensive. The servants who farmed their demesne lands were also cushioned, since they received food and clothing as part of their pay. The food allowance they were given often exceeded six quarters of mixed grains a year, which went a long way towards keeping a family in bread, pottage and ale. But smaller landholders like Hywel's great-uncle, the elderly Robert Boydell, were far more vulnerable. Robert owned a house and forty acres of land in Handley, as well as four acres of land in Bradley, near Frodsham, which he held with his wife Katherine. However, he had exchanged his lands in Catterich for a fixed lifetime annuity. So, shortly after Hywel received his inheritance, Robert sued him 'for a rent of 26s in Lacheford', which he claimed that his brother William had granted him.[14]

There were other calls on Hywel's purse, too – and not all of them as fair. No sooner had he obtained his lands than Thomas Young, the escheator, started chasing him for a full year's profit from the manor of

Dodleston during the period in which he had been a minor. In late 1355 or early 1356, Young seized some of Hywel's assets to cover the debt and Hywel was forced to appeal to the Black Prince again. He pointed out that, since he had been a ward at the time, he had never received the money. The scales of justice proved as unbalanced as before. On 5 June 1359, the prince ordered Young to let Hywel off paying the 10 marks that he had received 'for his sustenance' while he was underage. Hywel was also to be granted respite from payment of the remaining debt until the following summer. Nevertheless, he was still expected to pay up, despite the fact that it was Danyers who had enjoyed the profits.[15]

Danyers had come out on top yet again. Indeed, he had even been given a chance to reprise his custodial role. On 3 June 1359, the Black Prince had granted him the wardship of Hywel's nephew. Joan's sister, Matilda de Lymm, had married William Tranmere, lord of part of the manor of Tranmere in the Wirral. Tranmere was dead by October 1351, leaving a son who was now about 9 years old.[16] As his guardian, Danyers had the right to decide where the child would live and most guardians took their wards into their own homes, once the ward reached the age of 7. So Hywel had every reason to fear that his uncle would revert to his old tricks and there would be little he could do to protect the boy.

Danyers cast a long shadow. Yet slowly, very slowly, Hywel was beginning to break free and forge his own way. In November 1358, he stood surety for the good conduct of Robert Houghton, whom the Black Prince had just appointed constable of Beeston Castle, a magnificent fortress perched on a crag mid-way between Chester and Crewe. Among the other men to provide pledges for Houghton were David Malpas, lord of the manors of Hampton and Bickley, and his son Roger; Richard Cholmondeley, lord of Cholmondeley, and his cousin Kenrick; Nicholas Manley, the younger son of Robert Manley, lord of Manley; Philip Filkyn, lord of Tattenhall; and Robert Bellew, lord of Golborne Bellow.[17] For the most part these men were lesser players in Cheshire's hierarchy of power, compared to Danyers and his cronies, but several of them were to become Hywel's close friends and associates.

By late 1359, Hywel had also joined the Black Prince's military retinue. Edward III and his eldest son were superb martial commanders, moulded from the same clay as Edward I, and the men of Cheshire now played a major role in their foreign campaigns, as they had in the conflicts with Wales. This time it was the French whom they fought. Edward III had a strong claim to the French crown as the grandson and direct lineal descendant of Philip IV through his mother, Isabella. But the French nobility argued that a woman couldn't be anointed, thereby precluding succession via the female line. So, when the last of Philip IV's sons died in 1328 without leaving a direct male heir, the throne passed to his cousin, Philip VI. The 15-year-old Edward accepted the decision, but relations between England and France deteriorated over the next decade. In 1337, they took a sharp turn for the worse when Edward refused to pay homage to Philip VI for his lands in Aquitaine. The king promptly confiscated his territory. Edward retaliated by declaring himself, not Philip, the rightful ruler of France, precipitating what was later to be known as the Hundred Years War.

Edward had several objectives in pitching for the French crown. He was providing a focal point for disaffected nobles like the count of Flanders and duke of Normandy. He was protecting trade with Flanders, which imported large quantities of English wool. And he was defending the back door to England, since the French monarchs had supported the Scots in their struggle to remain independent. War also, of course, brought opportunities for adventure, glory and enrichment. Hundreds of knights and thousands of men of more modest means flocked to the king's banner, hoping to win fame and fortune. At the very least, knights could expect to get paid 2s and squires 1s a day, while foot soldiers and the most experienced archers earned 6d. But wages were as nothing next to war booty – and in the first years of the war there was plenty of booty to be had.

The English were stunningly successful in early campaigns. In 1340, Edward III won control of the waterways between England and France at the Battle of Sluys off the Flemish coast, ending the threat of a possible French invasion. In July 1346, he descended on Normandy with some 10,000 men and, on 26 August, he achieved a decisive victory at Crécy, with the help of the Black Prince. Edward followed up by marching on Calais and besieging it. On 3 August 1347, Calais finally succumbed, giving the king a base from which to make further forays. News of these triumphs spread rapidly. In the 1330s, Edward had introduced the practice of sending royal communications to the shires and parishes. His successes at Sluys and Crécy were broadcast from every pulpit in the country.

Two innovations – the mounted raid and the mounted archer – played a big part in the king's land victories. Edward III had learned from Robert Bruce's sudden swoops on northern England. Bruce had ravaged the area, terrorising the inhabitants, stealing their cattle and torching their crops. The king and his son used the same approach in France. Borrowing from techniques honed in the Scottish Marches, they rode through the French countryside pillaging their enemies' property and leaving a trail of devastation. In English hands, the *chevauchée* (as it was called) became a medieval weapon of mass destruction.

Edward had also discovered the value of putting archers on horseback. The longbow was a deadly instrument: it had a range of more than 600ft, was capable of penetrating plate armour and could be fired much faster than a crossbow (which had to be cranked or levered before each volley). A skilled longbowman could release ten to twelve arrows per minute. However, ordinary archers travelled on foot and couldn't keep up with the cavalry. Mounted archers, by contrast, rode to battle and then dismounted to fight. But they didn't need first-class horses. A charger robust enough to carry a fully armoured knight was very expensive. Lightly armoured archers could ride cheaper breeds and still move around very rapidly.

Combining the strengths of the longbowman with the mobility of the knight gave the king a much more versatile fighting force. Mounted archers, shooting on foot, could be used to scatter an enemy massed in a defensive position or to weaken an advancing foe. When they ran out of arrows, they could drop their bows and fight alongside the men-at-arms. They could also perform some of the lighter tasks traditionally performed by the men-at-arms, such as scouting, raiding villages for supplies and guarding prisoners. Their multi-purpose combat skills made them by far the most effective element in Edward's armies.

The men of Cheshire played a significant role in this tactical development. Between 1334 and 1343, the county supplied more than 2,000 mounted archers for the king's campaigns in Scotland, Flanders and Brittany. But even though the horses that mounted archers used were less costly than those required by knights, they still represented a substantial outlay. Horses of any kind needed harnesses and saddles and had to be fed. So the men who made up Edward III's armies were not the tattered throng who had served as foot soldiers in Edward I's militia. They came from the poorer ranks of the gentry or from wealthy yeoman families and were people of good standing in the local community.

Some of these landholders were obliged to provide military service. Others welcomed the chance to boost their incomes, since the cultivation of arable land wasn't as profitable in Cheshire as it was in southern England. The wet climate and heavy soil weren't good for growing grain, although the county's well-watered pastures and an abundance of acorns proved favourable for rearing cattle and pigs. The daily wage of 6d that a Cheshire archer could earn – twice the rate other archers earned – was a valuable supplement.

One member of the Boydell family had already taken the king's coin during the Poitiers campaign of 1355-57. John Boydell of Lymm had acquitted himself bravely. In November 1357, the Black Prince wrote to the county chamberlain and justice's lieutenant, ordering them not to put John on assizes or juries 'so long as he can be fairly spared'.[18] This was a reward for services rendered, as such duties prevented a man from earning money. John probably also brought home a sliver of the wealth the army had stolen or extorted. The English had taken 1,975 prisoners at the Battle of Poitiers, including the king of France himself. Jean II (who had been crowned after the death of his father, Philip VI, in 1350) was shipped to England, pending payment of a huge ransom. But many French nobles were able to buy back their freedom immediately. Plunder and pay-offs had more than covered the costs of the campaign and some of the loot eventually trickled out of the royal coffers into the purses of the lords, knights and lesser men who had taken up arms for their sovereign.

Even so, prices were rising and the Boydells of Lymm were struggling, although Hywel did his best to help. In July 1359, he granted John an income of £1 3s 4d out of the rents from his estates, together with the right to a rent of 6s 3d on the death of Ralph Boydell's widow, Elizabeth Davenport, who currently held it in dower. But Hywel wasn't rich himself. He had inherited only half of William Boydell's estates and those estates had been devalued by the Black Death. They had also, of course, dwindled substantially in his uncle's hands. Tempted, perhaps, by the prospect of winning some booty, Hywel decided to join the next expedition to France. On 24 September 1359, John de Burnham, chamberlain of Chester, was commanded to issue letters of protection for 'Howel ap Oweyn Voil and all the others' who were to accompany the prince with his knights and esquires.[19]

Hywel's luck proved as poor as ever; while the Poitiers campaign had been highly profitable, the Reims campaign was not. Edward III now had a completely different goal: to seize the throne of France for himself. He hoped to enter Reims without much resistance and have himself crowned at the cathedral, where French monarchs were traditionally invested. Despoiling the territory he aimed to rule would only reduce the taxes it produced and alienate his future subjects even further. So the king ordered that nobody was to set fire to any town, 'except for the odd house or two, to make it easier to extract ransoms from the rest', and threatened to hang anyone who disobeyed him.

Edward sent an advance guard to prepare the ground. In October 1359, two raiding parties pillaged Artois and Picardy, before returning to Calais, where the rest of the army was disembarking. Once his forces had landed, the king split them into two columns, taking command of the main body himself. The Black Prince led the rearguard of 2,500 men-at-arms and 4,000 archers, with Hywel among their ranks. The two divisions then marched along parallel routes to Reims, a strategy dictated by the need to forage for provisions.

They made slow progress. The French had stripped the surrounding countryside of food, so the English 'were in great want of bread and wine and meat'. The weather was also foul. Drenched in the rain that 'fell day and night', men and horses struggled miserably through a sea of mud. Worse still, when the army reached Reims on 4 December 1359 it discovered a well-stocked city with sturdy defences, amply prepared for a long siege. The inhabitants had learned from earlier disasters and spent the previous year building stronger fortifications. Edward blockaded the city, but after five weeks his supplies were running dangerously low. Weakened by cold and hunger, the English were forced to withdraw.

The French harassed them continuously as they retreated and managed to take a number of prisoners – including a certain merchant's son whose pen was to prove far mightier than his sword. Geoffrey Chaucer had been riding in the train of the Black Prince's younger brother, Lionel, earl of Ulster, when he was caught up in a skirmish, knocked down and captured. Fortunately for the youthful would-be poet, the king dipped into his own resources. On 1 March 1360, Edward paid £16 towards his ransom and Geoffrey was soon free again.

While Chaucer was anxiously awaiting his deliverance, the English headed south to Burgundy, where they raided the countryside until the duke of Burgundy bribed Edward to leave. Then, just as the king was turning towards Paris in March 1360, his messengers brought news that the French had launched a brutal attack on Winchelsea, a small town on the south coast of England. The raiders hoped to frighten the English into returning home to defend their own country and to rescue King Jean, who had been kept in comfortable confinement at Lincoln Castle, his enormous ransom still unpaid. They failed on both counts; Jean remained in his gilded prison, while a livid Edward marched on Paris. Yet, although he succeeded in sacking the suburbs, the city held out.

Frustrated – but unwilling to quit – Edward moved his forces to Chartres, 55 miles south-west of Paris. There, the chronicler Jean Froissart reports, disaster struck. On 13 April, 'such a storm and violent tempest of thunder and hail . . . fell on the English troops that it seemed as if the world was come to an end'. The hailstones were so large that they killed men and horses, the wind so ferocious that it ripped up the army's tents and the weather so harsh that scores of soldiers died of cold.

Edward saw the storm as a celestial warning. Papal legates had been trying for some months to negotiate a ceasefire between the English and the French. King Jean's son had also sent envoys and the duke of Lancaster had advised the king to settle. But Edward had obstinately refused to moderate his demands. With first-hand evidence of God's sentiments on the matter, he hastily changed his mind. Over the next few weeks his commissioners hammered out a pact with the French. The Treaty of Brétigny – named after the little village a few miles outside Chartres where the talks took place – was signed on 8 May 1360.

Edward renounced his claim to the French throne, reduced Jean's ransom to a still-massive three million gold écus (£500,000) and agreed not to make any additional territorial claims. In return, he was granted Guienne and Calais, together with other lands in Aquitaine and Gascony amounting in all to about a third of France. Edward insisted on retaining forty nobles as hostages to ensure that the French honoured the treaty. However, he undertook to return King Jean as far as Calais, where he would stay until a first instalment of 600,000 écus was paid on his ransom and the territories specified in the agreement were transferred.

On 24 October, the French made a down payment of 400,000 écus on Jean's ransom, after much scrabbling to raise the money. This was less than the stipulated sum, but Edward accepted the cash and the peace treaty was formally ratified. In the end, though, the Reims campaign had been a failure. Edward had acquired a large tract of land in France. Yet he had never had occasion to use the crown he brought with him in a baggage train reputed to be 6 miles long. Furthermore, many of the conditions of the treaty were never met and many of the ransoms he had been promised were never handed over. When King Jean died in April 1364, the French had only paid about a third of his ransom – a sore point in Anglo-French relations for years to come. So the Reims campaign brought little by way of loot or lucre and Hywel probably returned from France with nothing more than his wages.

Hywel had been to war – and once was enough. Waking up cold and stiff every morning, tussling with sodden boots, gnawing on stale bread for breakfast, riding until his arse ached, hurling himself into brief, terrifying interludes of fighting, shivering over fires painstakingly made by striking flint against steel, huddling under a damp cloak as he tried to sleep at night: he'd had a bellyful of France. When the Black Prince sailed for Bordeaux with his wife Joan in April 1363, planning to establish his court at Ombrière Castle, Hywel stayed at home.

But, whether or not they accompanied the prince, Cheshire's gentry were still expected to foot a share of the bill for his foreign ambitions. Fines were a crucial source of revenue and one local landholder had run into serious trouble. John Leycester had been involved in a bitter dispute with Hugh Chadderton over which of them was entitled to inherit the estate of his uncle, Sir Ralph Mobberley. In 1362, Leycester and his accomplices murdered Chadderton. They were captured in Coventry, brought back to Chester under armed guard and incarcerated in the castle to await trial, with strict orders from the prince that they be kept 'in separate chambers and in irons'.

Edward had personally arranged a grand jury to settle the dispute and was probably angry that Leycester had failed to abide by the court's decision. However, he eventually agreed to relax these harsh conditions when a number of local landowners undertook to pay him £1,066 13s 4d, at the rate of £100 a year, if Leycester or his friends escaped from the castle. Hywel was one of the men who stood surety for them.[20]

In the event, the culprits apparently made no effort to abscond. Nevertheless, Hywel could ill afford to take such a risk. He had just entered into another recognizance with David Hanmer, an up-and-coming Anglo-Welsh lawyer, Arthur Davenport and Jevaf' ap Jor' ap Madock (possibly the son of Iorwerth ap Madog, another eminent Welsh jurist) to the Black Prince for £100.[21] But one of the sources of revenue the Boydells had long enjoyed – the tolls from the wooden bridge that the family had eventually built to cross the River Mersey between Thelwall and Runcorn – was now drying up. The bridge had fallen apart or been swept away in a storm. So Sir John Boteler, lord of Warrington, wanted to build a rival bridge in stone near his own manor and collect the tolls himself.

On 6 July 1364, the king granted Boteler and his two co-investors, Sir Geoffrey Warburton and Matthew Rixton of Great Sankey, protection for a year during the construction of the new bridge. The carpenters, stonemasons and labourers they had hired, together with the ship they had chartered to carry stone, lime and other goods, were also to receive protection. Hywel knew Warburton and Rixton well. Warburton's younger sister, Margaret, had married Joan's brother Peter, while Rixton was Joan's first cousin, albeit on the wrong side of the blanket.[22] But as Hywel had discovered with Danyers, kinship didn't count for much when there was money to be made and his relatives' protestations that their motives were purely charitable probably rang distinctly hollow.

In fact, the project soon ran into problems. With no bridge in place, a number of enterprising local boatmen started ferrying passengers across the river. So, in October 1365, the Black Prince ordered that the offenders be imprisoned and their vessels impounded. Then Matthew Rixton was outlawed. As one of Lancashire's deputy sheriffs, Rixton had been charged with holding an election to choose two members of parliament for the county. But he and his partner had concealed the order and returned themselves as the members so that they could claim the attendance allowance of 4s a day. When rumours of their crime reached the king he launched an enquiry. Rixton was convicted of fraud and ejected from his seat.

Sir John Danyers, back from campaigning in France, barely waited for the judge's hammer to fall. He had already obtained permission to hold two annual fairs and two weekly markets in Latchford. Trading on his links with the Black Prince, he grabbed the chance to get involved in another potential money-spinner. On 20 October, the prince granted him the ship that had been used to carry materials for the new bridge, together with the stone Warburton had given Matthew Rixton, because Rixton had been declared a felon and all his goods were forfeit. Four months later, Edward III placed the three boats, their mariners and the victuals, timber and stone Danyers had assembled to construct the bridge under his protection for two years. Danyers pressed on with the project and the new bridge was finished in February 1369, when brother John, one of the hermit-friars of Warrington, received a licence to celebrate divine offices in the chapel at its foot.

In the meantime, Hywel's finances had improved. His cousin's widow, Elizabeth Davenport, had died, so her dower lands had reverted to his aunt and himself as Ralph's co-heirs. He and Joan had likewise each inherited half of his great-uncle Robert's modest holdings in Handley and Bradley, when Robert expired at a great age in 1366. Much to Hywel's relief, his nemesis was also beginning to fade in health and power. By March 1372, Sir John Danyers had passed away and, for all his driving ambition, there was one goal he had never achieved: he had no son to carry on his line. A second marriage, hurriedly contracted after his wife Joan's death several years previously, had proved fruitless. When Danyers died, he bequeathed the manor of Grappenhall to his two daughters, Margaret and Nichola, and his lands in Latchford and Handley to his widow, Alice. However, Margaret died very shortly afterwards, leaving Nichola her share of their father's estates.[23]

Hywel's Anglo-Welsh roots and fluency in the Welsh language were also coming in useful at last. By May 1373, the Black Prince had made him steward of Hopedale – one of the three Marcher lordships that Edward I had merged to form Flintshire and that had formerly belonged to Dafydd ap Gruffudd, last of the native princes of Wales. However, Hywel didn't have long in which to enjoy life liberated from the presence of his overbearing uncle. He was still alive on 25 September 1374, when he witnessed a lease of the manor of Bretton in Flintshire, where he continued to hold the lands he had inherited from his father.[24] But by January 1376 he, too, was dead. Generous, trusting and somewhat naïve, Hywel had been no match for the ruthless Danyers. Yet, as he lay dying, he could derive solace from the knowledge that, unlike Danyers, he had a male heir. He was leaving an adult son, William, who had already produced another son. The future of his family looked secure.

15

Venom in the Veins

The bolt slammed into his shoulder with such force that he pivoted before toppling to the ground. Stunned, dazed, speechless, William looked up at the clouds scudding across the sky. When he squinted to the left, he could see the shaft sticking out of his padded jerkin. It had maple vanes, neatly cut and glued into the grooves in the ash shaft. A well-made quarrel, he thought dispassionately. There was no pain. He simply felt cold, dizzy, as though the earth had turned to water, rolling beneath him like the Channel. He could hear men shouting and a horse screaming, but the sounds of battle faded as the water claimed him, a black riptide swirling over his head, drowning him in darkness.

His cousin Geoffrey found him. It was Geoffrey who staunched the flow of blood, helped him stand and half-walked, half-carried him to the surgeon's tent, Geoffrey who steered him to an empty pallet, forced wine down his throat and waited with him until the surgeon could examine the wound. The news wasn't good. The bolt head had driven through flesh and muscle, embedding itself deep in William's shoulder bone. It would have to be extracted rather than expelled, always a more difficult procedure.

William stared up at the canvas roof of the tent, teeth gritted, while the surgeon carefully sawed off the shaft a few inches above the entry point. Next he enlarged the wound and removed the shreds of fabric buried in William's tissue with a hooked metal probe. Then he started digging around for the bolt head with a diamond-shaped arrow spoon. God's bollocks, it hurt! William focused on the flies buzzing around the top of the tent pole in an effort to block out the pain. Finally, the surgeon managed to cup the bolt head with the spoon. Closing the pincers, he wiggled the spoon from side to side to loosen the head and tugged until it came free with a sudden squelch. William gasped.

Just when he thought the worst was over, the surgeon picked up a pitcher and tipped white wine directly into the open wound. William roared in agony as the alcohol seared his flesh. What was the crooknosed, boil-brained whelp of Satan doing? Trying to kill him? His curses subsided into a whimper as Geoffrey pushed him back down on the pallet. At last, the fire in his shoulder diminished. The surgeon covered the wound with a paste of barley flour and honey before wrapping a bandage around his shoulder and under his arm.

William sighed with relief. His whole shoulder throbbed. Thank Christ it was his left shoulder, not the right one, muscles bulging from all his years of practice with a longbow. Every able-bodied Englishman was required to train with a bow on feast days, instead of playing football or 'other vain games of no value'. But the men of Cheshire were renowned for their archery and William was proud of his skill. Geoffrey helped him clamber off the pallet and step outside. He inhaled deeply. The air was sweet and wholesome after the surgeon's tent, with its reek of blood and shit and fear-soaked sweat.

William had been named after the uncle from whom Hywel inherited his lands in 1349. He proved a resilient lad. A second outbreak of the plague, marked by the same distinctive buboes as the first, erupted in 1361. But unlike the Black Death, it carried off a disproportionate share of the young. 'There was a mortality of men, especially of adolescents and boys,' the *Chronicle of Louth Park Abbey* relates. Children who had escaped the earlier epidemic as infants, or who had been born after it ran its course, were now dying. A third bout followed in 1369: 'It was great beyond measure, lasted a long time and was particularly fatal to children,' the author of the *Anonimalle Chronicle* noted sorrowfully. Moreover, no sooner did this latest episode cease than severe floods 'drowned' the corn, ruining the harvest. Grain prices soared, peaking in the 'great dear year' of 1370, so that famine finished off many of those who hadn't perished from the pestilence.

William and his family emerged unscathed from both outbreaks of the plague, yet death had still visited their home. In about 1366, he had married Elizabeth, one of the two daughters of Adam de Buerton, lord of the manor of Buerton, near Audlem. Adam had expired in early 1365. His widow, another Elizabeth, held land in Buerton in her own right. So Adam seems to have left his estate to his girls – Elizabeth and her sister Alice, the wife of John Poole of Poole Hall in the Wirral.[1] But in the summer of 1370, Elizabeth also died, probably in childbirth. If the passage from womb to world was dangerous for a baby, it was hazardous for the mother, too.

A number of medical treatises provided detailed instructions for easing a difficult labour, dealing with a breech birth, extracting a dead foetus, removing the afterbirth and treating postpartum pain. The knowledge such texts contained was passed on by word of mouth and some of it was remarkably sound. Even so, roughly one in every fifty confinements ended in the mother's death – although it was often blood loss or infection, rather than the birthing process itself, that proved fatal. And the odds of experiencing complications were considerably higher if the mother was a teenager with an underdeveloped pelvis.

William may well have grieved for his young wife, but he had been wedded, bedded and widowed before the age of 20 and still had an heir to beget; he remarried within months of Elizabeth's death. His second wife, Cecily, was the daughter of Robert Bellew, lord of Golborne Bellew, with whom Hywel had long been friendly. Cecily had married Robert Huxley, the son of Richard Huxley, who held a moiety of the manor from which he took his name. However, Robert had also died, leaving his bride with a house and thirty acres of land in Huxley by way of dower. Cecily was soon pregnant and there was much rejoicing when she gave birth to a healthy baby boy at the family home in Handley on 11 July 1371. Thomas – named after Cecily's grandfather, Thomas Bellew – was baptised the very same day.[2]

Infants couldn't be carried into church until they had been 'instructed' because they were not yet Christian. So midwife, grandparents, godparents and William, proudly clutching his newborn son, gathered in the porch of the parish church, after sending word to John Assewell, the rector of Handley, to meet them there. Assewell began with the preparatory rites – exorcising Thomas from evil and infusing him with holiness – before ordering him to enter the temple of God. Then the baptismal party went into the church to stand by the font, where Thomas was stripped of his christening robe, asked various questions in Latin (which his godparents answered on his behalf) and immersed in holy water three times, 'in the name of the Father, Son and Holy Spirit'. After that, his senior godfather raised the spluttering baby from the font and held him while Assewell consecrated him with holy oil, wrapped him in a chrisolm (a garment to keep the oil in place), put a lighted candle in his hand and charged him with being a good Christian. Finally, once Assewell had directed father and godparents in their duties, the baptismal party trooped back to the manor house to celebrate.

Cecily, recovering from her ordeal in the birthing chamber, didn't attend the ceremony. Old Testament law stated that a woman who gave birth was unclean and shouldn't touch a holy object or enter a holy place for forty days after the birth of a son, or eighty following the birth of a daughter. She was then to make an offering to a priest and be purified. A variant of this custom had passed into Christian usage and, though the Church had officially relaxed the rule by the fourteenth century, society was often stricter in observing the period of exclusion. So Cecily almost certainly waited a full forty days before visiting Assewell to be cleansed.

She had probably given birth to at least one more child by the time William inherited Hywel's lands in 1375 – at which point he assumed the Boydell surname. Like his father before him, William enjoyed a warm relationship with his wider kinsfolk. He was particularly close to Geoffrey Boydell, the great-grandson of Sir John Boydell's younger brother William, who had settled in Hulme Walfield. Geoffrey was a few years older than Hywel and had served under the Black Prince in Aquitaine in 1369-70. He had subsequently married his third cousin, Joan, one of the great-granddaughters of Sir Vivian Standon and his wife Maud, the daughter of the first Sir William Boydell. Joan had inherited half of the manor of Standon in Staffordshire and Geoffrey had moved there. However, he still kept a house in Chester and made regular trips back home. On 10 January 1376, William – now calling himself Boydell – ceded all right to four burgages in Frodsham to Geoffrey. These were the same four burgages that his great-uncle William had acquired from Matilda de Camelsford in 1342. The latter had eventually given them to Matilda's daughter, Matilda de Hallum. But when Matilda's line died out, the properties had reverted to the main branch.[3]

As he rode around his estate on a frosty winter morning, William could afford to feel content. He had a dutiful wife, a thriving young son and enough land to keep his family in reasonable comfort. He also had a steadfast friend in Geoffrey, who lived only 30 miles away – no more than a day's hard ride, at the end of which he could always count on an enthusiastic welcome and a flagon of wine. Life must have seemed good. Yet, though Cheshire was far from the political intrigues of king and court, the news brought by messengers from the south was becoming increasingly worrying.

In 1367, the Black Prince had invaded Castile on behalf of the Castilian King Pedro, whose illegitimate half-brother Henry had deposed him. The prince defeated Henry, but the campaign bankrupted him. So, in an effort to repair his finances, he levied a tax on his subjects in Aquitaine and Gascony – the lands over which Edward III had been granted sovereignty in the Treaty of Brétigny in 1360, and which he had passed to his son. However, two Gascon lords petitioned the king of France, protesting against the tax. Charles V (who had ascended the French throne in 1364) seized the chance to repudiate the treaty. He heard the appeal and summoned the Black Prince to respond. When the prince refused to accept his authority, Charles declared Aquitaine forfeit. Three weeks later, Edward III reasserted his claim to the French crown and the war with France resumed.

The renewal of the conflict came at a terrible time for the English. The Castilian expedition had not only emptied the prince's pockets, it had also deprived the country of one of its greatest military commanders. During the campaign, the prince had contracted the mysterious illness that would ultimately claim his life. By early 1371, he was so sick that he was forced to return to England, where his health steadily deteriorated. Weakened by years of chronic illness, he died on 8 June 1376, aged 45. The heir to the throne of England and rock star of his generation – brave and dashing, albeit ruthless – was gone, bringing his father's hopes crashing down with him.

Edward III was old, tired and demoralised. He had ruled over the nation for nearly fifty years, leading it from turmoil to triumph on the battlefield. But his last years had been dogged by tragedy, with the death of his beloved wife, Philippa, and second son, Lionel, in 1369, followed by the untimely demise of his eldest son. His own health was also failing. When he died at Sheen on 21 June 1377 he had largely retreated from politics, leaving the direction of the country to a group of courtiers who were as incompetent as they were corrupt. It was a sorry end to a once glittering reign and an unhappy legacy to bequeath his 10-year-old grandson, Richard II, on whose head the English crown now weighed heavily.

The young king's accession could hardly have occurred under less auspicious stars. While the nobility were engrossed in preparations for the coronation and London was celebrating, England's enemies were gathering. Throughout the summer of 1377, the French and Castilians flitted across the Channel, raiding the south coast at will. Deeply alarmed by these incursions, the government ordered the tenants-in-chief to ready their retainers for battle. Yet such defensive measures were useless against an enemy that ruled the high seas. England needed a navy, but bad weather and mutiny had enfeebled the only fleet it could muster.

In January 1378, the king's ministers devised an ambitious plan to recover control of the Channel by capturing a chain of fortresses along the French coast and establishing a first line of defence in France itself. During the initial phase of the campaign, some 2,700 troops, serving under Richard Fitzalan, earl of Arundel, would attack the French fleet's home ports in Normandy. They would then return to England and join the rest of the army that had been raised. In mid-April 1378, the second phase would commence and the whole army would sail out of the Solent on a 'great expedition', to be led by the king's uncle, John of Gaunt, duke of Lancaster.

The preliminary arrangements went smoothly. By the end of March 1378, most of the troops assigned to Arundel had been mobilised and, by early April, the ships that had been requisitioned to carry them were ready. Among the soldiers assembled at Southampton were Geoffrey and William Boydell. Arundel had appointed Sir William Trussell of Kibblestone and Warmingham as one of his subcommanders. And Geoffrey, who was distantly related to Trussell through his wife Joan – whose great-granduncle, Sir John Hastang of Chebsey, had married Trussell's cousin Maud – promptly volunteered his services.

Egged on by Geoffrey, although they probably required little encouragement, William and his former brother-in-law, John Poole, rapidly followed suit. Geoffrey was granted judicial protection on 11 March 1378, while William and John's letters of protection came through ten days later.[4] Various other Cheshire and Staffordshire landholders who were related to Trussell in some way also volunteered to serve under his command. This was to be a tightly knit band of brothers.

But then, for reasons that aren't clear, the earl of Arundel's force was delayed. In late April, he and his troops were still waiting at Southampton. Gaunt's part of the venture had also stalled. He had originally intended to occupy Brest and take control of Brittany. However, he couldn't find enough ships to transport all the men, mounts and materiel he needed. Moreover, some of the vessels his admirals had requisitioned had no crews because many of the youths living along the south-eastern coast had gone into hiding to avoid the press gangs roaming the countryside for recruits.

On 1 June 1378, the king's counsellors met to review the situation. They ordered Arundel to press ahead with his attack on the French fleet and take Cherbourg. Meanwhile, Gaunt was to redirect his efforts from Brest to the port of St Malo. This would require fewer horses and thus less shipping, but it presented a major military challenge. St Malo stood at the western end of a long spit of land at the mouth of the River Rance, penetrating deep into the Channel. It was surrounded by sea and protected by great stone ramparts on all but the eastern side, where a citadel held by a large French garrison guarded the narrow strip of ground connecting the port to the mainland. In short, St Malo 'was

The port of St Malo in 1378

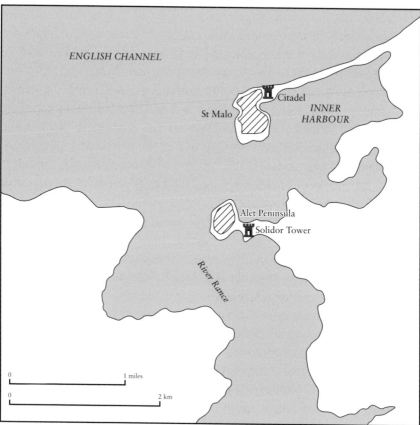

Source: J. Sumption, *Divided Houses* (2009), p. 326.

the best-fortified town in Brittany', the chronicler Thomas Walsingham dryly noted. 'So its capture would have seemed a great exploit.'

A few days later, the earl of Arundel set sail at last, with William and Geoffrey Boydell among the men-at-arms and archers crammed on board one of the eighty ships under his command. On about 7 June they arrived at Harfleur, where Arundel landed part of his force and began to attack the town. But though the French garrison at Harfleur was very small, it fought back valiantly and the English were unable to breach the town walls. After two weeks they withdrew, hotly pursued by the French, who inflicted heavy casualties on Arundel's troops as they waded through the water to scramble into their ships. Leaving Harfleur, Arundel sailed west to Cherbourg, where Ramón de Esparza, the Navarrese nobleman in charge of the port, let the English enter the harbour and handed over the keys to the castle.

Arundel had been fortunate. Although he had failed to capture Harfleur, he had encountered relatively little resistance at sea and had taken Cherbourg without a fight. In fact, Ramón de Esparza had been only too willing to cede the port. Cherbourg belonged to the king of Navarre, with whom the English had been secretly negotiating for some time. But, in March 1378, the French had learned of the king's scheming and decided to occupy the Navarrese fortresses in Normandy to prevent them from falling to the English. With an undermanned garrison and few supplies, Esparza was in no position to defend Cherbourg against a large French army.

Gaunt wasn't as lucky as Arundel. Nor, indeed, was he particularly competent. While he was completing his preparations for the departure of his fleet from Southampton the weather changed. Contrary winds pinned his ships in port until about 10 August 1378, when he finally sailed from the Solent with some 5,000 soldiers and 5,000 sailors – including Arundel's squadrons, who had returned to England at the end of June.

Despite the delay, when the English floated into the great bay at St Malo, they took the French totally by surprise. They boarded the merchant ships in the harbour, seized their cargoes of wine and burned the hulls. Then they disembarked on the eastern shore of the bay, occupied the spit of land linking St Malo to the mainland and set up the 400 cannon Gaunt had brought with him to pound the battlements.

The intimidated townsfolk offered to surrender, if the duke promised to protect them and their property from fire and pillage. However, Gaunt refused to do so – a decision that would prove a grave error of judgment. On about 14 August, the English launched their first attack. The fighting lasted all day, but the desperate inhabitants managed to repel them, inflicting severe losses on the soldiers who were climbing up ladders propped against the walls. Further assaults were equally unsuccessful.

In the meantime, word of the siege had reached the French king. Frightened that Brittany would be seriously weakened if St Malo fell, Charles sent reinforcements. Two forces converged on Dinan, at the head of the estuary of the River Rance on the opposite side of the river from St Malo. They had orders to avoid combat, but when the tide ebbed some of the young French gallants forded the Rance and attacked the rear of the English army.

While the English and French were skirmishing across the river that separated their camps, Gaunt continued to pummel the walls of St Malo with his cannon. He also ordered his sappers to start the slow business of tunnelling under the ramparts. Their mine was nearly finished when the townspeople guessed what they were doing. Realising that they would be defeated if the walls fell, the governor launched a night-time sortie and wrecked the mine. He and his men then attacked the English camp, slashing tents and slaying everyone they encountered, before escaping without a single casualty. A furious Gaunt blamed Arundel, whose soldiers were supposed to be on guard that night.

The duke was now in a very difficult position. He had a large army to feed and foraging for food had become far harder once the French held the shoreline opposite St Malo. Autumn was also setting in and it would be impossible to build another mine before winter arrived. Gaunt had already sent some of his troops home because of supply problems. In September 1378, he reluctantly abandoned the siege and issued orders to re-embark for England. The rest of the English soldiers re-boarded their ships in the middle of the month and sailed for Southampton. The 'great expedition' had turned into a great fiasco. Arundel was in disgrace, but most of the blame for the debacle fell on Gaunt as commander-in-chief.

William and Geoffrey were among those who returned to England, but William had been wounded during the campaign. Perhaps he was attacked while foraging for food. Perhaps he was hurt in the night-time assault on the English camp or in one of the many attempts on the walls of St Malo. All that can be said with reasonable certainty is that, in late August or early September 1378, he was injured – and, whether he was struck by the bolt from a crossbow, slashed by a sword or hit by a glancing blow from a lance, he survived the immediate trauma.

Many soldiers who were wounded on the battlefield pulled through, principally because they had worn armour and received good medical care. By the late fourteenth century men-at-arms usually wore plate armour, while archers wore padded doublets or thigh-length jackets reinforced with hundreds of overlapping iron plates or discs, known as brigandines or jacks. Most archers also wore open bascinets – conical metal caps that protected the side and back of the head – although some dispensed with helmets to avoid impeding their vision.

Armour provided effective protection for those who wore it. Many soldiers also had enough basic medical knowledge to wash and dress superficial flesh wounds. And the best surgeons were highly skilled. Various surgical manuals had been written, some of which drew on techniques acquired during the Crusades, when Islamic practitioners were more advanced than their European counterparts. Moreover, the vast majority of fourteenth-century surgeons saw military action. They were trained on such campaigns to treat all sorts of injuries, as well as experimenting with powders and poultices for closing wounds, inventing tools for extracting arrows and bolts, developing procedures for knitting fractured limbs together and learning how to amputate badly damaged or diseased ones.

However, many surgeons were poorly taught and illiterate. Those who *could* read usually possessed few surgical manuals and the few they owned might be out-of-date or garbled because they had been copied by scribes without any medical training. So the care wounded soldiers received on the battlefield was very haphazard. Furthermore, it was frequently complications like septicaemia that posed the biggest threat – and the treatment itself might cause an infection. Wine and honey were both known for their antibacterial properties and used to clean wounds, for example, but some surgeons believed it was necessary to make a wound suppurate by stimulating the production of pus, when the opposite was true.

William was shipped home soon after being injured – and perhaps he seemed to make good progress at first. If his wound ached and he tired quickly, that was normal. Yet, as the days passed, he must have felt increasingly ill. By the time he docked at Southampton his wound was probably angry and inflamed and, when he saw red streaks radiating from the incision, he would have known with stomach-churning certainty that it was infected.

Once he had disembarked, William still needed to get to Handley. The journey by road entailed going north from Southampton to Oxford, via Winchester and Newbury, swinging north-west to Worcester and Kidderminster and then following the main thoroughfare to Shrewsbury and Chester, a distance of nearly 200 miles. An able-bodied man could walk between 15 and 20 miles a day and ride 30 to 40 miles a day, if he changed horses. But William was no longer well enough to walk or ride and horse-drawn carts were slow. A two-wheeled cart usually covered about 12 miles a day, although it could cover more than 20 miles a day in fair weather on good roads. Thus, travelling by cart meant spending up to seventeen days jolting along rutted highways and byways, seeking lodgings every night from hard-headed innkeepers reluctant to shelter a desperately sick man.

Sailing around the coast was quicker, if conditions were favourable, although there was always the risk of being attacked by pirates. The Dee estuary had gradually been silting up and it was no longer possible to sail as far as Chester. But there were smaller harbours at Neston, Gayton, Shotwick and Burton, where a ship could unload, and at Neston one could charter a boat as far as the city. With a good wind in the right direction, Chester could be reached in as little as four to six days. From there, the journey to Handley was only 7 or 8 miles. So, rather than trying to get his cousin home via the long overland route, it is far more likely that Geoffrey paid for passage on one of the numerous fishing boats or cargo vessels that plied their trade around the coast. He may even have offered to pay the captain extra for sailing with all speed. For, by now, it must have been clear that William was dying.

Think of him lying on the hard wooden deck, venom coursing through his veins. Clinical texts show what he must have endured as his body slowly rotted. His wound leaked a foetid green pus, his heart pounded and his breathing was laboured. One moment he was burning up; the next he was cold, clammy and couldn't stop shivering. He vomited frequently and became increasingly confused. Perhaps he could hear the susurration of the waves and creaking of the ship's timbers. Perhaps he was also dimly aware of Geoffrey anxiously hovering over him. But as the infection raged inside him, he faded in and out of consciousness.

It takes quite a long time for a man to die of gangrene or septicaemia. Richard Marshal, third earl of Pembroke, lived for fifteen days after the wounds he had sustained at the Battle of the Curragh in Ireland turned gangrenous. And one Scottish knight survived for more than two months after being hit in the face by a crossbow bolt. William clung tenaciously to life until he reached Handley. There, he lingered for a day or two. Finally, on 14 September 1378, his heart stopped and his unmoored spirit slipped away.[5]

The writ for William's inquisition post mortem was issued on 15 September 1378 and the inquisition itself was conducted on 21 September. He had died holding 'two parks in the manor of Dodleston and Handley', worth £10 a year, by military service. These lands now belonged to his 7-year-old son, Thomas.[6] William had died fighting for king and country. But the country he fought for was England and the enemy he opposed resided only 40 miles from Avranches, where his ancestor Osbern fitz Tezzo had probably grown up. Their Norman roots long forgotten, the Boydells had become English through and through.

16

The Double Legacy

Thomas's heart beat faster as he entered the parish church at Handley. He'd prayed there on Sundays and feast days for as long as he could remember. He knew every painting on the walls, every inscription on the plaques commemorating his ancestors, every curlicue in the roodscreen separating chancel from nave. But he wasn't there to pray; he was there for a different purpose – and he was nervous. His wife Katherine squeezed his arm reassuringly as they passed through the porch and he smiled at her. Katherine was pregnant again, dress curved over her gently swelling stomach. She'd already produced two fine young sons. Perhaps the next child would be a daughter, Thomas thought fleetingly. Then, as his uncle hailed him, he was caught up in the business of greeting his neighbours.

It was Tuesday, 1 October 1392, and the church was filled with people. The escheator of Cheshire – the official responsible for administering property that was temporarily in the king's tenure – had arrived to determine whether Thomas was of age.[1] When a minor with lands held by military service was placed in wardship, he had to prove that he'd turned twenty-one before he could take over his inheritance. Since there were no official birth records, twelve local men had to confirm the heir's date of birth or baptism, as well as explaining how they had come by the information. Various relatives and acquaintances from nearby manors had assembled to testify on Thomas's behalf.

The church was the centre of community life and the nave served a wide range of functions. It was the place where local officers like the reeve, aletaster, constable and chief tithing-men were elected, the place where people traded, held meetings and settled disagreements. Men and women socialised and children played under the eyes of the chiselled saints gazing down from the wooden roof. Dogs, cats and pigs wandered around – much to the irritation of the parish priest, who complained about the piles of excrement they left behind. But the villagers had made a special effort for Thomas's proof-of-age inquisition, cleaning the church and strewing fresh, sweet-smelling rushes across the floor. A trestle table and two chairs had also been put out for the escheator and his clerk.

When the escheator sat down, the chatter died away. Thomas's uncle, William Bellew, was the first witness to be called. William swore on oath that Thomas was born and baptised at Handley on Friday, 11 July 1371, so he was now twenty-one. William could recollect the date vividly, he said, because he had just buried his eldest son. William's younger brother, Thomas, was next to testify. He, too, claimed to remember precisely when his nephew was born because he had fallen off his horse as it 'tottered' and broken his right shin-bone that same day.

Richard Harthill swore that he knew Thomas was twenty-one because his daughter Joan was born the Monday after Thomas was christened, while John Brescy recalled setting off on a pilgrimage to Santiago de Compostela the summer before Thomas was born. Four other local gentry testified that they were in the church mediating a dispute when Thomas was baptised and four more said that they were present because they were checking the accounts with the church proctors. So, yes, they were certain that Thomas was of age.

The escheator questioned each man carefully. He knew that witnesses often supplied stock answers and he was dubious about Thomas Bellew's evidence. If the claims he'd heard were to be believed, there had been a veritable epidemic of riding accidents resulting in fractured tibia. At last, satisfied with the answers he'd received, he declared that Thomas had indeed attained his majority and instructed the clerk to draft a writ discharging Thomas's two guardians, Robert and Peter Legh. The findings still had to be forwarded to one of the royal courts, but this was a formality. Five months later, on 6 April 1393, Thomas was granted control of his estates – and they had been considerably augmented since his father's demise.

The wardship of Thomas Boydell's lands and right to arrange his marriage had taken a circuitous path in the fourteen years between William's death and Thomas's coming of age. Both passed to the Black Prince's widow as part of her dower. But Princess Joan assigned her rights to Sir Lewis Clifford as a reward for the many years of loyal service he had given her husband and herself.[2] Clifford was among the most trusted members of Edward's household and had witnessed his will. When the prince died in 1376, Clifford stayed in Joan's service. In March 1378, she granted him custody of Cardigan Castle. That April, Clifford was also made a knight of the Garter, the chivalric order founded by Edward III and modelled on King Arthur's Round Table. To be chosen as one of the monarch's twenty-five knight-companions was the highest chivalric honour in the country.

Clifford was a man of many talents. He was a gifted soldier, polished courtier and intellectual. He counted the poet Geoffrey Chaucer among his close friends and was an ardent supporter of the religious reformer John Wycliffe, an Oxford theologian who had translated the Bible into English. However, Clifford was a southerner – his home lay in Kent – and had no interest in managing the estates of an insignificant youth living in far-off Cheshire. It was hard enough for absentee lords to enforce their rights at the best of times, but the county's palatine status presented additional obstacles; negotiating Cheshire's courts was a daunting prospect for any outsider. So Clifford leased the wardship of Thomas and his lands to Sir Robert Legh of Adlington and his half-brother Peter.[3]

Sir Robert had fought for the Black Prince, earning Edward's gratitude for the 'good services' he rendered in Gascony. Joan had subsequently made him bailiff of the manor of Macclesfield, which formed part of her dower. Moreover, Robert and his half-brother were related to Thomas, albeit rather tenuously, for Sir Robert's cousin, Katherine Honford, had married Thomas's cousin, William Tranmere. The princess may therefore have introduced the Leghs to Clifford or recommended them as competent local lords. In either case, the arrangement suited both parties perfectly: Robert and Peter would farm Thomas's lands and find him a fitting bride, while Clifford would receive an income from the wardship without having to worry about getting mired in legal disputes in a distant jurisdiction.

Everything proceeded smoothly until 1382, when two changes occurred. Sir Robert Legh died, leaving his rights under the lease from Sir Lewis Clifford to his son, another Robert. And Thomas inherited half of the property held by his cousin Margaret, the only grandchild of Sir John Danyers and his wife Joan. Margaret had married Alan Rixton, whose father Matthew had been involved in the project to build a bridge over the Mersey before disgracing himself. She had died without issue and, under

The descent of the Danyers family's estates

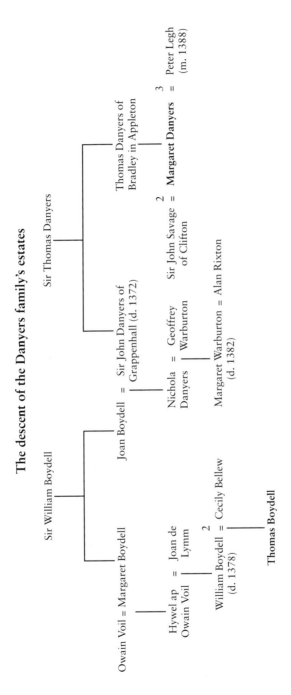

the terms of an entail Sir John and Lady Joan had set up in 1361, their estates were to be split between their respective families in the absence of any direct male descendants. Joan's share accordingly passed to Thomas, while Sir John's share went to his niece, Margaret Savage.[4]

The wardship of Thomas's second inheritance also fell squarely within Princess Joan's sphere. On 13 December 1382, she leased the manor of Grappenhall and all the property the Danyers family had held in Latchford and Handley to Alan Rixton, until Thomas came of age. Rixton was to pay £40 a year for farming the lands. But the escheator had mistakenly put the entire manor into wardship, ignoring Margaret Savage's claim. In June 1383, Margaret and her husband sued for her inheritance and, by January 1384, they had recovered her half of the estates, after striking a deal with Rixton.[5]

Alan Rixton continued to manage the lands Thomas had inherited from his cousin, while Robert and Peter Legh retained control of the lands he had inherited from his father. But by 1391, while Thomas was still under age, Rixton was ailing. That November, he surrendered the lease on Thomas's share of Grappenhall to the king, to whom Thomas's wardship had passed when Princess Joan died in August 1385.[6] In the meantime, Margaret Savage's husband had also died and she had married Peter Legh late in 1388. Thus, Peter now had a personal interest in the other half of the estates Margaret Rixton had left.

In the wrong hands, such a situation could have ended disastrously for Thomas. When Sir John Danyers had been presented with a chance to swindle the teenaged ward who held the rest of the lands belonging to his wife's family, he didn't hesitate. But Thomas was much luckier than his grandfather. Robert and Peter proved unusually benevolent guardians. By the time Thomas was granted possession of his estates in April 1393, the manors of Dodleston and Handley were said to be worth £10 a year more than they had been when his father died.[7] Robert and his wife Isabelle had also taken Thomas under their wing. A mere decade older than his youthful charge, Robert had treated the boy like a little brother rather than a chicken to be plucked – a kindness Thomas would not forget.

While Thomas Boydell was growing up in north-western England, another child of far more illustrious birth was growing up in the south-east. When Richard II came to the throne at the age of 10 in July 1377, the public welcomed him with open arms. Young and unsullied, the boy king represented the antithesis of his senile and embittered grandfather, Edward III. He was crowned in a glittering ceremony at Westminster Abbey and carried out of the church on the shoulders of his tutor, Sir Simon Burley, 'with crowds milling all round him and pressing upon him' so closely that he lost one of his consecrated shoes in the crush.

The festive mood didn't last long. A 'continual council' was established to rule the country during Richard's minority and, as soon as parliament met, it seized the opportunity to air past grievances. The House of Commons revived fifteen petitions dating from the reign of Richard's great-grandfather, Edward II. In October 1378, it also requested regular reports on the actions of the king's counsellors, for taxes remained (as always) a bone of contention. Parliament had already approved a poll tax in 1377, when all adults over the age of 14 were required to pay a groat towards the cost of the war with France. In 1379, it reluctantly agreed to a second levy, graduated according to individual wealth, and in 1380 it authorised a flat-rate tax of 1s on everybody aged 15 or more.

The heavy tax burden under which poor folk were labouring, together with continuing concerns about a French invasion and general disgruntlement over working conditions, proved a toxic brew. In May 1381, discontent erupted into outright defiance when the royal tax collectors began knocking on doors again. The people feared another poll tax, although the collectors were actually looking for those who had evaded the previous year's tax. Rioting broke out in Essex and Kent, and in June the protesters marched on London. Displaying remarkable courage for a boy who was still only 14 at the time, Richard met the mob at a 'handsome meadow' in Mile End, to the east of London, and encouraged it to disperse. But he was unable to defuse the situation before blood was spilled on the streets of the capital and the Savoy Palace, John of Gaunt's city residence, was destroyed. It took a second meeting, the death of the ringleader, Wat Tyler (who was killed when he drew a dagger in the king's presence), and the threat of force to quell the rising.

The Peasants' Revolt, as it was later known, reflected a general desire for change. It wasn't just browbeaten villeins who had joined the protest; prosperous villagers and manorial officials also downed tools to head for the capital. Nor was the unrest confined to southern England. Cheshire was supposed to be exempt from parliamentary levies, since it wasn't represented in the House of Commons. Nevertheless, in 1379, the justice and county chamberlain were ordered to appoint commissioners to collect the poll tax. The command was eventually revoked, but by then Cheshire had been caught up in the turmoil. That July, the serfs on the vast Wirral estates held by St Werburgh's Abbey mutinied. They were charged with destroying the abbey's property and terrorising the populace. Cecily Boydell's father, Robert Bellew, was one of the jurors who heard the case.

Popular rage – in Cheshire, as elsewhere – was largely directed at an oppressive Church and the gentry justices like Bellew who were responsible for enforcing the law. Richard's star still burned brightly, but by 1383 even his lustre was fading. The boy who had once been borne so informally through Westminster on his tutor's back had hardened into an imperious 16-year-old whose relationship with his barons was decidedly fractious. Richard had slowly been promoting his own circle of supporters, many of them drawn from families outside the established nobility. Ignoring the old guard, he lavished gifts and honours on the members of his clique with predictable results: those who were snubbed resented those who were richly rewarded. In October 1383, parliament voiced concerns about the king's behaviour, complaining that he 'clung to unsound policies' and failed to heed 'wholesome advice from his entourage'. Richard's response was polite but firm: while he would willingly listen to his lords, he would take counsel from anyone he chose.

The king also clashed repeatedly with his uncle, John of Gaunt, over the best way to manage the war with France. Richard and his allies wanted to negotiate, while Gaunt and his younger brother, Thomas of Woodstock, favoured launching a major campaign to protect England's continental assets. In May 1385, Gaunt's worst fears were realised when Charles VI (who had ascended the French throne in 1380) sent a force of 1,600 men to Scotland under the command of the formidable Jean de Vienne, admiral of France. Richard and his counsellors immediately started preparing for a counter-attack on Scotland, to be led by the king himself. That July, an army of nearly 14,000 men gathered at Newcastle-upon-Tyne.

On 6 August, the English troops entered Scotland. The king marked the moment by bestowing new honours on his friends and knighting 300 men in the hope of winning goodwill. Thomas's guardian, Robert Legh – who had ridden north at the head of ninety-two Cheshire archers – was among those who received the ritual blow on the shoulder.

In September 1385, when he collected the wages for the men under his command, he was described as 'Robert de Legh, knight', elevated from the plain 'Robert de Legh of Adlington' he had been only two months previously in a letter of protection for one of his archers. Robert had also brought a squire with him. The record of the levy doesn't name the youth, but Thomas had just turned 14 and was thus old enough to serve in such a role. Robert may have decided to give his ward a first taste of warfare. If so, it was a frustrating introduction.

As the English advanced, the Scots and French retreated before them, harassing their flanks without giving battle. On 11 August, Richard reached Edinburgh, only to discover it almost deserted. Infuriated by their enemy's will-o'-the-wisp tactics, his troops rampaged through the city, burning houses and churches. However, their supplies had run out and there was no food to steal. Weakened by hunger, the English started falling sick. Despite these difficulties, Gaunt wanted to press further north. The king disagreed. After a furious argument, he declared that he would take his men home before they starved to death. On 20 August, the English limped back to Newcastle, where they disbanded, having failed either to subjugate the Scots or to destroy Jean de Vienne's army. Fortunately for Richard, the French were in equally poor shape. Vienne had fallen out with his Scottish allies and his soldiers were also starving. Meanwhile, the citizens of Ghent had risen up against the French, throwing Charles VI's plans for invading England from the continent into disarray.

The following summer – his relationship with Richard in tatters – John of Gaunt left the country to make a bid for the Castilian throne, which he claimed through his wife Constance. The duke's departure left the king and his faction in the political ascendancy. But, in October 1386, the French threat resurfaced and Michael de la Pole – the son of a wool merchant from Hull, whom Richard had appointed as chancellor – asked for a huge levy to reinforce England's coastal defences. Parliament, already critical of the king's extravagance and suspicious that his ministers were lining their own pockets, bucked like an unbroken horse. Instead of consenting to the chancellor's demand, the Houses of Lords and Commons united to insist that de la Pole be sacked for mishandling the nation's finances.

Outraged by the audacity of his subjects, Richard haughtily replied that he wouldn't dismiss so much as the lowliest scullion in his kitchen at their request. Then he ordered parliament to get on with its proper business and retired to his manor at Eltham in Greenwich. But parliament held firm. Richard was finally forced to give way when the delegates it sent to Eltham to argue its case reminded him of an old edict stating that, if the king alienated himself from his people and refused to be governed by the advice of his lords, the people could depose him. This oblique reference to the fate of Edward II cowed Richard into submission; on 23 October 1386, he appeared at Westminster and dismissed de la Pole, who was then impeached. Richard was also compelled to accept the appointment of a year-long council to scrutinise the management of his household and realm.

The king didn't forgive the slight to his regal authority. In a gesture clearly intended to convey his disdain for parliament, he removed himself from London and embarked on an extended tour of England with his wife, Anne of Bohemia, to drum up political and military support for his cause. In July 1387, he spent a full week in Chester, where he commanded particular loyalty as its earl. He also secured a legal ruling that parliament's conduct had been unlawful and that September he installed his close friend Robert de Vere as justice of Chester, with orders to raise a royal force.

On his return to London, Richard discovered that his opponents had been equally busy. His uncle, Thomas of Woodstock, had spearheaded the parliamentary revolt against him, together with the earls of Arundel and Warwick. John of Gaunt's son, Henry Bolingbroke, and Thomas Mowbray, earl of Nottingham, had recently joined their side. In November 1387, all five magnates confronted the king to demand that de la Pole, de Vere and other members of his court be tried for treason. Richard played for time, while de Vere mobilised Cheshire's ruling elite. By mid-December, de Vere had assembled an army of 3,000-4,000 manorial lords and their retainers, which he was ready to bring south to the king's rescue. Sir Robert Legh was probably one of the many gentry who answered de Vere's summons, with the 16-year-old Thomas riding in his wake.

However, word of de Vere's plans had reached the five Lords Appellant (known as such after the legal procedure they had invoked to prosecute the king's favourites) and they headed north with their own followers to intercept him. On 20 December 1387, the two armies clashed at Radcot Bridge in Oxfordshire. The Appellants routed de Vere's force, although he managed to escape. Flinging off his armour, he plunged his horse into the River Thames and swam to the other bank, shrouded by the dense fog. But de Vere's lieutenant was captured and killed in cold blood, while the rest of his troops were stripped naked, plundered of everything they possessed and told to make their way back to Cheshire as best they could.

Cold, angry and deeply humiliated, the men of Cheshire raided the villages near Radcot Bridge, pilfered what clothing and food they could find and began the long trudge home. As Robert, Thomas and their companions struggled across country in the depths of winter, the king was left with no choice but to agree to the Appellants' demands. During the aptly named 'Merciless Parliament' of 1388, a number of Richard's supporters were tried for treason and executed, while de Vere and de la Pole (who had both fled the country) were sentenced to death *in absentia*. Several of the king's household officials were also impeached and exiled or executed. Richard's inner circle had been shattered.

The king licked his wounds and quietly set about rebuilding an entourage of men who would be loyal to him. When cracks in parliament's previously united front began to emerge, he also seized the chance to reposition himself as a peacemaker. Richard, it seemed, had matured from a prickly adolescent into a sensible young man, ready to heed his rightful advisers. In May 1389, when he announced that he would assume personal responsibility for governing the realm, having turned 22 the previous January, there was no dissent. The king immediately replaced the ministers whom the Appellants had imposed on him, promised to rule England wisely and outlined an extensive programme of reforms. Barely a month after he had asserted his right to rule as an heir of full age, English and French envoys concluded a truce that was to take effect in August and last for three years. And when Gaunt returned to England in November 1389, Richard embraced his uncle warmly.

Peace with France did not mean peace with Scotland, however. The Scots had raided northern England several times in 1388, and since they hadn't been included in the talks between the French and English they didn't feel bound by the ceasefire. In June 1389, Thomas Mowbray was ordered to lead an army into Scotland. The king of France also promised to issue an ultimatum; unless the Scots agreed to honour the treaty, he would foresake them. But money was so tight that when Mowbray set off, he had only 1,500 mounted men. Heavily outnumbered by the Scots, he was compelled to retreat to the English garrison at Berwick. That August, diplomacy at last succeeded where arms had failed. Fearful of having to face the English alone, Robert II of Scotland grudgingly agreed to the truce.

Meanwhile, Mowbray remained in Berwick. On 25 October, Sir Robert Legh and Thomas received letters of protection to serve under the earl's command for a year. When they reached Berwick, Geoffrey Boydell was waiting to greet them. Geoffrey had continued to pursue a part-time military career after fighting with Thomas's father at St Malo and had enrolled as an archer in Mowbray's standing force four months previously.[8]

Thomas was no longer the boy whom Geoffrey had reluctantly left in Cheshire all those years ago as a stricken child watching his father's life ebb away. At 18, he was a young man eager to prove his own worth in battle – although the period of calm following the truce produced few occasions to distinguish himself. When he wasn't touring the town walls to ensure the guards stayed awake, helping Robert, eating or sleeping, he whiled away his time playing dice or chess. Boredom was a regular feature of the garrison soldier's life. But the pay was good; as Robert's aide-de-camp, Thomas could expect to earn 1s a day. And the rations were generous. English soldiers stationed in Scotland were allocated a daily allowance of 2lbs of wheat bread, nearly a gallon of beer, a pound of meat or a pound and a half of fish, and 10oz of pottage made from dried peas, beans and oatmeal. On meat days they had beef or salt pork, and on fish days herring or stockfish, spiced with onions, garlic, pepper, saffron and cumin. So Thomas was well paid and well fed.

Nevertheless, he missed his family. His wife Katherine had already given birth to their first child, another Thomas. She conceived again shortly after Thomas senior returned from Berwick. Robert, named after Sir Robert Legh, was born in the winter of 1391 or first half of 1392. Within months Katherine was pregnant once more. And with a third child on the way, Thomas was eager to claim his patrimony; in May 1392, he entered into a recognizance for a neighbouring landholder and, in March 1393, he stood surety for the new deputy constable of Chester Castle – despite the fact that, officially, his assets weren't yet under his own control. Although the inquisition to prove that he was of full age had been completed in October 1392, the king had yet to grant him formal possession of the family estates.[9]

Two weeks later – probably soon after the birth of his daughter Margaret – Thomas finally received livery of the 'two parts of the manors of Dodleston and Handley' that he had inherited from his father and his share of the property that Margaret Rixton had left. But the Leghs still owed the king money for farming Thomas's estates and arranging his marriage. Moreover, Richard had somehow got wind of the fact that Thomas hadn't waited for permission to occupy his lands. Providentially, the king was in a forgiving mood. On 30 May 1393, he granted four of his servants in the royal butlery £40 from the sum due to him for Thomas's wardship and marriage. Then, on 5 June, he pardoned Robert and Thomas for having entered upon Thomas's inheritance prematurely. However, Richard still expected his cut. He ordered a number of men, including Robert, Thomas and Thomas's uncle, William Bellew, to recover any profits that had already been disbursed to other people.[10]

Thomas had probably benefited from the king's desire to tread softly at a time when Cheshire was in uproar. In early 1393, rumours were swirling around the county that Gaunt, Thomas of Woodstock and Henry Bolingbroke intended to surrender Richard's claim to the throne of France to secure a permanent peace with the French. The Cheshire gentry whose livelihoods were threatened by an end to their part-time soldiering were appalled. They were also worried by reports that the palatinate's ancient liberties were to be removed. Led by Sir Thomas Talbot and Sir Nicholas Clifton, both veterans of the French wars, a number of local squires rebelled. They nailed notices on church doors urging the populace to take up arms and quickly attracted a large following.

Richard hadn't forgotten that it was the men of Cheshire who came to his aid at Radcot Bridge. He responded with considerable sensitivity. In the spring of 1393, he sent the earl of Huntingdon and the Cheshire-bred Sir John Stanley north to suppress illegal gatherings. When this didn't work, he ordered Gaunt and Woodstock to quash the insurrection. Gaunt showed restraint, using force only when it was absolutely necessary. He also pardoned some of the rebels on the spot and made a point of recruiting them into the army he was about to take to Aquitaine. The ringleaders didn't get off quite as lightly. On 12 October 1393, Sir Robert Legh was told to arrest Talbot and Sir John Massey of Tatton, the county sheriff, who had sided with the insurgents. And, on 14 October, the king made Robert sheriff of Cheshire in Massey's stead. Yet even those who had headed the revolt were spared execution.

Thomas – loyal to his former guardian – had firmly aligned himself with the forces of law and order. He may also have been preoccupied with family matters, since his wife Katherine had recently given birth to another daughter, called Isabelle after Robert's wife. But when Gaunt was looking for men to go to Aquitaine with him, Thomas volunteered. The duchy of Aquitaine had passed to the English crown through Henry II's marriage to Eleanor of Aquitaine in 1152. Previous monarchs had promised that it would never be detached from the crown; it would always be held by the king or his eldest son. However, in 1390, Richard had conferred the duchy on John of Gaunt for life, probably as a reward for his support. The Gascons deeply resented Gaunt's appointment. Seen from their view, the grant was illegal, since Gaunt was the uncle – not the son – of the reigning monarch.

The Gascons complained volubly for some years. Then, in April 1394, as yet another round of negotiations with the French was beginning, their anger boiled over. A group of Gascon nobles and senior churchmen, headed by the archbishop of Bordeaux, refused to recognise Gaunt's authority and swore that henceforth they would only be governed by the king. Richard staunchly supported his uncle. In September 1394, he confirmed the terms of Gaunt's grant. The next month Gaunt set sail for Aquitaine with an army of 1,500 men.

Thomas and Sir Richard Aston, Gaunt's most prominent retainer in Cheshire, were among those who sailed under the duke's flag. On 9 September 1394, Aston appointed seven local gentry, including William and Thomas Bellew, to act as his legal representatives while he was away in Aquitaine in Gaunt's retinue. Thomas followed suit the next day, nominating the same men to look after his own affairs in his absence. He also contracted his son Thomas to Elizabeth, Aston's younger daughter by his second wife, Ellen. Once again, this was a case of intricate kinship connections coming into play; Ellen was a descendant of the same Hugh de Dutton whose sister Alice had married William Boydell, the parish priest turned manorial lord. On 29 September, Thomas received permission to grant his half of the manor of Grappenhall, together with some property in Warburton, Thelwall, Lymm, Tabley, Sale and Ashton, in tail to the two children. Mindful of the perils of fighting in a foreign campaign – this was, after all, how his own father had died – Thomas was obviously determined to order his son and heir's future, even though the boy was still only about 5 years old.[11]

In the event, Thomas's precautions proved unnecessary; there was no fighting, despite the fact that the Gascons continued to resist the duke's authority. In March 1395, Gaunt backed down and announced that he would reside in Bordeaux but wouldn't exercise his ducal rights while he was there. Gaunt stayed in Aquitaine for the rest of the year, while the army he had raised returned to England. By Easter 1395, Thomas was back in Cheshire, where he joined forces with his cousins, William Tranmere and John Tyldesley, in a lawsuit to recover some lands in Lymm that had once belonged to his great-great-grandfather, Gilbert de Lymm.[12]

Eighteen months later, Thomas's carefully laid plans were in ruins, for he and his elder son were both dead. Bubonic plague had become endemic. Sir Richard Aston had seen his first wife and all their children wiped out by an earlier outbreak. The king's wife, Anne of Bohemia, had also, perhaps, died of the pestilence on 7 June 1394. But 1396 is one of only two years in the last decade of the fourteenth century for which no mortalities from the plague are recorded in surviving coroners' rolls. So Thomas and his son presumably succumbed to one of the many other infectious diseases that could fell entire families.

Thomas met his end on Monday, 30 October 1396, aged 25. His inquisition post mortem shows that he died holding the manor of Dodleston, apart from the lands his mother Cecily held in dower. He also owned the manor of Latchford and the right to the tolls from Warrington Bridge, together with a house in Chester and lands in Handley, Stoke (near Picton), Godley, Newton in Longdendale and Stockport.[13] But he had already given much of his property to his elder son. Both estates would now go to his second son, Robert.

Priests repeatedly reminded their parishioners of the ephemeral nature of earthly existence. Murals and effigies depicted the grisly details of putrefaction and books elaborated on the art of dying well: surrounded by family, absolved of one's sins, anointed with holy oil and granted the final Eucharist. The rites that guided people through their last moments, and from the deathbed to the grave, were as clearly prescribed as those that marked their entry into the world. But familiarity with the Grim Reaper's embrace didn't lessen the grief of the bereaved.

Katherine doubtless mourned as she washed the naked bodies of her husband and child with warm water, wrapped them in linen sheets and prayed for their souls during the customary night-long vigil. The next day, under a sky the colour of pigeons' wings, her manservants brought parish coffins to the house and laid the corpses of Thomas and his son inside. They carried the coffins on biers into the church for the requiem Mass. Finally, the bodies of Thomas and his son were lifted out of their coffins and laid to rest in the chancel – the most prestigious burial place inside the church – as befitted the lord of the manor and his heir.

Clad head to foot in black, Katherine watched as the small shrouded body of her first-born was lowered into the ground on top of her husband's larger frame. She cannot fail to have recalled how – a mere four years previously – Thomas had stood proud and straight in the very same church, listening to the escheator pronounce him of age. Now 'Death's wither-clench' had turned her husband and son into worms' food. Thomas had received, and bequeathed, a double legacy. His paternal estates had been swelled by the property he inherited from his cousin. Yet his father had died at the peak of manhood and he had done the same. In fact, he was leaving an heir even younger than he himself had been when William breathed his last. Thomas had been twice blessed, twice cursed.

17

Fortune's False Wheel

Robert nestled against his mother as they sat on the wooden settle in the solar, savouring her familiar smell: a faint whiff of onions overlaid by the sweet scent of meadow grass from the little bags of dried woodruff she put in her clothes chest. Katherine had taken her Book of Hours out of the jewellery box in which she normally kept it and was absently stroking the silk cover. Dog-eared from use, it was one of her most prized possessions. She read from it every morning, quietly murmuring prayers for the souls of his father and elder brother. The ritual had eased her anguish during those first terrible days of loss, days in which grief had keened through their home like a winter wind, blasting everything it touched.

Robert's feelings about the slim volume of devotional texts were more mixed. He loved the picture of Mary teaching the Christ child how to read with an open Book of Hours resting on her lap, just as his own mother was teaching him to read with her copy. But he couldn't help hoping that Jesus had found it as hard as he did to decipher the squiggles on the page.

Katherine began the lesson by pointing to the illuminated capital letter at the start of the script and asking him which one it was. Robert recognised it immediately: an O made from a wheel with four figures perched around the rim. The first figure smiled as the wheel carried him upwards; the second sat at the top with a golden crown on his head; the third hung upside down, cap tumbling off; and the fourth clung desperately to the bottom of the wheel. Robert listened carefully while his mother explained what the picture meant. This was Fortune's Wheel, she told him, and it showed the fickleness of fate. When the blind goddess Fortuna spun her wheel, she might raise a man until he was as rich and powerful as a king or bring him low, stripping him of all the happiness he had formerly enjoyed.

Once Katherine had finished her explanation, she read the first few lines of text aloud, tracing the words with her index finger as she spoke. Then she pointed to each word in turn and asked Robert to pronounce it. He was puzzling over a particularly long word when Isabelle burst into the room, hair flying. Her cheeks were smudged with tears. 'Margaret hurted me,' she cried, sobbing passionately as she hurled herself at her mother and held up her arms to be lifted. Robert sighed. His sisters were always squabbling and now his mother would be distracted. The moment in which he held her undivided attention had passed.

Thomas Boydell's untimely death had left his family vulnerable. On 12 January 1397, six weeks after he died, his wife Katherine was granted a third of his estates, excluding the lands her mother-in-law Cecily still held by virtue of being widowed herself. Later that year Katherine also sued Elizabeth, the child bride of her deceased elder son, for a third of the lands that Thomas had vested in the young couple for life.[1] In the meantime, arrangements were being made for the management of her son Robert's inheritance during his minority.

Robert's wardship had passed automatically to the king, as earl of Chester. On 9 January 1397, Richard II leased the rights to the tolls from Warrington Bridge and a fishery at Latchford to Robert Holden of Haslingden for £8 a year. Six weeks afterwards, he granted Sir William Mainwaring, lord of Baddiley and Peover, custody of the rest of Robert's assets and the right to arrange the boy's marriage. Mainwaring was ordered to agree a price with Roger Walden, whom the king had appointed as his treasurer on 20 September 1395.[2]

Mainwaring was distantly connected to the Boydells through his cousin, John Honford. But it was mercenary considerations, rather than kinship or kindness, that motivated him to buy Robert's wardship – and he soon concluded that he had struck a bad bargain. In the spring of 1398, he complained to the king that he was expected to provide security of £400 before he could enter Robert's lands, yet they were only worth £130. Richard wasn't willing to haggle; on 10 May, he instructed the escheator to take Robert's wardship back into the hands of the crown.[3] Mainwaring actually had a valid point. With three widows – Cecily, Katherine and Elizabeth – each entitled to her dower for as long as she lived, a sizeable chunk of Thomas's estates was tied up. However,

The connection between Sir William Mainwaring and Robert Boydell

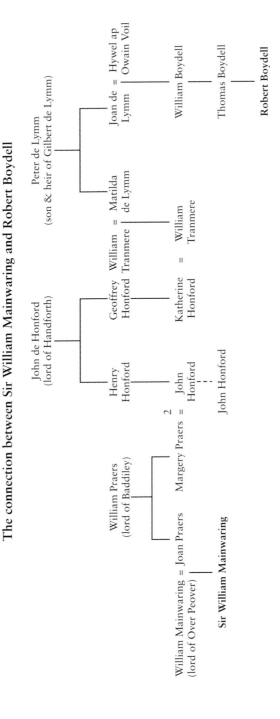

Katherine was probably grateful for the delay in resolving Robert's custody, since it ensured that he remained in her care.

Besides, Mainwaring had other things to preoccupy him; the political situation had become highly volatile again and Cheshire was caught up in the furore. From 1389 to 1397 there had been relative harmony between Richard and his advisers and within the country as a whole. The insurrection of 1393 had been an isolated incident and even that had ended without bloodshed. By March 1396, the king's envoys had also clinched a truce with the French and negotiated a second royal wedding. Richard's first marriage had been childless and he knew that he needed to remarry. When Charles VI of France offered him the hand of his 6-year-old daughter, Richard decided that the advantages of peace outweighed the girl's youth and the inevitable delay in producing an heir.

Richard had learned to behave more moderately, showed greater consideration in his dealings with his subjects and paid heed to his counsellors' advice. Nevertheless, he hadn't forgiven the Appellants for humiliating him. Nor had he changed his earlier beliefs. He remained convinced that kingship was a God-given office and regarded it as his duty to preserve the rights of the crown. His defeat at Radcot Bridge in December 1387 and the Merciless Parliament of 1388 had exposed the limits of royal power. Without an army to enforce his will, Richard knew that his authority was very restricted.

By mid-1397, the king was ready to act. On 10 July – completely without warning – he had the three senior Appellants arrested. Thomas Beauchamp, earl of Warwick, was detained at the end of a banquet in London to which he had been lured by a ruse. Thomas of Woodstock, duke of Gloucester, was seized before dawn the next morning and Richard Fitzalan, earl of Arundel, was persuaded to surrender. Two months later, Warwick and Arundel were put on trial by a parliament Richard had ensured would be pliable. That summer he had ordered Sir Robert Legh, as sheriff of Chester, to assemble 2,000 archers and bring them down to Kingston-upon-Thames, near London, by 'high morn' on 15 September. From Kingston they marched on the capital, where Richard had them arrayed around Westminster.

Surrounded by a large force of flint-faced Cheshire soldiers with strung bows, parliament soon saw the error of its ways and convicted both earls of treason. Arundel was beheaded the same day, while Warwick was sentenced to life imprisonment. Thomas of Woodstock was already dead – murdered, it subsequently transpired, on Richard's orders. According to John Hall, one of the men who later stood trial for the crime, the king had commanded the earls of Nottingham and Rutland to kill Woodstock and they had arranged for him to be suffocated with a feather mattress in the back room of a Calais hostelry.

Richard had waited ten years to strike, but he knew that he was treading a dangerous path. So, rather than disbanding his entire army, he retained some of the best troops to protect him. By the autumn of 1398, he had an entourage of 312 archers grouped into seven watches. They included Cecily's nephew, Ralph Bellew, and William Boydell (possibly Geoffrey's son, now a young man of about 19). Both were granted the right to wear the livery of the crown – the badge of gold and silver crowns that the king gave the most favoured members of his retinue – together with the customary wage of 6d a day. Richard kept another cohort of handpicked veterans as a reserve force in Cheshire, on annuities of £5 a year. Cecily's brother William, who had testified at Thomas's proof-of-age inquisition, Thomas's cousin, William Tranmere, and John Boydell of Lymm were among them.[4]

The king's bodyguards accompanied him everywhere. They ranged around him in a protective circle whenever he ventured out and took turns standing watch with axes outside his bedchamber at night as he slumbered. Richard, grateful for his archers' fidelity, allowed them a remarkable degree of licence. He permitted them to call him 'Dickon', a mode of address that would have earned most men a thrashing. He also looked the other way when they routinely abused their position. 'By nature bestial, these Cheshire men were ready to commit every sort of crime, and their shamelessness soon increased to the point where they regarded only the king as their equal, treating everybody else, however powerful or noble he was, with contempt,' the chronicler Thomas Walsingham raged. They beat, wounded, murdered, raped, ravished and stole from the king's subjects with impunity.

Richard simply ignored the complaints. Backed by a squad of crack troops whose loyalty was assured, he began building a 'wider realm', with Cheshire at its core. In September 1397, he promoted the county from a palatinate to a principality and expanded it by incorporating large swathes of land formerly belonging to the earl of Arundel. In October 1398, he set up a fund of 4,000 marks, to be distributed among those who had fought at Radcot Bridge – one of many signs of preferment he showered on the people of Cheshire. And he amassed a huge war chest, amounting to £43,964 (about £28.5 million in today's terms), at Holt Castle on the Welsh border, supplementing the wealth he had confiscated from Arundel with wagonloads of jewels and bullion transported from London.

By 1399, the centre of political gravity was shifting north, yet storm clouds were slowly gathering. Loved in Cheshire and Wales and surrounded by his faithful archers, Richard had dissociated himself from parliament and focused on the provinces where he felt most at ease. This had caused resentment in the shires he didn't favour. The king had also alienated many of his barons and one individual – Richard's first cousin, Henry Bolingbroke, duke of Lancaster – had particular cause for anger. Richard had exiled Bolingbroke from England in April 1398 and confiscated his father's estates after John of Gaunt's death in February 1399. When the king mounted an expedition to Ireland in June 1399, taking a large contingent of Cheshire archers with him, Bolingbroke seized his chance.

In early July, as Richard and his archers were battling Irish chieftains, the duke returned from exile to reclaim his patrimony. He had won over another powerful regional magnate, Henry Percy, earl of Northumberland, and when he landed at Ravenspur in Yorkshire he found further support in his father's Lancastrian heartlands. Meanwhile, the king was stranded abroad. Some of the vessels that had carried the royal army to Waterford in June had sailed on to Dublin; others had returned to their home ports. On 17 July, worried by the reports filtering across the sea, Richard sent a small advance guard to north Wales under the earl of Salisbury's command. But another week passed before he could procure all the ships he needed to bring back the rest of his troops. The delay was disastrous; by the time the king disembarked in Wales on 24 July, many of his retainers had laid down their arms, believing that he had died or fled, and Bolingbroke controlled much of England.

Chester capitulated without a fight. On 5 August 1399, Sir Robert Legh, who was still serving as county sheriff, met Bolingbroke at Shrewsbury and agreed to surrender the city. More than 1,000 of Cheshire's best soldiers were away in the king's army, so its military strength was greatly depleted. But Legh had also, apparently, become alarmed by Richard's increasingly tyrannical rule. In August 1397, the king had given him a stipend of £40 a year. By May 1399, Richard clearly questioned his loyalty. At a meeting in Cardiff he made Legh swear allegiance and promise to reveal any plots that came to light while he was in Ireland.

Perhaps Legh had concluded that the king's cause was lost, or perhaps he thought that Richard needed to be brought to heel. In either case, he ceded Chester without a struggle, although he was probably aghast at what happened next. During the twelve days Bolingbroke spent in the city he sacked the castle. He also had Legh's half-uncle Peter, the man who had been responsible for recruiting many of the king's Cheshire bodyguard (and who had also been Thomas Boydell's other guardian), arrested and summarily beheaded. Bolingbroke's soldiers simultaneously looted the city and roamed the countryside, trampling the cornfields and pillaging people's homes. Katherine and her children must have been utterly terrified. Handley was only 2 miles from Coddington, where the freebooting Lancastrian army set up camp on its way to Chester and rampaged through the nearby villages, probing water cisterns and other hiding places with their spears in their search for plunder.

The news that his 'inner citadel' had fallen came like a hammer blow to Richard, who was still in Wales. He had just learned that his uncle, the aged Edmund of York – whom he had put in charge of the realm in his absence – had deserted to Bolingbroke's side. Word of Chester's bloodless submission left him reeling. Shocked and frightened, he fled to Conway Castle in the dead of night, disguised as an itinerant priest. Then, on the advice of the few friends who had accompanied him, he sent emissaries to Chester to find out what the duke wanted. But when his envoys arrived in the city on 9 August, Bolingbroke had them arrested. The next day he sent the earl of Northumberland's son, Sir Harry Percy (known as Hotspur because of his fearlessness in battle), to negotiate with the king.

Hotspur told Richard that Bolingbroke was willing to reach a peaceful settlement on three conditions: that his inheritance was restored to him; that a parliament was called over which he would preside as steward; and that the counsellors whom he blamed for bringing down his uncle, Thomas of Woodstock, were put on trial for treason. Hotspur also offered to swear upon the sacrament that the duke had no desire to steal Richard's throne. What he *didn't* say was that he had left a large force concealed behind some rocks a few miles outside Conway, with orders to stay hidden until he had prised the king out of his fastness. Hotspur had deliberately brought only five soldiers into the castle with him to lull Richard into believing he was safe. Still, the king was cautious. He spent several days considering Bolingbroke's terms and insisted that Hotspur swear he meant 'no deceit', before agreeing to go to Flint to meet his foe. But when he reached the rocks where Hotspur had secreted his troops he realised that he had been tricked. By then it was much too late. Hotspur had chosen his hiding place well and Richard could neither flee back to Conway nor make his escape. He was compelled to accept Hotspur's protestations that the army was there to protect him.

On Saturday, 16 August 1399, the king met his adversary in the great hall at Flint Castle. There, according to one eyewitness – the young French courtier Jean Creton, who had been travelling with the royal party – Bolingbroke bowed low, doffed his cap and pledged to help Richard govern his people better. The king replied, 'If it pleases you, fair cousin, it pleases us as well.' Then Bolingbroke ordered horses to be readied and the entire entourage rode to Chester. But once they arrived, Richard's treatment was far less respectful; he was confined in the castle's highest tower under the hostile watch of the sons of the duke of Gloucester and earl of Arundel, who hated him for having had their fathers put to death.

Four days afterwards, Bolingbroke and his royal prisoner set off for London. On the first night, as they paused for shelter outside Nantwich, some of Richard's former bodyguards tried to rescue him. The king made another attempt to get away several nights later by climbing out of a window in the tower where he had been lodged. But he was caught in the act and, from then on, he was kept under armed surveillance all the time. His last chance had gone, for Bolingbroke's goals were slowly changing as he registered the warmth of his reception on the journey south. On 20 August 1399, when Sir Robert Legh stood surety for the good behaviour of John Legh of Booths, who had been one of the watch captains in Richard's bodyguard, Bolingbroke was still calling himself 'steward of England'. By early September, when he arrived in the capital with the captive king, what had begun as a struggle to recover his birthright had become a bid for the throne.

On 29 September, Richard relinquished his crown and a record of his 'renunciation' was presented to parliament the next day. Charged with thirty-three counts of tyranny, perjury, extortion, duplicity, theft, murder, harassment and condonation of the violence committed by his

Cheshire archers, the king had allegedly abdicated of his own accord. In fact, there had been nothing willing about it. Incarcerated in the Tower of London and subjected to enormous pressure, Richard had grimly hung onto his kingship, insisting that it was a sacred and inalienable role conferred by God. But the duke of Lancaster now held all the chips, as Richard well knew, and neither legal nor spiritual arguments would stop him. On 13 October 1399, Henry Bolingbroke was crowned Henry IV of England in Richard's stead.

When Richard's overthrow was confirmed, his Cheshire bodyguards resigned themselves to the situation and returned to their homes. Henry also embarked on a policy of conciliation by hiring some of the soldiers who had been prominent in Richard's service and restraining those of his supporters who were baying for blood. But the mood of the Cheshire gentry and yeomen was still volatile; in January 1400, anger erupted into violence, ignited by a last-ditch effort on the part of some of Richard's friends to restore the deposed king.

The Epiphany Rising – so called because it took place during the traditional feast to commemorate the visit of the Magi – lasted barely a month, but the conspirators had already sent agents to Cheshire asking for help. The hotheads eagerly responded. On 10 January, an armed band of citizens wearing Richard's sign of the white hart descended on Chester Castle to demand that it be handed over in his name. When the garrison refused to submit, they proceeded to the Eastgate and removed Peter Legh's head from the spike on which it had been left to rot. Then they marched around the city proclaiming that all able-bodied men should rally to liberate the true king. Some of Richard's archers soon joined them and, abandoning their efforts to capture the castle, the insurgents rampaged through the countryside, exhorting the populace to rise up on the king's behalf. However, when they headed back to Chester to wreak further havoc, they discovered that the rising had failed.

The rebels quickly disbanded. Yet, if they hoped to escape the usurper's wrath by making themselves scarce, their hopes were in vain; Henry sent his 12-year-old son Harry to deal with the culprits. Harry had been made prince of Wales and earl of Chester on the day of his father's coronation and was expected – like earlier princes – to play his part in defending the realm. But investing him with the authority to govern the earldom he had been granted was also a clear statement that the succession was resolved; unlike the childless Richard, Henry had a manly and vigorous heir who would be ready to assume his father's monarchical responsibilities when the time came.

On 23 January 1400, Prince Harry appointed conservators of the peace in each of the county's administrative units. Robert's great-uncle, William Bellew, was among them, although he had actually taken part in the events of the previous fortnight. Robert himself was still only 8 or 9 and much too young to participate in the revolt, but it was obvious where his family's sympathies lay. In early February, the prince ordered a preliminary enquiry. A more detailed investigation followed in March and, on 22 May, the king issued a general pardon to the people of Cheshire, from which 125 men were specifically excluded. William Bellew was among those required to sue individually for Henry's forgiveness. He was pardoned on 1 June, after his sureties pledged a hefty 200 marks for his good conduct – more than three times the amount most men were required to put up.

By that point Richard was in his grave. He had been moved from the Tower of London to Henry's Lancastrian stronghold at Pontefract, where he died in mid-February 1400. His body was brought down to the capital for a solemn requiem Mass at St Paul's Cathedral. Then, on the night of 5 March, it was transported to the Dominican friary at Kings Langley in Hertfordshire and quietly interred there the next morning. The ornate tomb Richard had built in Westminster – where his beloved first wife, Anne of Bohemia, was buried – lay vacant, too dangerous a reminder of the king's status and of Henry's dubious claim to the throne.

Conflicting rumours about Richard's end rapidly started circulating. Some people persisted in believing that he was alive, even though Henry had ordered that his face be displayed as his corpse was carried down to London. Others accepted that he was dead but questioned the cause, since he was only 33 years old. Thomas Walsingham, one of Henry's chief admirers, insisted that Richard had pined away from grief. John Hardying, who served in the Percy household, thought that he had been starved to death at Henry's command, lingering in hunger, filth and cold for fifteen days until he passed away. Meanwhile, Adam Usk, a clerk who had been involved in deposing the king, hedged his bets. Richard, he wrote, 'mourned even to death, which came to him most miserably', as he lay in chains in Pontefract Castle, 'tormented . . . with starving fare'. The sceptics were almost certainly right. Richard would always have posed a risk to the new regime, as the Epiphany Rising had shown, and the temptation to remove him probably proved overwhelming.

Richard's death elicited the usual flurry of obituaries and reviews, many of which made passing reference to the capriciousness of fate. 'Now consider, ye kings, lords, dukes, prelates and earls, how very changeable the fortunes of this world are,' the court historian Jean Froissart observed, reflecting on Richard's downfall. Adam Usk was less sympathetic. The king had been endowed with great gifts. Yet he had fallen 'in the midst of [his] glory, as Fortune turned her wheel, . . . amid the smothered curses of [his] people'.

Destiny's deity had brought Richard low. The Boydells of Grappenhall and Handley were also sinking – as they had risen – by her decree. Katherine had clung to her three surviving children, trying to shield them as much as possible from the consequences of their father's premature death, and she had been lucky that Robert's wardship slipped through the cracks in the system as the Ricardian regime collapsed. In the ensuing chaos, Robert's lack of a guardian had passed unnoticed for some time. But Fortune's wheel was still turning. On 4 June 1400, the system finally caught up with Robert when Prince Harry demanded that Katherine deliver her husband's heir to the escheator, since his custody belonged to the prince as the new earl of Chester. This was clearly not the first attempt the prince had made to get hold of Robert and he was fast running out of patience. In a courteous, but uncompromisingly worded, missive he ordered his 'beloved Katherine' to hand over Thomas's heir, just as he had previously directed. He now expected her to comply 'at once' or explain why she was unable to do so. If she failed to respond, she would be fined £100.[5]

Katherine, terrified that her defenceless young son might be placed in the care of an abusive guardian, approached Sir Robert Legh for help. Legh had been genuinely fond of her husband and was well aware of the compliment Thomas had paid him in naming his second son Robert. But the writ could hardly have come at a worse moment. An earlier treaty with Scotland had expired on 29 September 1399, the very day on which Richard had been deposed, and the Scots had immediately resumed raiding in the northern Marches. Henry had written to Robert III of Scotland, attempting to extend the truce. However, Robert had pointedly replied to him as duke of Lancaster, even though Henry had been crowned more than two weeks earlier. So Henry planned to lead a large army into Scotland, hoping to discourage further raids and force the Scots to recognise him as England's legitimate ruler.

The king had made it abundantly plain that he expected the men of Cheshire to fight for him. On 25 June 1400, while he was travelling north, he wrote to John Massey of Puddington, who had replaced Legh as county sheriff, confirming a previous order to send sixty men-at-arms and 500 archers to Newcastle, where he would 'arrange such wages as will content them'. The promise of pay was actually a major concession. When parliament met in late 1399, the House of Commons had demanded that Richard's former watch captains repay the 'great sums of gold and silver' they had supposedly been given. Henry tactfully replied that, since they couldn't do so, he would require them 'to provide service for a certain time at their own cost'. But though he had softened his stance in the intervening months, Cheshire's governing elite knew their loyalty was being tested.

Legh was busy mustering troops from the hundred of Macclesfield and preparing to lead them up to Scotland. Nevertheless, when the question of Robert's custody resurfaced, he stepped forward. There is no direct record of the purchase of Robert's wardship, but a deed in which Legh later bound himself to pay part of the money he still owed for purchasing the right to manage Robert's lands and marriage suggests that he offered the prince £300.[6] This was £100 less than Richard's treasurer had hoped to extract from Sir William Mainwaring in 1397. Even so, it was far more than the £130 that Mainwaring had claimed Robert's estates were worth. Much to Katherine's relief, the prince accepted the offer.

No sooner had the arrangement been made than Legh set off for Scotland. In the event, he and William Bellew, who had also volunteered to fight for the king, were back in Cheshire barely two months later. Henry's expedition to put the Scots in their place had been an abject failure. He and his army had crossed the border into Scotland in mid-August. However, as the English advanced, the Scots simply reverted to their usual tactic of retreating in the face of the enemy. They knew from long experience that the English would eventually run out of food and that all they had to do was wait. Two weeks after entering Scotland, his supplies exhausted, Henry returned to England with nothing to show for his efforts.

Indeed, far from enforcing his royal will, the king had made a serious misjudgement. On 29 August, as he was resting at Leicester on his journey back to London, a courier reached him with urgent news. Pausing only to dismount from his sweat-lathered horse, the messenger announced that a Welsh squire called Owain Glyn Dŵr had just launched another rebellion. Glyn Dŵr had destroyed many castles and was burning and pillaging the towns in which the English dwelled. Henry had been looking in the wrong direction.

The king hastily assembled the remains of his army and set off to deal with this new menace, but a full year was to pass before he realised the scale of the threat Glyn Dŵr represented. By then disaster had befallen the Boydell family once more. On Saturday, 20 August 1401, Robert died after a brief illness.[7] Like his father and brother, he had probably succumbed to something other than the plague. Although northern England had been hard hit by another outbreak of the pestilence in the summer of 1399, there were no significant recurrences at the start of the fifteenth century. Katherine – who presumably nursed her son during his last days – appears to have perished with him. There is no further trace of her in the records; she simply vanishes into the past, yet another casualty of time's obliterating flight. But it was Robert's death that marked the real turning point in the family's affairs. When Ralph Boydell had fallen prey to the Black Death in 1349, his cousin Hywel stepped into his shoes. When Robert died, there was no male heir to carry on the line. Three generations of the Boydell family had expired in less than twenty-five years, leaving only Cecily and her two granddaughters alive. Fortune's whirling wheel had proved false indeed.

18

Ashes and Dust

The flickering torches drew nearer. There were easily a hundred men, a few of them mounted but most on foot. Some had longbows slung across their backs; others brandished swords, sickles and homemade spears fashioned from billhooks, metal glinting in the ruddy glow from the flames. It was quiet except for the occasional clink of a harness and the muffled thud of booted feet. When the moon broke through a slit in the clouds, it shone on the rider at the front of the line, illuminating his tattered banner: Owain Glyn Dŵr's four lions snarled in the watery silver light, rearing up on their hind legs with teeth bared and claws unsheathed.

The captain of the garrison watched grimly as the Welsh advanced. He'd herded the women, children and old folk into the keep, along with the pigs, sheep and dogs, and sent an archer up to the lookout post. He and the rest of his guards had formed a circle around the edge of the motte, with the fittest villagers placed between them, nervously clutching old and rusty weapons. He'd done what he could, but the situation was hopeless; with only a handful of soldiers and poorly armed peasants, he couldn't hold the castle against such a large force.

The Welsh paused just out of arrowshot, while the archers strung their bows and their leader spoke to them, clapping one man encouragingly on the back. Then, as they resumed their march, they started chanting: Glyn Dŵr, Glyn Dŵr, Tywysog Cymru. *The sound rang out in the clear evening air:* Glyn Dŵr, Glyn Dŵr, Prince of Wales. *At first the attackers walked, but soon they picked up speed until they were running. A few stumbled and fell, struck by arrows. Most reached the palisade, where they hacked at the planks covering the spaces between the uprights and tore away the slats. Then they poured into the bailey.*

The archers positioned on the motte fired with disciplined precision, but their supply of arrows was pitifully small. When they ran out, the Welsh clambered up the scarp. The din of clanging weapons and agonised screams filled the night. Swords and spears pierced soft flesh, scythes mowed through limbs, and sickles with cruelly sharp curved blades ripped through men's torsos. Desperately though they fought, the defenders were gradually overwhelmed. At last only one soldier stood, surrounded by mocking Welshmen. Terrified, he attempted to surrender; they fell on him like starving wolves thrown a hunk of meat.

Glyn Dŵr's followers didn't try to break into the keep; they simply laid burning brands around the base and waited. The summer had left the timber bone-dry and all it took was a slight gust of wind for the flames to catch. Within minutes the tower was ablaze. The Welsh jeered as the blistering heat drove out the panicked villagers who'd sought refuge inside, but their leader spoke sharply. Then, in heavily accented English, he ordered the villagers to leave. He would take the animals, but he wouldn't kill women, children or greybeards.

When the sun rose the next morning, a pall of black smoke hung over Dodleston. The motte was littered with corpses: soldiers sprawling on the hard-packed soil in blood-soaked jerkins; peasants lying in a tangle of broken limbs and rucked tunics red with gore. Flies buzzed around the carcases and the smell of charred wood permeated the air. All that remained of the fortress Osbern fitz Tezzo had built was a pile of glowing embers.

In the autumn of 1403, a messenger pounded on the door of the manor house in Handley. When one of the maidservants let him in, alarmed by the sound of urgent knocking, he hastily asked for an audience with Cecily Boydell. He bore grave news from Sir Robert Legh: Dodleston Castle had fallen and the whole village had been destroyed. Moreover, Glyn Dŵr himself was reputed to be nearby, preparing to invade Cheshire. Faces scrubbed and hair neatly braided, Margaret and Isabelle listened solemnly as the messenger told their grandmother that the revolt had now spread into Flintshire and Glyn Dŵr's supporters had attacked numerous English settlements. The king was assembling an army to march into Wales and launch a counter-assault, but that would take time.

The past seven years had been very difficult for the Boydells. First, Thomas and his elder son had died. Then his wife Katherine and younger son, Robert, had followed them to the grave. Margaret and Isabelle could barely remember their father, but their mother's death must have been a

The major administrative and lordship divisions of north Wales, *c.* 1400

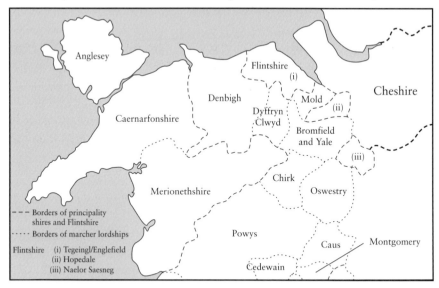

Source: J.B. Smith and L.B. Smith, 'Wales: Politics, Government and Law', in *A Companion to Britain in the Later Middle Ages*, ed. S.H. Rigby (Oxford, 2003), p. 343.

devastating blow. Although more than a fifth of all children in medieval England lost a parent before reaching adulthood, relatively few were full orphans. In most cases, it was the father who died; despite the perils of giving birth, the prevalence of fatherless children was more than twice that of motherless children. But while the loss of a father could be traumatic, the loss of a mother was even harder. A father's death might cause economic privation. A mother's death threatened the very fabric of the family. It was she who maintained the household, fed the children, cared for them when they were sick and taught them before they were old enough to leave home. Margaret and Isabelle were materially secure, yet they were still completely dependent on adult authority and susceptible to abuse.

In fact, Robert's death had left the two girls even more exposed because they were now the joint heiresses to their father's estates. When there was an underage male heir to feudal lands he entered into wardship, while his siblings normally stayed in their mother's custody, to be raised on the income from her dower lands. But if the ward died and there were no more sons, the daughters took the deceased boy's place.

Their guardianship passed automatically to the man who had bought the original rights. So Margaret and Isabelle had both become Sir Robert Legh's wards.

Fortunately, he had allowed them to continue living with their grandmother. It was a mutually convenient arrangement. Legh's first wife, after whom Isabelle had been named, had died in about 1401. Legh had remarried and his second wife, Margery, had recently given birth; she wouldn't welcome another two children to care for. More importantly, Legh had his hands full, as England lurched from one crisis to the next. Since ousting Richard II from his throne in September 1399, Henry IV had faced several challenges to his rule – the most serious being in Wales. Owain Glyn Dŵr had proved a surprisingly formidable foe.

Glyn Dŵr was not a natural rebel. He could trace his lineage back to the ancient princes of Powys and Deheubarth, but he had almost equally strong English links. He had trained as a barrister in London. His wife was the daughter of Sir David Hanmer, the renowned Anglo-Welsh lawyer with whom Margaret and Isabelle's great-grandfather, Hywel, had done business. And he had fought for the English crown. In 1384, Glyn Dŵr helped to man the garrison at Berwick; in 1385, he enlisted in the army Richard II assembled to invade Scotland; and, in 1387, he served in the retinue of Richard Fitzalan, earl of Arundel. He may have remained in the earl's service until Arundel was executed in 1397. If not, he certainly kept in touch with the earl's relatives; when Henry IV restored Arundel's disinherited son to his earldom in October 1399, Glyn Dŵr was acting as his squire. In short, Glyn Dŵr was a highly educated man who mixed freely with England's border gentry and enjoyed the patronage of one of the nation's greatest nobles. Yet, on 16 September 1400 – during a meeting at his ancestral home in Glyndyfrdwy, a small village near Llangollen – he took the extraordinary step of proclaiming himself prince of Wales and declaring war on the English. Two days later, he and his supporters descended on the Vale of Clwyd and torched the town of Ruthin.

The ostensible cause of the revolt was the bad blood between Glyn Dŵr and Reginald Grey, lord of Ruthin and Dyffryn Clwyd. Conflicting accounts claim that Grey had used deception to cast Glyn Dŵr in a bad light with the king and that the pair had become embroiled in a territorial dispute. But far wider grievances underpinned their personal animosity. Fifteenth-century Wales was two countries in one. The Wales outsiders saw was a country of castles and walled towns built by English colonists, oases of safety in an alien landscape. England's aristocratic families held vast blocks of land and their stewards ruled with a rod of iron, ensuring that most of the profits went to the absentee lords they served. However, under the surface lay another Wales: a country steeped in myth, bound by genealogical ties and deep-rooted customs of hospitality. This was the country from which Hywel's father had come – and it was a country whose people profoundly resented being treated as inferiors.

The barriers between the two realms were not just ethnic or cultural; they informed almost every aspect of life. There were separate law courts for English and Welsh litigants, with different laws and procedures; separate administrative systems, with different rules and office-holding hierarchies. The distinctions had originated in an effort to respect the traditions of a conquered populace, but over time they had become an excuse for blatant discrimination. Thus, by 1400, the Welsh were ripe for revolt – and in Owain Glyn Dŵr they finally had a champion with the magnetism and martial skills to lead them.

For five days, between 18 and 23 September 1400, Glyn Dŵr's followers attacked English towns in north-east Wales. After burning down Ruthin, they sped north to assault Denbigh and Rhuddlan, before crossing east to Flint and sweeping south to Hawarden, Holt, Oswestry and Welshpool. Henry was sufficiently alarmed to divert his army from its journey back from Scotland. In late September, he led a campaign into north Wales and rapidly quashed the resistance. Eight of the men who had been involved in the attack on Ruthin were executed. Several prominent rebels, including one of Glyn Dŵr's sons, also abandoned his cause and the government offered pardons to those who submitted. The uprising appeared to be over.

Yet Glyn Dŵr and his closest companions were still at large. They had fled to the mountains, where it was impossible to find them. Moreover, the principality was seething; Welsh scholars from Oxford and Cambridge were returning home and the peasants were surreptitiously arming themselves. Parliament's response made matters worse. In March 1401, it passed the first of several laws intended to make the Welsh toe the line. Welshmen were banned from buying land in England and no Englishman could be tried or convicted on the word of a Welshman. This only fanned the flames of Welsh wrath. On 1 April 1401, the rebellion flared up again when two of Glyn Dŵr's kinsmen captured Conway Castle. They had been denied pardons for participating in the initial revolt and hoped to force the government to settle with them. But by July, when they had been pardoned and the castle was back under English control, the uprising had spread to central and southern Wales.

The pattern of the next few months followed that of the previous year. As summer turned to autumn the English slowly reasserted their authority and Glyn Dŵr melted away into the mountains – aided, so it was said, by a magical stone that rendered him invisible. However, the rebel leader was merely biding his time. In April 1402, he ambushed his arch-enemy, Reginald Grey, and carried him off to his craggy hideout, to be kept there until a huge ransom was paid for his release. Then, on 22 June, Glyn Dŵr won a major victory at Bryn Glas, only 18 miles from Leominster, one of the most important English garrisons in the Welsh Marches. Sir Edmund Mortimer, the king's cousin, was captured and many of Herefordshire's leading gentry were slain in the battle.

When news of the disaster reached Henry, the king immediately took steps to safeguard the most vital border castles. In September 1402, he also led an English army into north Wales, but torrential rain and terrible gales forced him to return to Shrewsbury having achieved very little. Even so, the government remained reluctant to negotiate with Glyn Dŵr. It also dragged its feet over ransoming Mortimer, a mistake for which it soon paid dearly. On 30 November, Mortimer married Glyn Dŵr's daughter Catrin and, on 13 December, he announced that he had joined the Welsh cause. Glyn Dŵr had pulled off a remarkable diplomatic triumph. Mortimer's defection had brought his own extensive retinue under Glyn Dŵr's banner and given the revolt a validity it previously lacked. Mortimer's nephew, the 12-year-old earl of March, descended from Edward III's second surviving son, Lionel of Antwerp, whereas Henry descended from Edward's third surviving son, John of Gaunt. So the Mortimers arguably had a better claim to the English throne than Henry himself.

Heartened by his success, Glyn Dŵr changed tack. Rather than holing up in the mountains during the winter as they had previously done, he and his rebels continued to fight throughout the bad weather. By early 1403, his forces were amassing on the edges of Cheshire and, on 22 February, they burned down the town of Hope, only 10 miles west of Handley, where Cecily Boydell and her two granddaughters were anxiously following the course of the war. But instead of continuing east, Glyn Dŵr turned south. Men flocked to his cause and castles fell like ninepins as he pushed deep into Carmarthenshire. What had once been a series of localised insurrections had become a national revolt infecting the entire principality.

It was in this febrile atmosphere that Hotspur arrived in Chester on 9 July 1403 to launch a second uprising. The Percys had become increasingly disenchanted with the monarch they had helped to make. They were close to the Mortimers – Hotspur was married to Sir Edmund's sister, Elizabeth – and had been incensed by Henry's refusal to hear their pleas for aid in securing Edmund's release. They were also disappointed by the rewards the king had doled out. Although Henry had granted them various offices, including key roles in the defence of the realm, the profits had been less than they expected. When Hotspur asked for more money to guard the Marches, Henry tried to brush him off. Hotspur would have none of it and in the ensuing argument the king struck him in the face. Henry's decision, in April 1403, to create a new command structure in Wales and put Prince Harry rather than Hotspur in charge, probably destroyed any last vestiges of loyalty the Percys felt towards the king.

Hotspur thought that Cheshire would be sympathetic to his cause, since it was home to some of the men most adamantly opposed to Richard II's deposition. His hopes were realised when many of the gentry, including Sir Robert Legh, rallied to his summons – swayed by Hotspur's claim that Richard was still alive. Legh was no firebrand; he had swiftly transferred his allegiance to Henry once Richard was unseated. But when Hotspur's call to arms came, Legh switched sides. Others were more cautious. The Boydells of Lymm were noticeably absent from the rebels' numbers. William Bellew also kept his distance – made wary, perhaps, by memories of the abortive Epiphany Rising in 1400. If so, he was wise.

The Battle of Shrewsbury on 21 July 1403 was one of the bloodiest confrontations ever to take place on English soil and the outcome was calamitous for Cheshire's ruling elite. The Percys were soundly defeated. Hotspur was cut down as he led a last desperate charge against the king, while his uncle, Thomas Percy, was captured. Nineteen of the county's foremost gentry also died on the battlefield, two succumbed to wounds sustained in combat and two were beheaded with Thomas Percy. Another thirty-one men whose inquisitions post mortem were held shortly afterwards were probably likewise among those who fell fighting for Hotspur. Many of the casualties were people with whom Thomas Boydell had socialised.

Yet, even as the survivors were hobbling home, the Welsh were on the move again. In July 1403, the men of Flintshire joined Glyn Dŵr's revolt. On 4 August, they plundered Flint and razed Rhuddlan to the ground. Over the next few weeks they swept through the plains on the Welsh side of the River Dee, ransacking English towns and villages. Pulford, Poulton, Dodleston, Kinnerton, Marleston, Lache, Claverton, Eccleston, Eaton and Hawarden were all 'destroyed by the rebels, some of them burnt, and nobody dared to remain in them'.[1] Dodleston Castle was reduced to a smouldering wreck. There had been no uprising in north Wales for more than a century and the castle had been allowed to fall into a state of disrepair. Run-down, roof leaking, timbers rotting, it had only been garrisoned during the occasional emergency – and, even then, the force stationed in it had been tiny. When the Welsh descended on the castle, it was poorly equipped, undermanned and soon overrun.

As reports that Glyn Dŵr was planning to invade Cheshire spread like wildfire, the county prepared for war. Prince Harry commanded the keepers of the Wirral to 'appoint watches and make ditches, hedges and other impediments' against Glyn Dŵr's coming, while Chester readied itself for a siege. The mayor was ordered to expel every Welsh resident from the city and impose a curfew: no Welshmen could stay within the city walls at night and those who entered the city in the daytime were banned from carrying any weapons other than a knife to cut their meat, using the taverns or meeting in groups of more than three.

In mid-September 1403, the king also led another expedition into Wales, but Glyn Dŵr's guerrillas simply retreated, disappearing into their mountain lairs as if they could truly invoke the power of magic. Henry returned to Hereford less than two weeks afterwards, angry and frustrated. Providentially for those of the Cheshire gentry who had fought for Hotspur at Shrewsbury and survived the carnage, it was clear that expunging the rebellion would be a difficult process. Much as Henry might have wanted to punish the culprits, he knew that he needed their military skills. Teeth gritted, he adopted a conciliatory tone. On 7 September, Sir Robert Legh was forgiven for his part in the revolt. Indeed, by 30 September, he had even been restored to his post as one of the justices for the three hundreds of the eyre at Macclesfield.

Margaret and Isabelle's guardian was back in royal favour. A month later, the people of Cheshire were granted a general pardon, subject to paying a fine of 3,000 marks – although the citizens of Chester had to pay a separate fine of 300 marks – and, by early 1404, most of Hotspur's former supporters had been rehabilitated.

They had been spared on the understanding that they would help to guard England's borders – and never had those borders been more in need of protection. As soon as Henry set off for London again, Glyn Dŵr renewed his attacks. Worse still, French and Breton volunteers joined him. On 11 January 1404, Prince Harry responded to the growing danger by commanding Sir Robert Legh and all the other Cheshire gentry with lands nearest to the enemy to hasten to the Marches and reside there 'for the defence of the realm'.

In April 1404, the situation deteriorated even further with the death of Philip the Bold, duke of Burgundy, who had advocated peace with England. Glyn Dŵr was quick to exploit the opportunity his demise presented. That May, he sent two of his most trusted confidantes to the French court to negotiate an alliance. Two months later, on 14 July, Charles VI of France and Owain, 'Prince of Wales', entered into a mutual oath to oppose their common enemy, Henry of Lancaster. Glyn Dŵr had pulled off another major political coup; he had been accepted as ruler of Wales by one of Europe's reigning monarchs and assured of military aid.

Charles kept his word. The English waited apprehensively, as a fleet of sixty French vessels assembled at Harfleur. However, ineptitude or bad weather prevented the ships from setting sail until the late autumn and, when the French tried to land at Falmouth because the seas were too rough to sail around Cornwall, they were easily repelled. Glyn Dŵr would have to wait until the following spring for the help he had been promised.

As it happened, the Welsh war leader was doing remarkably well without French assistance, partly because the 16-year-old Prince Harry was still recovering from the grave wound he had received at Shrewsbury, when a stray arrow struck him below the eye while his visor was raised. Glyn Dŵr had also found another powerful ally in Hotspur's father, Henry Percy, earl of Northumberland. The earl had reached Shrewsbury too late to support his son. Hastily denying any knowledge of Hotspur's plans, he had narrowly escaped being convicted of treason. Henry had stripped him of office, ordered him to surrender his main castles and taken three of his grandchildren as hostages – lenient treatment in the circumstances. But the earl was not the kind of person to accept the death of his son or the curbing of his ambitions quietly. In February 1405, he entered into a secret pact with Glyn Dŵr and Sir Edmund Mortimer to overthrow Henry. The trio agreed that, once they had toppled the king, they would divide the country into three dominions. Percy was to have northern England, Mortimer southern England and Glyn Dŵr a greatly enlarged Wales.

However, the tide was slowly beginning to turn Henry's way. In the spring of 1405, Prince Harry resumed his role as the king's lieutenant in north Wales. On 11 March, he wrote to his father, reporting that he and his household knights had killed between 800 and 1,000 rebels at Grosmont in Monmouthshire. Then, in early May, the Welsh suffered a crushing defeat at Usk, when Glyn Dŵr's brother Tudur was killed and his son Gruffudd taken prisoner. The victorious English beheaded 300 of Glyn Dŵr's followers before carrying Gruffudd off in chains to be locked up in the Tower of London for the rest of his life.

The king was cock-a-hoop. Declaring that he would lead an expedition into Wales to finish off Glyn Dŵr, he headed for Hereford. But just as he was finalising his plans, he learned of yet another insurrection. The earl of Northumberland and Thomas, Lord Bardolf, had apparently joined forces with an army of northerners led by Richard Scrope, archbishop of York, and Thomas Mowbray, earl marshal of England. In fact, Percy and Bardolf may have been plotting independently of Scrope and Mowbray, although a letter Henry sent his Privy Council shows that he believed they were in cahoots. On 22 May, the king reluctantly abandoned the Welsh campaign and ordered his supporters in the Midlands to assemble all the men they could find to deal with this new threat. Four days later, Prince Harry directed Legh to meet him 'with 100 defensible, honest, able bowmen, in good array for war'.

In the event, the Yorkshire Rising was soon suppressed; badly organised and backed largely by disgruntled peasants, it was doomed from the start. Scrope and Mowbray were captured, tried for treason and convicted on 7 June 1405. They were paraded through the streets of York the next day and then executed outside the city walls. Meanwhile, as Henry pressed north, Northumberland and Bardolf fled to Scotland. By mid-July the king had seized all of the earl's castles, including Alnwick, the huge fortress on the Anglo-Scottish border that had been in the Percy family for nearly a century. Within two months of hearing of the conspiracy, Henry had stamped out every last shred of northern resistance to his rule.

Sir Robert Legh had already returned to Cheshire, where he was completing the nuptial arrangements for his two wards. On 24 June 1405, the 12-year-old Margaret married Hugh Reddish, the second son of Richard Reddish, lord of the manors of Little Heaton and Reddish. Four months later, on 11 November, her 11-year-old sister, Isabelle, married Nicholas Langton, the second son of Ralph Langton, baron of Newton in Makerfield. Both men were much older than their brides. Hugh's elder brother had just turned 30, while Nicholas's elder brother was nearly 40, so Hugh was probably in his late twenties and Nicholas in his thirties.[2] But Legh had done his best for the girls. He had mined his extensive social network to pair them with the junior scions of two established Lancastrian families – a shrewd move, given that Henry's usurpation of the throne had placed the Lancastrians in the ascendancy. Besides, Legh still owed Prince Harry the £300 he had agreed to pay for custody of Thomas Boydell's heir and lands. Any affection he felt for Margaret and Isabelle had to be weighed against the money their marriages could fetch.

In July 1406, Legh promised to pay the prince £40 towards the arrears on the bill for the girls' wardship. As Glyn Dŵr's fortunes continued to wane and his revolt fizzled out, the administration of Cheshire was gradually returning to normal and old debts were falling due. There was a substantial bureaucratic backlog; another ten months passed before the escheator found time to conduct Robert Boydell's inquisition post mortem. But on 26 May 1407, nearly six years after Robert's death, his lands were formally divided between his two sisters. Legh had already given Margaret's half to her husband Hugh, when they married. Isabelle was still a minor, although she had also come of age by 13 June 1408. On 18 June, she and Nicholas were granted possession of her share of Robert's lands.[3] Legh had fulfilled his custodial duties – and not a moment too soon. He was only 47 years old, but an action-packed life had taken its toll. By 18 August 1408, he was dead.

The rest of Margaret and Isabelle's inheritance was still tied up. Some of it remained in the hands of their brother Thomas's widow. Elizabeth had married Thomas Danyers of Over Tabley, the son of Sir John Danyers' much younger half-brother, forming yet another link in the many complex familial bonds that connected Cheshire's manorial gentry. However, Margaret and Isabelle didn't have to wait long. Elizabeth herself died on 6 October 1409. Seven weeks later, on 29 November, the sisters were declared Thomas's rightful heirs.[4]

Cecily Boydell also held a modest estate in dower – and was proving far more vigorous than certain members of the Reddish family would have liked. Between 27 August and 13 October 1411, Hugh Reddish and his kinsman Thurstan were required to enter into three separate recognizances that Thurstan would stop harassing Cecily. Quarrels over dower were quite common in the litigious society of late medieval England, but Cecily was a survivor. She had already coped with the loss of a husband, son and two grandsons; putting the belligerent relative of an ambitious in-law in his place was a trivial challenge by comparison. In the end, Hugh had to wait another thirteen years for Margaret's share of her grandmother's dower lands. When Cecily finally died in the spring of 1425, she was in her seventies – an age very few of her contemporaries attained.[5]

Dramatic changes had occurred in that time. The two political figures who had dominated Margaret and Isabelle's childhood were gone. Henry IV died in March 1413, after a long illness. He had contracted a disfiguring skin condition, accompanied by bouts of acute sickness, which was widely thought to be divine punishment for executing Archbishop Scrope. Owain Glyn Dŵr probably died in 1415, a broken man. He had eluded capture and his last days were shrouded in mystery, inspiring tales that he lived on and would return – like King Arthur – to save his people. As for Prince Harry, he too had perished. Crowned Henry V after his father's demise, he had reigned for just nine-and-a-half glittering but brutal years when he died at Vincennes, outside Paris, on 31 August 1422.

Death had also come calling for Nicholas Langton and Isabelle had remarried; indeed, she and her new spouse, John, the eldest son of Gilbert Abram, lord of the manor of Abram in Lancashire, had risked their souls to wed. Under canon law, when a man and woman married, the husband's blood relatives became those of his wife. Similarly, the wife's blood relatives became those of her husband. The Church had established strict rules on the degrees of affinity that were prohibited. However, couples who fell within the more remote degrees of affinity could still marry, if they obtained a papal dispensation. Isabelle and

John were related 'in the third and third degrees of affinity': in other words, they were second cousins or stood to each other as second cousins through a prior marriage. They had knowingly ignored this impediment, but the Vatican was prepared to be merciful. On 1 July 1418, the bishop of Lichfield was ordered to absolve 'John Aburham, donsel [squire], and Isabel Boydelle, noblewoman', from excommunication, provided that they did penance and temporarily separated before going through another marriage ceremony.[6] Perhaps Isabelle had been pressurised into marrying John, or perhaps theirs was a rare medieval love match.

She and John had already struck a deal with Margaret and Hugh. By March 1318, they had sold Isabelle's share of the Boydell lands to her sister and brother-in-law. The two couples sold the manor of Bache, near Chester, at much the same time. William and Felicia Doncaster had acquired the manor in 1307 and given it to their daughter Margaret in 1323. But Margaret's line had failed and the property had passed to the Boydells. On 17 December 1425, Margaret and Isabelle, and their respective husbands, also disposed of four houses in Chester – possibly the last of the fifteen messuages attached to the manor of Dodleston.[7]

Hugh may have used some of the proceeds to start rebuilding Dodleston Castle, although his heart clearly wasn't in the task. Archaeological evidence suggests that base stones were laid for a new semi-timbered structure, but it was never finished.[8] With Glyn Dŵr's defeat, Wales was quiescent again. The castle had outlived its purpose and Hugh preferred to spend his wife's money creating an elegant family home. He chose a site just outside Grappenhall, where he had a fine moated residence constructed. The house would be tangible evidence of his seigneurial status – and lest anyone forget who was now in charge, it would be called Reddish Hall.

The Boydells had been utterly eclipsed. Margaret was dead by 2 April 1438. Hugh was allowed to keep her lands until he expired in February 1448, at which point everything went to their son Thomas.[9] Isabelle may still have been alive when her sister died, but she had long since moved to Abram, where no trace of her remains. Helto and Idonea's offspring had perpetuated the Boydell name for 250 years and retained the Cheshire estates Idonea's grandfather had won nearly 100 years before she married Helto. With Margaret's death, Osbern fitz Tezzo's lineage – like his castle – had apparently crumbled into ashes and dust.

The Norman Conquest replaced the existing Anglo-Saxon nobility with a new ruling class, men who spoke French, drank wine and built castles. But though their roots lay in mainland Europe, they diverged from their neighbours. While every medieval European nation had a patrician elite, it was generally a single, broad caste. The aristocracy held formal titles and enjoyed much the same privileges, no matter how rich or poor they were. They also split their estates among their children, albeit in unequal shares, thereby creating numerous heirs who claimed blue-blooded status long after family fortunes had been scattered.

In England, by contrast, the nobility were divided. There was a small coterie of titled magnates who held vast swathes of territory directly from the king and a much larger group of lesser landowners – the gentry – who held land from the barons they served. The former enjoyed greater privileges than the latter, although all possessed fewer privileges than their continental counterparts. And virtually all followed the Norman custom of passing their inherited estates to their eldest sons, leaving younger sons to make their own way in life. Both the barons and their followers were required to defend the kingdom. The magnates also attended the royal councils that William established to replace the Anglo-Saxon Witan. But over time England's middling landholders became increasingly involved in the running of the country, too – as constables, sheriffs and keepers of the peace, local jurors and knights of the shire in the counties that were represented in parliament.

Thus, the Conquest tethered power to the possession of real estate because many of the invaders owed their rank to the lands they held rather than their pedigree. It also changed the basis on which landed wealth was handed down, ensuring that the English aristocracy gradually became less numerous but financially stronger than their European peers. And it sowed the seeds for a two-tier parliamentary system in which titled magnates sat, by right, in the House of Lords, while the gentry were only eligible for election to the House of Commons as emissaries of the counties in which they resided.

Yet just as the Normans transformed England, so England transformed the Normans. The descendants of those who had crossed the Channel in 1066 slowly shed their Norman identity as immigrants married indigenes, administrators of Anglo-Saxon origin entered noble service, the English language displaced French in common parlance and literate monks (often of mixed parentage) spoke up for the nation in their chronicles. By 1204, when Normandy fell to the French, it was impossible to tell who was Norman and who was English.

Osbern's military exploits secured his heirs a place among the gentry. The Boydells held lands and office in the small corner of the country they had made their own. They intermarried with other families of similar social standing, did business with them, stood surety for them and sometimes quarrelled with them – disastrously on occasion. Like many other seigneurial houses, they eventually discarded the formal trappings of chivalry as other avenues to power emerged. However, they remained a part of north-western England's governing class, embedded in a world of personal connections and collective responsibilities. Such people didn't direct the course of the state. While sovereigns and aristocrats swaggered across the national stage, the gentry usually acted out their roles in the local arena. But they might assist the great players, as the Boydells did. Osbern's offspring fought in the armies of monarchs and magnates, oversaw royal garrisons and held royal stewardships, travelled abroad on the king's business and helped to administer the laws of the land. They were among the many knights and squires who quietly nudged history along.

And their story wasn't over. As Margaret Reddish lay dying in the house her husband had so ostentatiously named after his own ancestors, the Boydells of Lymm were rising in the world. Lacking the lands their distant cousins possessed, they had left far fewer tracks. That would change in the centuries to come. One member of the family would produce a daughter whose descendants included two English queens: Mary II, co-monarch with her husband William of Orange, and her younger sister, Anne. Another would attain high office in the Order of the Knights Hospitaller, the great military order charged with defending Christendom from the Muslims. Still other members of the family would become well-known artists, engineers and inventors. Not all of them prospered. Bankruptcy and scandal shaped their lives, too. But by the middle of the eighteenth century the wealthiest branch of the clan owned a magnificent country retreat in Rossett, just 3 miles from Dodleston. The Boydells had returned to the land of their forefathers as a force to be reckoned with.

Abbreviations

(Unless otherwise indicated, the place of publication is London)

BPR	*Register of the Black Prince*, ed. M.C.B. Dawes, 4 vols (1930-33).
CDF	*Calendar of Documents Preserved in France, Illustrative of the History of Great Britain and Ireland: 918-1206*, ed. J.H. Round (1899).
CDS	*Calendar of Documents Relating to Scotland,* ed. J. Bain, G.G. Simpson and J.D. Galbraith, 5 vols (Edinburgh, 1881-1986).
CALS	Cheshire Archives and Local Studies.
Chart. Chester Abbey	*The Chartulary or Register of the Abbey of St Werburgh, Chester*, ed. J. Tait, 2 vols (Manchester, 1920-23).
CCHR	*Calendar of Charter Rolls* (1903-27).
CCR	*Calendar of Close Rolls* (1892-).
CFR	*Calendar of Fine Rolls* (1911-62).
CIM	*Calendar of Inquisitions Miscellaneous* (1916-2003).
CIPM	*Calendar of Inquisitions Post Mortem* (1904-2010).
CPR	*Calendar of Patent Rolls* (1906-).
CRR	*Curia Regis Rolls* (1922-).
DIWD I	'Calendar of Deeds, Inquisitions and Writs of Dower, enrolled on the Plea Rolls of the County of Chester, Henry III and Edward I', Appendix 4, *26th DKR* (1865).
DIWD II	'Calendar of Deeds, Inquisitions and Writs of Dower, enrolled on the Plea Rolls of the County of Chester, Edward II', Appendix 4, *27th DKR* (1866).

DIWD III	'Calendar of Deeds, Inquisitions and Writs of Dower, enrolled on the Plea Rolls of the County of Chester, Edward III', Appendix 6, *28th DKR* (1867).
DIWD IV	'Calendar of Deeds, Inquisitions and Writs of Dower enrolled on the Plea Rolls of the County of Chester, Richard II to Henry VII', Appendix 6, *29th DKR* (1868).
DKR	Reports of the Deputy Keeper of the Public Records.
GB 133 ARL	Warburton of Arley Charters, University of Manchester.
GB 133 RYCH	Rylands Charters, University of Manchester.
GB 133 TW	Tatton of Wythenshawe Muniments, University of Manchester.
LCRS	Lancashire and Cheshire Record Society.
Ormerod	G. Ormerod, *The History of the County Palatine and City of Chester*, revised and enlarged by T. Helsby, 3 vols (1882).
Pipe Roll	*The Great Rolls of the Pipe, 1169-1180* (1892-1908).
RRC I	'Calendar of Recognizance Rolls of the Palatinate of Chester, to the end of the reign of Henry IV', Appendix II, *36th DKR* (1875).
RRC II	'Calendar of Recognizance Rolls of the Palatinate of Chester, from the beginning of the reign of Henry V to the end of the reign of Henry VII', Appendix II, *37th DKR* (1876).
RRC III	'Calendar of Recognizance Rolls of the Palatinate of Chester, from the beginning of the reign of Henry VIII to 11 George IV', Appendix I, *39th DKR* (1878).
TNA	The National Archives.

Notes

This book draws on numerous scholarly works but, as a popular history, its primary purpose is to capture the general reader's imagination. The story of the Boydells forms the spine of my narrative, so I have included all sources relating to the family below. Otherwise, I have conformed to the convention of using minimal endnotes.

Winner Takes All

1. Various unpublished pedigrees suggest that Osbern was a member of the family of Tesson or Taisson, lords of Cinglais. I have found no evidence to support these claims.

The Wages of War

1. J.B. Yates, *The Rights and Jurisdiction of the County Palatine of Chester* (Manchester, 1856), p. 4.
2. *The Domesday Book: A Complete Translation*, ed. A. Williams and G.H. Martin (2003), pp. 908-09, 959, 732-35. (Part of the land Osbern held in Maidenwell was in dispute.)
3. R. Swallow, 'Palimpsest of Border Power: The Archaeological Survey of Dodleston Castle, Cheshire', *Cheshire History Journal* 54 (2014-15), pp. 36-39.
4. *CDF*, No. 1240; *The Ecclesiastical History of Orderic Vitalis*, III, ed M. Chibnall (Oxford, 1983), pp. 237-39.
5. R. Power, 'Magnus Barelegs' Expeditions to the West', *Scottish Historical Review* 65, 180, Part 2 (1986), pp. 119-20.

An Undone Land

1. *CDF*, No. 1239.
2. *CDF*, No. 1240.
3. *The Lincolnshire Domesday and the Lindsey Survey*, ed. C.W. Foster and T. Longley (Lincoln Record Society 19, 1924), p. 255.
4. *Chart. Chester Abbey*, I, pp. 52, 59.
5. *Chart. Chester Abbey*, I, No. 371; *CPR, 1399-1401*, p. 300.

What's in a Name?

1. *Liber Feodorum: The book of fees commonly called Testa de Nevill,* II (1923), p. 1002; British Library Harley charter, 54-A-45, cited in G.R. Sitwell, *The Barons of Pulford in the Eleventh and Twelfth Centuries and their Descendants* (Scarborough, 1889), p. 78.

2. *Report on the Manuscripts of Lord Middleton, preserved at Wollaton Hall, Nottinghamshire* (1911), p. 19; 'Chartulary of Dieulacres Abbey', ed. G. Wrottesley, *Staffordshire Historical Collections,* new series IX (1906), No. 86; 'Chartulary of the Gresleys of Derbyshire', ed. J. Harland, *The Reliquary* 6 (1865), p. 83.

3. *The Charters of the Anglo-Norman Earls of Chester, c. 1071-1237,* ed. G. Barraclough (LCRS 126, 1988), No. 128; *CCHR, 1300-1326,* p. 251; *Chart. Chester Abbey,* I, Nos. 39 and 40.

4. *CPR, 1399-1401,* p. 301; *Charters of the Honour of Mowbray, 1107-1191,* ed. D.E. Greenway (Oxford, 1972), p. 83.

5. *Charters of the Anglo-Norman Earls of Chester,* No. 171.

6. *Pipe Roll, 1169-70,* p. 147; *Pipe Roll, 1170-71,* p. 103; *Pipe Roll, 1174-75,* p. 156; *Pipe Roll, 1175-76,* p. 85; *Pipe Roll, 1176-77,* p. 109.

7. *Pipe Roll, 1175-76,* p. 81; *Pipe Roll, 1179-80,* p. 50.

8. British Library Harley charter, 54-A-45, cited in Sitwell, The Barons of Pulford, p. 78; CALS DLT/B1.

9. *Charters of the Anglo-Norman Earls of Chester,* Nos. 131 and 187.

10. Hugh attested Nos. 203, 208, 240, 242, 250, 267 and 321; Alan, Nos. 260 and 267: William, Nos. 256 and 257; and Richard, Nos. 203, 240, 250, 256 and 257. Barraclough concluded that several of these charters are forgeries but that all are based on authentic earlier grants; see relevant charters in *Charters of the Anglo-Norman Earls of Chester.*

11. See, for example, 'Chartulary of Dieulacres Abbey', No. 92; *The Coucher Book or Chartulary of Whalley Abbey,* I, ed. W.A. Hulton (Manchester, 1847), No. 16; CALS DCH/E/246 and DCH/E/247.

12. *Records of Early English Drama: Cheshire including Chester,* I, ed. E. Baldwin and others (Toronto, 2007), p. 42-44.

13. Ibid.

14. *Charters of the Anglo-Norman Earls of Chester,* No. 270; RRC III, p. 281.

15. Ormerod, II, p. 440; Ormerod, I, pp. 567, 595, 602.

16. *Report on the Manuscripts of Lord Middleton,* pp. 43-44. Barraclough thought this a fourteenth-century forgery based on a genuine earlier deed; see *Charters of the Anglo-Norman Earls of Chester,* No. 330.

17. *Chart. Chester Abbey,* I, Nos. 42 and 82; *The Registrum Antiquissimum of the Cathedral Church of Lincoln,* VII, ed. K. Major (Lincoln Record Society 46, 1953), No. 2089.

18. *CRR, 1203-1205,* pp. 172, 233, 257, 263, 317; *CRR, 1205-1206*, p. 59; *Feet of Fines for the County of Lincoln, 1199-1216*, ed. M.S. Walker (Pipe Roll Society 67, 1954), pp. 98-99.

19. P. Leycester and T. Mainwaring, 'Tracts Written in the Controversy Respecting the Legitimacy of Amicia, Daughter of Hugh Cyveliok', ed. W. Beamont, *Remains Historical and Literary Connected with the Palatine Counties of Lancaster and Cheshire* (Manchester, 1869), p. 42.

Family versus Flock

1. *The Chartulary of Cockersand Abbey,* II, Part 2, ed. W. Farrer (Manchester, 1900), pp. 736-37; *Chart. Chester Abbey*, I, No. 41.

2. *The Registrum Antiquissimum of the Cathedral Church of Lincoln,* IV, ed. C.W. Foster and K. Major (Lincoln Record Society 32, 1937), No. 1111; *CPR, 1399-1401,* p. 302.

3. *CCHR, 1257-1300*, pp. 395-98. Sir John Boydell was still alive in 1239 when he was summoned to serve as a juror in a dispute between Croyland Abbey and Spalding Priory, on the one hand, and William d'Albini, earl of Arundel, on the other; *CRR, 1237-42,* p. 182. He was dead by 1242, when Hugh fitz Ralph and William Woodthorpe held his lands; *Liber Feodorum,* II, pp. 1054, 1062, 1090-91. So John probably died without issue – as did his brother Robert, who would have been his heir if John had no children. A branch of the Boydell family settled in Walmsgate, Lincolnshire, but they were most likely the descendants of one of Helto's brothers.

4. *Descriptive Catalogue of the Charters and Muniments of the Gresley Family*, ed. I.H. Jeayes (1895), p. 5; *Registrum Antiquissimum of the Cathedral Church of Lincoln,* VII, No. 2089.

5. Apart from William, two members of the Boydell family feature in Cheshire in early thirteenth-century records. Geoffrey witnessed a grant to Adam de Dutton, before 1212; GB 133 ARL/1/7. He was probably named after Henry II's son Geoffrey (*fl.* 1158-1186) and is most likely to have been William's first cousin. John settled in Lymm and is named in a lawsuit of 1337; TNA CHES 29/48, m. 10. John may have been Geoffrey's son, but the close links between the Boydells of Lymm and Dodleston (reinforced by various intermarriages) suggest that he was Richard's child.

6. *Concilia Magnae Britanniae et Hiberniae*, I, ed. D. Wilkins (1737), p. 477.

7. Ormerod, I, p. 567; *Coucher Book*, I, No. 16.

8. G. Wrottesley, *Pedigrees from the Plea Rolls, 1200 to 1500* (1905), p. 265; CALS DLT/B3.

9. *Chart. Chester Abbey*, I, No. 43; Ormerod, II, p. 845; *Chart. Chester Abbey*, II, No. 553.

10. *CCHR, 1327-1341*, p. 156.

11. *CCHR, 1327-1341*, p. 156; Ormerod, II, p. 865.

12. Lancashire Archives DDCL 72.

The Path of Chivalry

1. 'Chartulary of Dieulacres Abbey', No. 42. The deed is undated but the witnesses included Sir William Vernon, 'then justice of Chester' (the position he held from 1229 to 1232).

2. Ormerod, I, p. 632 and III, p. 198. The grant is undated but Maud probably made it soon after her brother's death, c.1228.

3. GB 133 RYCH/1263; GB 133 TW/92. William's son, Sir John Boydell, also witnessed a deed with William de Brexis (sic), probably the son of Hugh's son, Sir Hugh de Brexes; see GB 133 RYCH/1267.

4. 'Chartulary of Dieulacres Abbey', No. 60; Ormerod, I, p. 567; G. Ormerod, 'Calendar of Enrollments', in *Miscellanea Palatina: Consisting of Genealogical Essays Illustrative of Cheshire and Lancashire Families* (privately printed, 1851), p. 14; GB 133 RYCH/1263; *Chart. Chester Abbey*, I, No. 26.

5. *CPR, 1232-1247*, p. 464.

6. *CPR, 1247-1258*, p. 70; *Cheshire in the Pipe Rolls, 1158-1301,* trans. M.H. Mills and ed. R. Stewart-Brown (LCRS 92, 1938), p. 128.

7. *CCR, 1247-1251*, p. 185; Ormerod, *Miscellanea Palatina*, pp. 5-10; *Calendar of County Court, City Court and Eyre Rolls of Chester, 1259-1297*, ed. R. Stewart-Brown (Manchester, 1925), p. 31; *Chart. Chester Abbey*, I, No. 331 (with addendum in II, pp. xxx-xxxi).

8. *Chart. Chester Abbey*, II, No. 480; CALS WMS 301.

9. 'Chartulary of Dieulacres Abbey', Nos. 48, 61 and 62; *The Coucher Book or Chartulary of Whalley Abbey,* II, ed. W.A. Hulton (Manchester, 1847), No. 29.

10. *Cheshire in the Pipe Rolls, 1158-1301*, p. 128; J. Tait, 'Knight-Service in Cheshire', *English Historical Review* 57, 228 (1942), p. 440.

11. *CIPM*, II, p. 130.

12. J.R. Studd, 'A Catalogue of the Acts of the Lord Edward, 1254-1272', unpublished Ph.D. thesis, University of Leeds (1971), Acta 844.

13. *CIM,* I, p. 116.

14. Staffordshire Archives M9/3.

15. *CIPM*, II, p. 130.

One Welshman's Head

1. 'Annales Prioratus de Dunstaplia', in *Annales Monastici*, III, ed. H.R. Luard (1866), pp. 293-94.
2. *CCR, 1272-1279,* p. 402.
3. *CIPM*, II, p. 130; *CCR, 1272-1279,* p. 402.
4. P. Morgan, *War and Society in Medieval Cheshire, 1277-1403* (Manchester, 1987), p. 30, citing TNA E372/124.
5. 'The Hope Castle Account of 1282', ed. A.J. Taylor, *Flintshire Historical Society Journal* 33 (1992), pp. 25-28.
6. Ibid., pp. 28-29, 41, 44-47.
7. *Calendar of County Court, City Court and Eyre Rolls of Chester,* pp. 52-53.
8. Ibid., pp. 56-57.
9. *Calendar of Various Chancery Rolls, 1277-1336* (1912), pp. 281-82.
10. Margaret held three burgages (rental properties) in Frodsham 'by gift and feoffment' of Nicholas de Frodsham. In October 1329, Nicholas's son John quitclaimed all right in the houses to Margaret, suggesting that the two were related; see CALS DCH/F/37.
11. J.C. Parsons, *Eleanor of Castile* (New York, 1995; paperback edn, 1997), pp. 109, 114, 133, 162-63.
12. N.M. Fryde, 'A Royal enquiry into abuses: Queen Eleanor's ministers in North-East Wales, 1291-92', *Welsh History Review* 5 (1971), pp. 366-76.
13. *Calendar of County Court, City Court and Eyre Rolls of Chester*, pp. 56-58, 60, 63-64, 118, 120, 140.
14. *Calendar of County Court, City Court and Eyre Rolls of Chester,* p. 144; GB 133 RYCH/1267.
15. *Chart. Chester Abbey*, II, No. 893; *Calendar of County Court, City Court and Eyre Rolls of Chester,* pp. 122, 149.
16. *CIPM*, III, p. 3.
17. Eaton Charter No. 26, Edward I, in *A Calendar of Ancient Charters Preserved at Eaton Hall, Cheshire*, ed. W. Beamont (Warrington, 1862). The transaction took place before 29 September 1299, when the abbot of Dieulacres leased the manor to William Doncaster with a clause to this effect.
18. *CIPM*, III, pp. 144-45.
19. *CIPM*, II, pp. 478-79; CALS WMS 306.
20. TNA CHES 29/7 m. 1; CHES 29/9 m. 7, CHES 29/9 m. 6, CHES 29/9 m. 4, CHES 29/10 m. 11, CHES 29/10 m. 10 and CHES 29/10 m. 12.
21. TNA CHES 29/8 m. 10, CHES 29/8 m. 6, CHES 29/8 m. 1, CHES 29/8 m. 3d, CHES 29/9 m. 17; CHES 29/9 m. 15 and CHES 29/8 m. 2d.
22. TNA CHES 29/9 m. 11; *Chart. Chester Abbey*, I, No. 44 and II, No. 481.

Blade and Trade

1. TNA CHES 29/7 m. 16d; Hawarden Deeds/5 and 6; CALS DLT/B7; 'Flintshire Genealogical Notes', ed. E.A. Ebblewhite, *Archaeologia Cambrensis*, fifth series 12 (1895), p. 259. John also attested two grants of land in Newton to Hugh and Mary Brickhill; see GB 133 ARL/25/10 and GB 133 ARL/25/17.
2. Eaton Charters No. 17 and No. 26, Edward I; *Accounts of the Chamberlains and Other Officers of the County of Chester, 1301-1360*, ed. R. Stewart-Brown (LCRS 59, 1910), p. 27.
3. William Boydell and Nichola Doncaster were married before 20 June 1303, when their respective fathers entered into a covenant; see TNA CHES 29/17 m. 4d.
4. TNA CHES 29/13 m. 9.
5. TNA CHES 29/17 m. 4d. All further references to the dispute between Sir John Boydell and William Doncaster come from this source.
6. Ormerod, I, p. 448.
7. TNA CHES 29/15 m. 11d.
8. TNA CHES 29/17 m. 4d.
9. TNA CHES 29/17 m. 14; CHES 29/17 m. 17; CHES 29/17 m. 21, CHES 29/19 m. 5, CHES 29/19 m. 8 and CHES 29/19 m. 9.
10. RRC I, p. 47.
11. TNA CHES 29/20 m. 15d and CHES 29/20 m. 16d.
12. Ormerod, I, p. 604, note a.
13. TNA CHES 29/21 m. 3d; *CIPM,* V, p. 38.
14. *CFR, 1307-1319*, p. 34.

On the King's Business

1. *Vita Edwardi Secundi: The Life of Edward the Second*, ed. W.R. Childs (Oxford, 2005), p. 9.
2. *CPR, 1307-1313*, pp. 102-03.
3. TNA CHES 29/17 m. 14; CHES 29/17 m. 17; CHES 29/17 m. 21, CHES 29/19 m. 5, CHES 29/19 m. 8 and CHES 29/19 m. 9.
4. TNA CHES 29/19 m. 3d.
5. CALS DCH/F/803; TNA CHES 29/22 m. 10, CHES 29/22 m. 19 and CHES 29/22 m. 19d.
6. TNA CHES 29/22 m. 1r and CHES 29/22 m. 47r.
7. TNA CHES 29/21 m. 16, CHES 29/21 m. 18d and CHES 29/21 m. 22; CALS WMS 304 and WMS 309; W. Beaumont, *A History of the Castle of Halton and the Priory or Abbey of Norton* (Warrington, 1873), p. 169.
8. TNA CHES 29/22 m. 13d; *CCR, 1307-1313*, p. 281.
9. *CFR, 1307-1319*, p. 100.

10. TNA SC 8/70/3488.

11. CALS DLT A30/10; *CPR 1348-1350*, pp. 5-6.

12. *CCHR, 1300-1326*, p. 194.

13. *A Calendar of the Register of Henry Wakefield, Bishop of Worcester 1373-1395*, ed. W.P. Marret (Worcestershire Historical Society, new series 7, 1972), p. 143; *CPR, 1313-1317*, p. 47.

14. RRC I, p. 47.

15. *CDS*, V, No. 3248.

16. CALS DAR/D/69/1.

17. *CPR, 1321-1324*, p. 72; *South Lancashire in the Reign of Edward II as illustrated by the Pleas at Wigan Recorded in Coram Rege Roll No. 254*, ed. G.H. Tupling (Manchester, 1949), pp. xxxii, xxxiv-v and 86-87.

Floating in Blood

1. *South Lancashire Pleas*, pp. xxxiv-v, 77, 86-87; *CFR, 1319-1327*, 102, 109; *Rotuli Parliamentorum, ut et Petitiones et Placita in Parliamento*, I, ed. J. Strachey (1767), p. 438.

2. *South Lancashire Pleas*, pp. 87-88; *Calendar of Chancery Warrants, 1244-1326* (1927), pp. 574-75.

3. *South Lancashire Pleas*, pp. xlii-l, 46-47.

4. Ibid., pp. l-li, 46-47.

5. Ibid., pp. li, 95.

6. Sir Ralph Vernon of Hanwell was the eldest son of Sir Ralph Vernon, baron of Shipbrook. He married Margaret, daughter of Urian de St Pierre, but was dead by 1319-20, when his widow sued for her dower; see Ormerod, III, pp. 246-48, 252, 697.

7. CALS DCN 1984/63/25; TNA WARD 2/47/169/3; DIWD II, p. 123.

8. DIWD II, p. 113.

9. *CPR, 1330-1334*, p. 364; 'Townships: Duxbury', in *Victoria County History of Lancashire VI*, ed. W. Farrer and J. Brownbill (1911), pp. 208-09, note 15.

10. *CPR, 1327-1330*, p. 110; *CPR, 1330-1334*, p. 364.

11. T. Barns, 'The Architectural Antiquities of the Parish Church of St. Wilfrid, Grappenhall', *Transactions of the Lancashire and Cheshire Historical Society* 33 (1881), pp. 98-101, 108.

12. Ibid., pp. 99-100.

13. RRC I, p. 47; Barns, 'Architectural Antiquities', p. 99.

14. CALS DCN 1984/63/30.

15. Wrottesley, *Pedigrees from the Plea Rolls,* pp. 115, 265; GB 133 RYCH/1742.

16. Beamont, *A History of the Castle of Halton*, p. 172; Barns, 'Architectural Antiquities', p. 101.

Illicit Amour

1. Robert of Avesbury, *De Gestis Mirabilibus Regis Edwardi Tertii*, ed. E.M. Thompson (1889), p. 284; *The Brut, or The Chronicles of England*, I, ed. F.W.D. Brie (1906), pp. 261-62.
2. DIWD I, p. 38; Ormerod, II, p. 842; Eaton Charter No. 35, Edward III.
3. CALS DCN 1984/63/31; DIWD II, p. 120.
4. DIWD III, pp. 36-37.
5. RRC I, p. 47; DIWD III, p. 39.
6. Modern animal studies show that wormwood delays ovulation and interferes with implantation; see J.M. Riddle and J.W. Estes, 'Oral Contraceptives in Ancient and Medieval Times', *American Scientist* 80, 3 (1992), p. 231.
7. *BPR*, III, pp. 39-40.
8. RRC III, p. 281.
9. *BPR*, III, p. 2.

Cornered and Constrained

1. When William died his lands were valued at £24 7s 8d per annum, but their worth had declined by £16 as a result of the plague. William had also given his son property valued at £40 a year.
2. CALS DCH/F/37, DCH/F/45 and DCH/F/51.
3. Robert Boydell transferred the property his father had given him to Thomas de Dutton in 1340-41. William joined with Peter Legh of Betchton to redeem the land two years later. See DIWD III, pp. 39, 41; CALS DCN 1984/63/24.
4. RRC I, p. 135.
5. *BPR*, I, p. 37.
6. Evidence of this marriage comes from a lawsuit in which William's uncle sued Ellen Legh for some tenements in Handley that Ellen held 'for the life of Elizabeth, late the wife of Ralph Boidell'; see *BPR*, III, p. 214.
7. TNA SC 8/155/7701; *BPR*, I, p. 94.
8. RRC I, p. 48.
9. *BPR*, III, pp. 93-94.
10. *BPR*, I, pp. 94, 118, 158.
11. TNA SC 8/155/7701; *BPR*, I, pp. 94, 118.
12. *BPR*, I, p. 158; *Accounts of the Chamberlains*, p. 124.
13. *Accounts of the Chamberlains*, pp. 126, 163; *CCR, 1349-1354*, p. 2.

Black Smoke

1. RRC III, p. 281.
2. TNA CHES 3/2 No. 3.

3. *BPR,* III, pp. 1, 20, 33, 459; Ormerod, III, pp. 298, 707; RRC III, p. 281; TNA CHES 3/2 No. 3.
4. *Accounts of the Chamberlains,* p. 157.
5. *BPR,* III, pp. 108, 114; *Accounts of the Chamberlains,* pp. 157-58.

An Unequal Contest

1. DIWD II, p. 97; Wrottesley, *Pedigrees from the Plea Rolls*, p. 198; Ormerod, I, p. 452.
2. *The Extent of Longdendale, 1360*, ed. J. Harrop and others (LCRS 140, 2005), pp. 94-95, 98; *BPR,* III, p. 106.
3. *BPR*, III, pp. 70-71.
4. For details of Hywel's petition, see *BPR*, III, pp. 93-94. According to William Boydell's inquisition post mortem, Hywel was 19. But Hywel actually turned 21 in early 1354, so he was three years younger than Danyers had alleged; see RRC III, p. 281 and *BPR*, III, p. 149.
5. *Accounts of the Chamberlains,* p. 163.
6. *BPR,* III, pp. 93-94.
7. Ibid., pp. 99, 101.
8. Ibid., pp. 106-07.
9. RRC III, p. 281; Ormerod, I, p. 732.
10. *BPR,* III, pp. 120, 149; TNA WARD 2/47/169/4.
11. *BPR,* III, p. 143.
12. Ibid., p. 159.
13. Ibid., p. 160.
14. Ormerod, II, pp. 845-46; DIWD III, 41; CALS DCN 1984/63/24; Wrottesley, *Pedigrees from the Plea Rolls*, p. 116.
15. *BPR,* III, pp. 223, 346.
16. Wrottesley, *Pedigrees from the Plea Rolls*, p. 198; *BPR*, III, pp. 44-45, 344.
17. RRC I, p. 107.
18. *BPR*, III, p. 282.
19. TNA WARD 2/47/169/6; *BPR,* III, pp. 367-68.
20. *BPR,* III, p. 455.
21. RRC I, p. 218.
22. For Peter de Lymm's marriage to Margaret Warburton, see GB 133 ARL/4/65. Matthew Rixton was one of the three natural sons of Richard Rixton, younger son of Alan Rixton and brother to Joan's mother, Emma; see 'Townships: Great Sankey', in *Victoria County History of Lancashire III*, ed. W. Farrer and J. Browbill (1907), pp. 409-10, note 11.
23. *BPR,* III, p. 459; Ormerod, I, p. 473 and II, pp. 845-46; GB 133 ARL/4/30.
24. Flintshire Record Office D/G/2698; Ebblewhite, 'Flintshire Genealogical Notes', p. 261.

Venom in the Veins

1. *BPR*, III, p. 475; H.F. Burke, 'Some Cheshire Deeds', *The Ancestor* 6 (1903), p. 41; DIWD III, p. 66.
2. TNA CHES 3/8 No. 8.
3. *The Controversy between Sir Richard Scrope and Sir Richard Grosvenor in the Court of Chivalry*, I, ed. N.H. Nicolas (1832), p. 275; *CIPM, XXI*, p. 153; *A Descriptive Catalogue of Ancient Deeds*, VI, ed. H.C. Maxwell Lyte (1915), p. 202; CALS DCH/F/94; British Library Add. MS. 6032, f. 30.
4. The Soldier in Later Medieval England database, TNA C76/62 m. 17.
5. TNA CHESH 3/8 No. 4.
6. Ibid.

The Double Legacy

1. Details taken from Thomas Boydell's proof-of-age inquisition, TNA CHES 13/13 No. 8.
2. *CCR, 1377-1381,* p. 185; RRC I, p. 499.
3. RRC I, p. 499.
4. Ormerod, III, pp. 655, 661; RRC I, p. 48; *BPR*, III, 437; Ormerod, I, pp. 595-96.
5. RRC I, pp. 406, 421.
6. Ibid., p. 202.
7. Ibid., p. 48.
8. *CDS,* V, No. 4438; The Soldier in Later Medieval England database, TNA E101/41/17 m. 5d.
9. RRC I, pp. 3, 538-39.
10. RRC I, pp. 48, 290; *CPR, 1391-1396*, pp. 270, 279.
11. RRC I, pp. 13, 48.
12. Wrottesley, *Pedigrees from the Plea Rolls*, p. 198.
13. Ormerod, II, p. 846.

Fortune's False Wheel

1. RRC I, p. 48; DIWD III, p. 61.
2. RRC I, p. 237; *CFR, 1391-1399,* p. 208.
3. RRC I, p. 317.
4. Ibid., pp. 33, 48, 475.
5. TNA CHES 2/74 m. 13d.
6. RRC I, p. 295.
7. Ibid., p. 49.

NOTES

Ashes and Dust

1. J.E. Messham, 'The County of Flint and the Rebellion of Owen Glyn Dŵr in the Records of the Earldom of Chester', *Journal of the Flintshire Historical Society* 23 (1967-68), pp. 14-18, citing Chamberlain's Accounts (SC 6/775/3 f.).
2. RRC I, p. 49; *Abstracts of Inquisitions post Mortem made by Christopher Towneley and Roger Dodsworth,* I, ed. W. Langton (Manchester, 1876), p. 80; 'Townships: Walton-le-Dale', in *Victoria County History of Lancashire VI,* p. 292, note 32, citing Towneley MS. DD, no. 1501.
3. RRC I, pp. 49, 295.
4. RRC I, p. 400; Ormerod, I, pp. 472-74.
5. RRC I, p. 400; RRC II, p. 152.
6. *Calendar of Entries in the Papal Registers Relating To Great Britain and Ireland, Vol 7, 1417-1431*, ed. J.A. Twemlow (1906), p. 87.
7. Ormerod, II, p. 846; TNA WALE 29/247; Congleton Borough Charter CTH 4/119, cl. 19, trans. D. Roffe, available at http://www.roffe.co.uk/charters/b4/119.htm
8. Swallow, 'Palimpsest of Border Power', p. 37.
9. RRC II, pp. 611-12.

Select Bibliography

All sources pertaining to the Boydell family are cited in the endnotes. Summaries of many of these sources are now available in the online catalogues of the National Archives, relevant county archives and various libraries with special collections. Digitised versions of a growing number of chronicles can also be found at HathiTrust, Internet Archive and Google Books, although Oxford Medieval Texts has produced more modern editions in some instances.

Other valuable research tools include the Prosopography of Anglo-Saxon England (PASE) website, where users can map and quantify the estates of all the landholders named in the Domesday survey; The Soldier in Later Medieval England database, which contains the names of soldiers serving the English crown between 1369 and 1453; and British History Online, a digital library of key printed primary and secondary sources. In addition, the University of Houston Law Center maintains a vast collection of medieval English court rolls at Anglo-American Legal Tradition (AALT). These are digital scans of the original Latin manuscripts, so they are difficult to use. However, some of them have been indexed.

For those who wish to read more about the period this book covers, I have included further recommendations below. The place of publication is London, unless otherwise stated.

ALLMAND, C.T., *The Hundred Years War: England and France at War c. 1300-c. 1450* (Cambridge, 1988; revised edn, 2001).

BARLOW, F., *The Feudal Kingdom of England, 1042–1216* (third edn, 1966).

BELL, A.R., CURRY, A., KING, A. and **SIMPKIN, D.,** *The Soldier in Later Medieval England* (Oxford, 2013).

BELLAMY, J.G., *The Criminal Trial in Later Medieval England* (Toronto, 1998).

BENNETT, M.J., *Community, Class and Careerism: Cheshire and Lancashire Society in the Age of Sir Gawain and the Green Knight* (Cambridge, 1983).

BEVERLEY SMITH, J., *Llywelyn ap Gruffudd: Prince of Wales* (Cardiff, 1998; new edn, 2014).

BOOTH, P.H.W., *The Financial Administration of the Lordship and County of Chester, 1272–1377* (Manchester, 1981).

BULLOUGH, V.L. and **BRUNDAGE, J.A.** (eds.), *Handbook of Medieval Sexuality,* (New York, 1996).

CARPENTER, D., *The Struggle for Mastery: Britain 1066–1284* (2003).

CLANCHY, M.T., *From Memory to Written Record: England 1066–1307* (third edn, Oxford, 2013).

COSS, P., *The Origins of the English Gentry* (Cambridge, 2003).

CROUCH, D., *The Image of Aristocracy: In Britain, 1000–1300* (1992; e-edn, 2005).

DAVIES, R.R., *The Revolt of Owain Glyn Dŵr* (Oxford, 1995; paperback edn, 1997).

DYER, C., *Standards of Living in the Later Middle Ages: Social Change in England c. 1200–1520* (Cambridge, 1989; revised edn, 1998).

GILLESPIE, J.L., 'Richard II's Cheshire Archers', *Transactions of the Lancashire and Cheshire Historical Society* 125 (1974).

GOODMAN, A., *John of Gaunt: The Exercise of Princely Power in Fourteenth-Century Europe* (1992; reprinted 2013).

GREEN, D., *The Black Prince* (Stroud, 2001).

GREEN, J.A., *The Aristocracy of Norman England* (Cambridge, 1997).

GUMMER, B., *The Scourging Angel: The Black Death in the British Isles* (2010).

HATCHER, J. *The Black Death: The Intimate Story of a Village in Crisis, 1345–1350* (2008; paperback edn, 2009).

HEWITT, H.J., *Cheshire under the Three Edwards* (Chester, 1967).

HORROX, R. and **ORMROD, W.M.** (eds.), *A Social History of England,* (Cambridge, 2006).

JUPP, P.C. and **GITTINGS, C.** (eds.), Death in England: An Illustrated History (Manchester, 1999).

LAUGHTON, J., *Life in a Medieval City: Chester 1275–1520* (Oxford, 2008).

MCNIVEN, P., 'The Cheshire Rising of 1400', *Bulletin of the John Rylands Library* 52, 2 (1970).

MILLER E. and **HATCHER, J.,** *Medieval England: Rural Society and Economic Change, 1086–1348* (1978; reprinted 2014).

MORGAN, P., *War and Society in Medieval Cheshire*, 1277–1403 (Manchester, 1987).

MORRIS, M., *A Great and Terrible King: Edward I and the Forging of Britain* (2009).

MORRIS, M., *King John: Treachery, Tyranny and the Road to Magna Carta* (2015).

MORRIS, M., *The Norman Conquest* (2013).

MORTIMER, I., *The Perfect King: The Life of Edward III, Father of the English Nation* (2008).

ORME, N., *Medieval Children* (New Haven, CT, 2001; paperback edn, 2003).

POUNDS, N.J.G., *The Medieval Castle in England and Wales: A Social and Political History* (Cambridge, 1994).

PRESTWICH, M., *Edward I* (Berkeley & Los Angeles, CA, 1988).

RUBIN, M., *The Hollow Crown: A History of Britain in the Late Middle Ages* (2005).

SAUL, N., *Richard II* (New Haven, CT, 1997; paperback edn, 1999).

SHAHAR, S., *The Fourth Estate: A History of Women in the Middle Ages* (1983; revised edn, 2003).

SUMPTION, J., *Divided Houses: The Hundred Years War III* (2009).

THIBODEAUX, J.D., *The Manly Priest: Clerical Celibacy, Masculinity, and Reform in England and Normandy, 1066–1300* (Philadelphia, PA, 2015).

THOMAS, H.M., *The English and the Normans: Ethnic Hostility, Assimilation and Identity 1066-c.1220* (Oxford, 2003; reprinted 2005).

TRACY, L. and **DE VRIES, K.** (eds.), *Wounds and Wound Repair in Medieval Culture* (Leiden, 2015).

TUCHMAN, B. W., *A Distant Mirror: The Calamitous 14th Century* (New York, 1978; paperback edn, 1979).

VINCENT, N., *A Brief History of Britain 1066–1485: The Birth of a Nation* (2011).

WARREN, W.L., *Henry II* (Berkeley & Los Angeles, CA, 1973).

Index

INDEX

INDEX